AMERICAN EDUCATION

Its Men

Ideas

and

Institutions

Advisory Editor

Lawrence A. Cremin
Frederick A. P. Barnard Professor of Education
Teachers College, Columbia University

Lectures on School-Keeping

*

Lectures to Female Teachers on School-Keeping

Samuel R. Hall

ARNO PRESS & THE NEW YORK TIMES
New York * *1969*

Reprint edition 1969 by Arno Press, Inc.

*

Library of Congress Catalog Card No. 76-89185

*

Reprinted from a copy in
Teachers College Library

*

Manufactured in the United States of America

Editorial Note

AMERICAN EDUCATION: *Its Men, Institutions and Ideas* presents selected works of thought and scholarship that have long been out of print or otherwise unavailable. Inevitably, such works will include particular ideas and doctrines that have been outmoded or superseded by more recent research. Nevertheless, all retain their place in the literature, having influenced educational thought and practice in their own time and having provided the basis for subsequent scholarship.

Lawrence A. Cremin
Teachers College

Lectures on School-Keeping

*

Lectures to Female Teachers
on School-Keeping

LECTURES

ON

SCHOOL-KEEPING.

BY SAMUEL R. HALL.

BOSTON:

PUBLISHED BY RICHARDSON, LORD AND HOLBROOK.

No. 133, Washington-Street.

1829.

PREFACE.

Of nothing are the people of the United States more disposed to boast, than the free government, free institutions and free schools, which they have established. By the latter, it is designed to place within the reach of every child, the means of acquiring an education, sufficient to prepare him for the duties of a citizen. In a large number of the states, the establishment and support of free schools, has been a prominent object with the Legislatures. In some, the system adopted is, perhaps, better than in any other part of the world.

But still there is a very general opinion, that the amount of benefit desirable, is not obtained from these primary fountains of knowledge. Many plans have been formed to increase their usefulness. Some of these have been put in operation, and others have ended in theory.

It is highly desirable to every patriot, philanthropist and christian, that " the strong desire manifested to render this moral engine of social happiness and political security, as extensive, as complete and efficacious, as the vast resources of our intelligence and wealth will permit," may not cease, till something effectual shall be accomplished. No subject has stronger claims upon us, " for on the correct and early education of youth, depends the ultimate success of every rational enterprise for the intellectual and moral improvement of man."

In order to raise common schools to that standard of excellence it is desirable they should attain ; the defects, which exist, must be sought out. Nothing effectual can be done till these, with the causes of them are ascertained. The remedies may then be proposed, applied and tested. There is a very general belief, that one of the most common defects is the improper character and superficial qualifications of teachers. It is well known that many who are employed to teach our primary schools, are deficient in almost every necessary qualification. While this defect is so prominent, all the efforts to increase the usefulness of schools, can be attended with only partial success. But let the character of teachers be improved, and improvement in the schools will follow of course. To accomplish this object, it is desirable that institutions should be established for educating teachers, where they should be taught not only the necessary branches of literature, but, be made acquainted with the science of *teaching* and the mode of *governing* a school with success. The general management of a school should be a subject of *much study*, before one engages in the employment of teaching.

However important such institutions are to the success of common schools, as yet, very few of them exist. This has led to the inquiry whether a publication of very practical character, containing such directions to instructers, as might be easily understood and applied, would not be of essential service. This inquiry has led to the publication of the following volume.

The substance of the Lectures, has been given at various times, to classes of young men, who were qualifying themselves to become teachers, in the Institution of which the Author has charge. He has selected such subjects of remark, as have appeared to him the most important, and has endeavoured to give all the directions as much of a practical character, as possible.

The object, in lecturing and writing, has been to present the nature of their employment, to those who are preparing themselves to instruct ; and to impress them with the importance of being properly qualified, and faithful in their employment, as well as to give such directions for governing and teaching as might be useful to them.

The Author does not expect that *all* will correspond with him, in the views he has taken of various subjects, nor, does he dare to believe that all his directions are the best that could be given. But, they are the best, that he could give. And he does firmly believe, that by attentively following them, teachers will be able to accomplish *much more* than has been usual, in training children and youth to habits of application, and in assisting them to gain necessary knowledge.

The work is designed not only to be *studied* by those at Academies, who are anticipating the work of the teacher, but to be carried by the master into his school, and be a directory in the performance of his daily labour.

The Author solicits the candid remarks of such as have had extensive acquaintance with the business of teaching, and hopes thereby to improve the character of the work, if a subsequent edition is demanded. He contemplates the work as an experiment, and as he has had no track to guide him, and only his own judgment and experience to depend on, he is solicitous for the result. Be that what it may, he will have the pleasure of reflecting, that his ardent desire to see the character of teachers improved, and a method of teaching more practical and better adapted to the capacities of children adopted, is laudable. If he has failed of furnishing such a work as is needed, it is owing to want of capacity—not to want of a desire to benefit the rising generation, and through them, his country.

Boston, August, 1829.

1*

ADVERTISEMENT.

The questions in *italics* are designed to call the attention of those, who are qualifying themselves to become teachers, to a practical application of what is said previously. They must of course form an answer according to their own judgment. Answers to many of the questions will be better given in the scholar's own words, than by committing to memory the sentence or sentences, to which the quotation refers. The questions are made very general, in order that they may not be too much depended upon. The intelligent instructer, who puts them to a class, will not be confined to them; but will ask many others.

It may be useful for such as *have been* in the habit of teaching, to have occasional meetings, and question each other on a given portion of the book. Those who may be employed in a town, may occasionally meet for the same purpose. They might also be able to make each other acquainted with the results of their experience and efforts, and mutually benefit each other.

CONTENTS.

———

LECTURE I.

LECTURE II.

LECTURE III.

LECTURE IV.

1. The importance of learning the nature of the
   teacher's employment—means of acquiring it.
2. Responsibility of the teacher—importance of
   realizing and understanding it.

LECTURE V.

1. Importance of gaining the confidence of the
   school—means of gaining it.
2. The instructer should be willing to spend all of
   his time when it can be rendered beneficial to
   the school.

LECTURE I.

Young Gentlemen,

I am induced by various considerations to address you in the following course of Lectures. You expect soon to assume the responsibilities and care of the district schools, in which your services may be needed. It is, therefore, highly important, that a portion of your time *now* should be devoted to the subject which is about to occupy your whole attention. Indeed, all the progress you may be able to make in *science* will not be a sufficient preparation for the work before you. Without some knowledge of the *nature of your business,* how can you be qualified to engage in it? Without having made the *" science of teaching"* a study, how can you be better prepared for success in it, than you would be to succeed in law or medicine, without having studied either? It is true, that many have engaged in teaching school, without having gained any knowledge of the nature of their work, save what they had acquired in the schools which they attended while children. But that others have pursued a course inconsistent and unreasonable, is no reason why you should imitate their bad example, and thus render your labours useless, or even injurious, to the children placed under your care. A moment's attention to the subject, is, it would seem to me, sufficient to show, that no one ought to assume the office of teacher, without having endeavoured first to obtain some correct views of the subject; of the obstacles in his way—the manner in which they may be overcome—the labour he is to perform—and the most probable means of benefiting, in the highest degree, his youthful charge.

I engage in the labour before me, with interest, as involving that which is highly necessary to you, and impor-

2

tant to the community through which you will shortly be dispersed.

Before proceeding to the subject more immediately before us, it will be necessary for me to animadvert on some circumstances in the existing state of our community, which have an important bearing on the character and success of schools.

There is generally no lack of conviction, that *education* is important. Very few are found, even among the ignorant, who are slow to acknowledge, that learning is necessary to enjoyment and usefulness. Among the well educated, no one remark is more frequently heard, than that a good education is necessary for every citizen in a land of civil and religious freedom. But it is equally obvious to me, that while the importance of education is generally acknowledged, the immense value of common schools is not realized. When it is recollected, that from these minor fountains of knowledge, and from these only, the great mass of the community receive all their instruction in science, the marked indifference to their character and usefulness which so often appears, is truly astonishing. "Most of our legislators, our judges and governors have commenced their preparation for the high stations they have filled in society, by drinking at these simple springs of knowledge. We see the magic influence of our schools, in the habits of industry, sobriety and order which prevail in the community; in the cheerful obedience yielded to the laws, and in the acts of charity and benevolence, which are every day multiplied around us. Rarely have we seen a native of our state, paying his life to her violated laws,"* if his early years were spent in the schools of our land. These are facts known and generally acknowledged. But still, with many, there is a criminal indifference to the character and usefulness of common schools.

This is not an indifference which the *stranger* would so readily discern; for much is said in public bodies, by editors and professional men, of their importance, and much interest is felt by such. But still, there is a degree of indifference which it is not hard to detect. It is exhibited in various ways, one of which is the inattention to

* Burnside's Address, at Worcester, Massachusetts.

school meetings at which arrangements are made for the schools of the year. When such a meeting is notified, it is not unfrequently found that but very few attend. From one tenth to one half of the voters are usually present. Almost any article of business is sufficient to detain a voter from attending. When the meeting is organized, some arrangements are made in relation to the board of the teacher, and fuel for the school; and a committee is appointed to provide a master. This committee is often directed by a vote, not to employ an instructer above a certain price, which is frequently very inadequate. The instructer is engaged with a reference to his cheapness, or he is selected on account of relationship, or something equally unconnected with his character for morality, literature or ability to teach. The school commences, and parents seem to feel quite satisfied without further effort, or even inquiry, unless it be to know whether their children are severely punished. The business of the shop or the farm, claims as usual, the chief attention; and the question, whether their children are making all the progress they ought, is very seldom asked. Little is known of the character of the school, beyond the report of the children themselves, or perhaps the remarks of the visiting committee.

I am happy to say that there are many exceptions to the above; but am constrained still to believe, from actual observation, in the Eastern and some of the Middle States, that the exceptions are not sufficient to make these remarks untrue. Whole towns may be found where an interest has been excited on the subject of schools, commensurate with their importance. I am happy to believe that this is true of the city of Boston. Some others have set a good example. But these are not a majority.

The indifference complained of, and which is so perceptible after all the legislating there has been on the subject, is yet great; and requires only to be mentioned to be condemned by the reflecting and judicious. It may have its origin in habit, in ignorance, and in want of reflection.

Habit effects a part. The parent who never visits the school which his children attend, will perhaps hardly give as a reason, that he never saw his father within the walls

of a school room, though it is very possible this may be a
chief reason.   Still, if interrogated on the subject, he will
probably say he lacks time, or does not feel competent to
judge of the character of the school, &c.   The fact, however, may be, that he has, from his very youth, formed a
habit of considering the school a subject of far less
consequence than it is.   He has imperceptibly imbibed
the sentiments of his own parents, and as they appeared
but little interested in the character of the schools which
they maintained, so the habit has come down to him.   It
may also have been induced from others.   We are strongly
inclined to go with the multitude whether right or wrong.
When the greater part of parents are indifferent to the
character of the school, this feeling is very naturally extended to those who at first might have felt some solicitude on the subject.   Thus habits of indifference have extended from family to family, from neighbourhood to
neighbourhood and from district to district.   The effect
becomes permanent, and year after year continues or in-
creases it.   But other circumstances have an influence in
producing these lamentable effects.   It is very apparent
that the value of primary schools is not duly considered.
A large proportion of parents very seldom sit down to reflect on the influence which their own actions will have on
the general happiness of the country, or the influence to be
exerted by themselves on the character, usefulness and
enjoyment of their children.   Few realize as they ought,
that their indifference to these subjects is a sin against
their country's welfare, their own, and that of their families.   They see not the connexion between the institutions in which the character of their children is moulded,
and the future welfare of their children.   There are men,
who would consider themselves deeply insulted, if accused
of lacking patriotism ; men, who at the first encroachment
of a foreign foe, would seize the sword and, " shoulder to
shoulder" rush impetuously on the assailant,—men, who
would not turn away from the field of battle, while they
had blood to spill and an enemy to face,—who still are suffering an enemy to make fearful inroads on the happiness
and safety of the republic ; an enemy more dangerous
than a Philip or a Burr, a Cæsar or a Bonaparte.   Inattention to the means of extending knowledge through the

land, is undermining the beautiful pillars of our republican government. But we have reason to believe numbers never think of this. Reflection is wanting; hence they do not discover the effect, which their indifference to these subjects may produce on the welfare of the country. It *should be known* by all, that the best institutions of our country can be perpetuated no longer than intelligence and virtue continue among the common people. We may as well expect liberty in Turkey, as in these United States, when the common people cease to be enlightened. We may as well expect virtue in a band of robbers, as among our citizens, when ignorance is the characteristic of the common people.

If " to send an uneducated child into the world is like turning a mad dog into the street,"* all are under obligations to regard with high interest, those institutions which furnish the means of mental culture to the great mass of people. That parent, who is indifferent to the intellectual food of his children is certainly as guilty as he, who, through indifference, permits his offspring to feed on poisonous food, or should disregard the calls of nature, and make no provision for them in meat and drink. He disregards *his own* happiness as well as that of his children. What comfort can he expect to take in them in age, if he neglect to lay the foundation of their usefulness while they are under his control? Parents can rationally expect but little from children of riper years, if they have neglected to furnish them when young, with such knowledge as would direct them in the path of virtue and filial duty. I see no object more revolting to me, than an undutiful and unkind son. I see no distress more acute, than that of a parent, whose child is brought into shame and disgrace. Parents who are indifferent to the character of the schools which their children attend, do not reflect how severe the consequences may be to their own happiness. How pungent have been the feelings of a father or mother, when attending the trial of a son indicted for some high crime committed against the laws of the land, when, after conviction the wretched criminal

* Parkhurst's Moral Philosophy.

2 *

has upbraided them as the cause of his ruin, by having
been negligent of his education !

It is unquestionably the duty of every one, to promote
as far as may be the happiness of those around him. But
those who disregard the character and usefulness of primary schools, are neglecting to secure the happiness of
the neighbourhood. Slander is often owing to the want
of mental culture and hardly any thing produces greater
misery, where it extensively prevails. Insubordination
and a disregard to every law and to the necessary regulations of society, is always the result of ignorance and
vice. By these, the peace of society is disturbed and its
quiet broken up. The effect is not less unfavorable to
domestic peace—for he who enters the family state uncultivated, ungoverned, and unqualified for its duties, will
make others unhappy as well as himself.

Want of reflection on these subjects, certainly occasions some of the indifference exhibited, but not all. A
want of natural affection has a share of influence. There
are parents, so greedy of gain, that this becomes the all
absorbing object, and when the child is found to afford
the least aid in accomplishing this object, to this service
he is dedicated, and very little time is allowed for any
other purpose. In such a man's estimation, to clothe and
feed his children seems to be the whole of the parent's
duty, and when that duty is performed, he rests contented,
as to those placed under his care; but seems to consider it
a duty to *himself* to obtain as much benefit as is possible
from their earnings before manhood. I am happy to believe that the remarks here made are not applicable in
their full extent, to a *majority* of parents. But I am still
forced to believe, that with many, there is a want of proper love to children, which shows itself, by the entire
unwillingness manifested to give the time, furnish the
books, or provide the instruction needed. Can that parent be said to *love* his child who seems to have little
thought of his future character or usefulness ?

Many, it is to be feared, have no proper sense of the
moral obligation resting upon them, in relation to teaching
their children what is most important for them to know.
If we are to judge from the conduct of many, we should
be led to conclude they had never seen that requisition

in the word of God, "Train up a child in the way he should go," or that the apostolic injunction, "Bring up your children in the nurture and admonition of the Lord," had never fallen upon their ears. Is it more than facts and common observation will justify, if I say, that multitudes of parents seem to realize very little of the moral obligation that rests upon them, or, of their accountability to God! The thought, that they must soon meet the children, God has committed to them, at the bar of Infinite Holiness and render a full and impartial account to Him for the manner of treating them while under their care, is not so often realized as its solemnity requires. And, moreover, the intimate connexion between the character of paternal intercourse and the happiness or misery of the child, is as little considered. That man who regards it as a matter of indifference, whether his children can read the sacred Scriptures understandingly or not— whether they form their moral taste from the writings of inspired men, or heathen philosophers, must be considered as not realizing his own moral accountability. When a man appears to have very little concern whether his children form or not, such habits of mental discipline, as will enable them to investigate the evidence of those things which have the most important bearing upon their present and future welfare, it cannot be that he has a proper sense of his or their moral obligation.

To some or all of the above causes, is to be attributed a large part of the manifest public indifference to the character and usefulness of common schools. There are however, others which have a share of influence, but which will be more properly embraced in the subjects of the next Lecture. When so many circumstances combine to produce indifference to the subject, it is not strange that a great part of the benefit, that might be derived from schools, is lost to the community. In order to point out a remedy, the nature of the disease should be fully known. However malignant it may be, it cannot be presumed to be without remedy, till the best have been faithfully applied. That there is a remedy, has, I conceive, been fully proved, by the fact that in some places, where once the school seemed to be a nuisance rather than a blessing—where many within sight of the school room

were growing up in utter ignorance, and in habits of insubordination and crime ; such a change has been effected as to put a new face on almost every thing connected
with schools. Disorder has given place to decorum ;
idleness to industry ; and misimprovement of time, to a
faithful application to books, and the means of intellectual
culture.

LECTURE II.

I have in a preceding lecture adverted to the fact,
that there is a delinquency on the part of many parents,
in considering the value and importance of primary
schools. This is owing to various causes, and has the
effect to render schools far less useful than they otherwise
might be. In connexion with the former remarks, I shall
now advert to several other causes which have had an influence to prevent the usefulness of our schools.

1. There is a backwardness on the part of many parents to furnish the necessary apparatus. It is not known
or not realized, that a few dollars expended in obtaining
some very cheap apparatus, would probably add very
greatly to the usefulness of the institutions at which their
children are placed, to obtain the first rudiments of knowledge. Hence the house is left empty—there are no
globes and maps, or any other means for illustrating those
common things, which every child should be made fully
to comprehend. Curiosity is not excited, and there is
but a dull and formal round of labour, in which young
and volatile minds appear to feel but very little interest.
I am led to believe that a few dollars applied yearly in
supplying a general apparatus for the use of all the scholars, would frequently do more to increase the usefulness
of a district school, than five times the amount expended
in lengthening the school without it.* While with some

* Teachers and School Committees would do well to examine the articles of apparatus prepared by Mr. Josiah Holbrook of Boston, and for sale by most of the

parents there is a continual thirst for innovation, with many, there is a fixed aversion to change. ' There was no such thing when I was young—no such thing when I attended school, therefore it is not necessary now.'—Such is the thought, and sometimes the language of parents, when the necessity of furnishing means for the benefit of schools is urged upon them. The books, to be used by the scholars themselves in pursuing their studies, are frequently inadequate. Of what character soever, if they are possessed they must be used. In the estimation of many, it is an object of greater consequence to save a dollar, than to facilitate in an important degree, the progress of children in knowledge. Thus, there is often important loss both to parents and children. If the child might make double the progress in the same time, there is a loss of half of his time, his board, his tuition and the wear of his apparel ; all of which might be saved to the parent, and the child be as well instructed, if there were a due attention to furnishing things necessary for him in the school. This, in a series of years, would amount to no inconsiderable sum. The direct effect is to retard the progress and prevent the usefulness of the school ; the indirect effect to injure both child and parent.

The evil now under consideration proceeds sometimes from ignorance and sometimes from parsimony. There are not a few ignorant of this subject, who, were they made acquainted with it fully, would at at once be engaged to make the necessary provision for the usefulness of their school. They read no works on education—they associate very little with men of science, and especially with those who are taking a deep interest in education and making provision for the best interest of youth. So complete has this ignorance appeared in some instances, where I have had personal acquaintance, that the smile of derision could scarcely be withheld, when I have urged the subject of furnishing means for rendering the school useful, and have mentioned certain articles of apparatus that ought to be furnished for every school.

booksellers in that place. They are ingenious, simple, and not expensive. With the aid of them, every teacher might be qualified to give his pupils interesting lectures, upon the most useful principles in Geometry, Mechanics, Astronomy, &c. They are furnished at so cheap a rate as to be within the means of almost every school district.

Parsimony has its effect. The very thought of expending a few dollars in this way is sufficient to call forth the strongest opposition to every proposal for supplying the school with what is necessary for the benefit of its members. I could feel better reconciled to this state of things, if there were consistency in it. But when I see a father prevailed on to purchase finery for his children, to five times the amount asked for this object; or furniture, not to add to the comfort of his family, but only for display ; or, for luxuries, which, instead of benefiting any one, injure the health of all, I am inclined to a severity of reprehension, which prudence perhaps would not justify. I have solicited a parent to furnish his son with nothing more than a necessary book, and was repulsed with a sigh and the plea of poverty ; and the next hour I heard the *poor man* giving orders to go to the store and get a quantity of *rum* for family use, which would cost three times the amount of the book. The next hour, he was rich enough to furnish money to this very son to attend a party of pleasure, to double the amount I had asked him to pay for the book, and for all this and much more he was *rich enough.* " Will you take this little paper for your children ?" I said to another, " it will cost but a dollar." " No, I am not able." " But I am persuaded you will find it a very great benefit to your family, and you may contrive to save the amount in some way, by curtailing expenses less necessary." " I should be glad to take it, but I am in debt, and I cannot." —The next day the same parent was able to pay two dollars for his children and himself to see the " *shows*" which were exhibited ten miles off, besides the loss of a day, from their accustomed labour.

I might, were it necessary, mention a hundred illustrations of a similar kind which have occurred under my own observation. But they will be observed by yourselves, and I need only advert to them in this place.

2. Another cause of injury to the usefulness of district schools is the existence of parties within the district. There is but a minority of school districts, where there is not from some cause or other, a disagreement among parents, that eventually grows into a " party thing." This has originated, often, from causes at first very trifling, and has been in some instances continued from father to son.

Sometimes difference of religious opinions, has caused it. Sometimes parties have arisen from different political views—at other times merely the location of the school house, or of the families that compose the district, has originated difficulties and discussions that have been kept up for many years. One part of the district is more wealthy than another, or more enlightened, or a part of the families may be connected with each other by consanguinity, and combine to form a party, and in this way strife is engendered. There is sometimes a party that wishes great severity in the school, and another that wishes great laxness of government—one party is in favor of having an instructer from college, and another wishes one who has never been in sight of it. One party wishes to give high wages, and another cares only for an instructer who will keep " cheap." A thousand trifling causes give rise to these ever varying divisions; and, go where you will, you may be told of the " Congregational party," the " Baptist party," the " Presbyterian," or " Methodist," or " Universalist," or some other " party," formed by disagreement in religious opinions. You will be told of the " Democratic party," the " Federal party"—the " Administration party," or some other, growing out of political disagreement. You will be told of the " hill party"— the " meadow party," the " river party," the " school house party," &c. &c. Now the influence of all these " party divisions" and feelings, is to obstruct the usefulness of the school. Happy would it be if they were confined to parents; but our children imbibe the same feelings, which are carried to the school, and cause dissension there. All are seldom pleased with the same instructer, or, with the same mode of teaching. Where such things exist to any considerable extent, the effect is unhappy, and the benefit derived from the school is comparatively very small.

3. Another source of injury to common schools is the disposition of the more wealthy to place their children at some Academy or High School. Many are able to be at the expense of sending their children to some seminary of higher order, and hence feel but little interest in the common school. Its character is a subject of little interest. A few unsuccessful efforts, to have the school what they wish, end in discouragement, and they often say,

"Well, if we cannot have a good school at home, we *can*
send to the Academy." Such institutions are now so numerous, that there is little difficulty in carrying into execution this resolve. In this respect, it is undoubtedly
true, that Academies and Grammar schools are exerting
an unfavourable effect on the common schools of our
country.* In many other respects their influence is favourable. It is certainly a subject of great importance
to the success of elementary institutions, that the wealthy
should strive to increase their usefulness, and elevate
their character. The influence of the example of this
class does a great deal to injure these institutions, for
many are governed very much in their estimate of things,
by the opinion and conduct of the rich. By withdrawing
their influence and assistance, the work is left to those who
have not the means, and often to those who have not sufficient weight of character to afford the requisite support.
Hence the public sustain much injury, and, though it is
not the design of the rich to do wrong in this way, yet a
very little reflection must show, that an evil to the community, of considerable magnitude, is unquestionably the
result. Every thing is a public evil that serves to depre-
ciate the value of those institutions, in which the stamp of
character is fixed on the great majority of people.

4. I wish here to allude to another cause, which has
appeared to me to have an influence in preventing the
usefulness of primary schools. It is an evil of a negative

---

* A committee of the legislature of Massachusetts, in their Report on education,
have the following remarks on the influence of multiplying Academies.

"The legitimate effects of such institutions are to engross the attention and care
of the more wealthy and influential portions of the community, and proportionably
to withdraw their aid from the common free schools. The free schools in consequence, languish under the feeble and irregular efforts to maintain them, of the
poorer and less enterprising portions of the community. It is with learning as with
riches, the higher it is prized, the more it is accumulated, and as the poorer part of
the community, is also in general the less learned, the stimulus to enterprize, in
this behalf, as well as the pecuniary ability, is altogether inadequate. Had
the same efforts of the more wealthy, interested and enterprising portions of the
community, which have been devoted to the interests of academies and incorporated seminaries, been directed to the interests of the common schools, who will believe that they would not, long since, have attained a much higher character, than
they now sustain ? It is by no means improbable, that the combined efforts of the
whole community, to elevate the character of the common schools, might ere this,
have rendered them as profitable for the acquisition of a good practical education,
as are now the incorporated academies. But while that class of the community,
which has enlisted its principal efforts in favour of those academies, has by those
efforts, thus indirectly injured the cause of common education ; and also, while it has
least needed the fostering care of government, it has largely shared in its munifi-
cence, to the utter exclusion of the poorer class of the community."

character, and might, perhaps, have been better introduced in another place, and in another shape. But, still, I will give it a moment's attention here. There is a want of christian effort to raise the standard of moral influence in schools. The impulse of christian enterprise, of the present day, has led to associations for benevolent effort on almost every subject but this. We hear it mentioned, as a cause for lamentation and regret, by christians and clergymen of almost every denomination, that schools are so often schools of vice. It is a remark which has often fallen on my ear, that "Our children learn more of bad, than of good; increase in vice faster than they gain in knowledge." Indeed, so general is this feeling in many places, that christian parents are accustomed to say, when any new vicious habit is discovered in a child, "He learned it at school." Is it not surprising, that, with these facts so prominent, no combined effort among professed christians has been exerted on this subject? Is it one, on which effort would be hopeless? Is there no ground to believe, that exertion, on the part of christians, would be successful in raising the moral character of our schools? I know that individuals have felt, and have acted. Individual districts have used their best efforts to obtain moral instructers. But this is by no means sufficient. "*Union is strength.*" United and persevering effort is needed on this, as well as on other subjects with which the happiness of society is so intimately connected; and deserves attention, if the *literary* improvement of the young is alone regarded. The most orderly, the most moral school, will make the best progress in study. Moral motives are the best inducement to a faithful improvement of time. It may always be expected by committees of visitation, to find the most subordination, the best progress in learning, and the most correct deportment, where the greatest interest has been awakened in regard to the moral character of the school. I will not undertake to say, that every effort of combined christian influence would be productive of all the effect desired. But it does seem to me just, to attribute a portion of the defect, in the character of schools, to this cause.

5. A very prominent reason, why common schools are not more useful, is the imperfect qualifications of in-

tions? There may be found some exceptions to the truth of these statements, but, so far as my acquaintance has extended, these are very few.

Another class of teachers are those, who, in addition to the benefits of the district school, have resorted to an academy for a single season. Some, after attending but a few weeks, and others, after a few months, engage in the capacity of instructers. In this class there is a diversity. Some are instrumental in raising the character of their schools, while others do more hurt than good. Yet all lack instruction in those things which regard the business of teaching.

There is another class who engage in teaching for a season, for the sake of pecuniary compensation. They are preparing for college, or are members of college, when they are from twelve to sixteen years of age, and while they are paying exclusive attention to classical studies. The knowledge, which they have been able to gain of common school studies, is limited ; and when they wish to be employed as teachers, they find themselves greatly deficient. They have perhaps fine talents, and are esteemed as young gentlemen of high promise. But their qualifications for instructing a district school with success, are not better than those who were included in the class before mentioned, and they are perhaps even inferior. An example may serve to show the subject in a clearer light. Mr. Z. is a member of one of our most respectable colleges. He is a young gentleman of good talents, and ranks among the first in his class; and to good scholarship adds a very amiable temper, and strict morality. He was invited to keep a school, and engaged it. But the first day he entered it, was the first time he was ever in a common school in his life! After a few weeks of great anxiety and fatigue, he found it impossible for him to benefit the scholars, or to govern them, and asked a dismission from his employment. Similar instances, though not so strongly marked, are often occurring. The deficiency of qualifications for their business, prevents the usefulness of many teachers, and has an influence unfriendly to the character and success of our schools. There are many who are well qualified for the office among the two latter classes, but I am induced to believe they constitute but a minority.

6. Another reason why the standard of education in
common schools, has not been more elevated, "is to be
found in the unwillingness, on the part of school districts,
to make adequate compensation to teachers of approved
talents and qualifications. How else does it happen, at a
time when the merchant is overstocked with clerks, and
the professions of law and medicine are thronged with
students, there is such a lamentable deficiency in the
number of those who have the inclination and ability to
engage in the business of instruction? Is it not to be ascribed to the more liberal encouragement offered to other
employments, compared with the compensation of school
teachers? Institutions for the formation of teachers.are
desirable; but the education of teachers would be unavailing unless the districts could appreciate the importance
of affording such compensation as would command their
services. There could be no other guarantee, that those
who were educated for the purpose, would engage in the
business of teaching. Other causes have their influence,
but much of the difficulty may be traced to a disinclination on the part of districts, to make adequate compensation for the required talents and services. This is de-
monstrated by the fact, that those districts which adopt a
liberal course, have able teachers and good schools. The
business of education should be committed to the best
talents in the country; and it is vain to expect the
choicest fruits, without paying the market price. The
monthly wages of the teachers of district schools, are frequently one third less, than the amount paid to experienced clerks and journeymen mechanics in the same vicinity. In consequence of this state of things, many of
the schools are taught by those who resort to the employment as a temporary expedient, to help them in acquiring
some other profession. These persons are without experience, and can have little excitement to establish a character in a business they have resorted to as a temporary
employment. It is desirable that the inhabitants of districts should feel a deeper interest in the character of the
schools, where the characters of their children are to be
in some measure formed. If under the charge of an able
instructer a child may be advanced as far at twelve years,
as is usual at eighteen, then there is a gain of six years, to

be devoted to further improvement, or to aid the parent. It is evident that such results are attainable under the improved systems of the best instructers; and it is the part of wisdom to adopt such improvements as have been tested and sanctioned by experience."* When suitable compensation is allowed for the services of teachers, we may expect that there will be a great improvement in the character of those employed, and consequently, in the usefulness of district schools.

The next thing I shall mention, as having an influence unfriendly to the progress of common school education, is a want of books of the character needed. Many of the school-books in common use in the country, have been, and still are, entirely unfit for use. To mention one : a *Spelling-Book*, of very different orthography and pronunciation from the dictionary in common use, is now found in many, and, till lately, has been found in almost all the country schools.† Many of the books are not adapted to the capacity of children, or do not present a satisfactory view of the subjects on which they treat.

But this difficulty is in a degree obviated, by improvement in the character of some of the books designed for common schools. Could all the best books extant, be introduced extensively, great improvement would ensue. It is a subject of congratulation, that much effort is using for this purpose.

The last thing of which I shall treat in this connexion, is the improper construction and the inconvenient location of school-houses. Many are cold, so that in the winter a part of the scholars must either be very uncomfortable, or make constant disturbance by going to the fire. In others the chimney is defective, and the house is constantly filled with smoke. The seats and desks, in a majority of school-rooms, are badly constructed, so that it is very tedious to sit in them. They are often so narrow as to make it impossible to write with convenience. The desk is usually put so far from the seat that small scholars can scarcely write without putting themselves in a very uncomfortable posture.

* A. C. Flagg, Superintendent of Common Schools, N. Y.
† As a substitute for this, *The National Spelling-Book*, by *Mr. Emerson,* recently published at Boston, may be strongly recommended for adoption.

3*

The location of school-houses is often governed by a regard to the centre of the district, without regard to any thing else. We often observe them built on some eminence where the bleak winds of winter have no obstruction, and where there is no screen from the intense heat of summer; when at the same time some inviting grove is near, of which such advantage might have been taken as to have prevented both wind and heat from causing any annoyance. There are but few districts where some convenient place might not be found for the site of the school-house, which would promote the comfort of the scholars in both seasons of the year.

The health and convenience of the scholars should be regarded as very important objects in the construction and location of school-houses, and it is just to attribute a part of the failure in the usefulness of schools, to the negligence in these particulars, manifested by many districts.

LECTURE III.

HAVING adverted in the preceding lecture, to certain existing evils, unfriendly to the character and usefulness of common schools, I shall, in this, call your attention to *the requisite qualifications of an instructer*. The subject is one of high importance. It is not every one of those, even, who possess the requisite literary attainments, who is qualified to assume the direction of a school. Many entirely fail of usefulness, though possessed of highly cultivated minds. Other ingredients enter into the composition of a good schoolmaster. Among these *common sense* is the first. This is a qualification exceedingly important, as in teaching school one has constant occasion for its exercise. Many, by no means deficient in intellect, are not persons of common sense. I mean by the term, that faculty by which things are seen as they are. It implies judgment and discrimination, and a proper sense of propriety in regard to the common affairs of life. It leads us to form judicious plans of action, and to be governed by our circumstances, in such a way as men in general will approve. It is the exercise of reason, uninfluenced by passion or prejudice. It is in man nearly what instinct is in brutes. It is very different from genius or talent, as they are commonly defined, but is better than either. It never blazes forth with the splendour of noon, but shines with a constant and useful light.

2. *Uniformity of temper* is another important trait in the character of an instructer. Where this is wanting, it is hardly possible to govern or to teach with success. He, whose temper is constantly varying, can never be uniform in his estimation of things around him. Objects change in their appearance as passions change. What appears right in any given hour may seem wrong in the next. What appears desirable to-day, may be beheld with aversion to-morrow. An uneven temper, in any situation of life, subjects one to many inconveniences. But when placed in a situation where his every action is observed, and where his authority must be in constant exercise, the man who labours under this malady is especially unfortunate. It is impossible for him to gain and preserve respect among his pupils. No one who comes under the rule of a person of uneven temper, can know what to expect or how to act.

3. A capacity to *understand and discriminate character*, is highly important to him who engages in school-keeping. The dispositions of children are so various, the treatment and government of parents so dissimilar, that the most diversified modes of governing and teaching need to be employed. The instructer who is not able to discriminate, but considers all alike, and treats all alike, does injury to many. The least expression of disapprobation to one, is often more than the severest reproof to another ; a word of encouragement will be sufficient to excite attention in some, while another will require to be urged, by every motive that can be placed before him. All the varying shades of disposition and capacity should be quickly learned by the instructer, that he may benefit all and do injustice to none. Without this, well meant efforts may prove hurtful, because ill-directed, and the desired object may be defeated, by the very means used to obtain it.

4. It is desirable that teachers should possess much *decision of character.* In every situation of life this trait is important, but in none more so than in that of which I am treating. The little world, by which he is surrounded, is the miniature of the older community. Children have their aversions and partialities, their hopes and fears, their plans, schemes, propensities and desires. These are often in collision with each other, and not unfrequently in collision with the laws of the school, and in opposition to their own best interest. Amidst all these, the instructer should be able to pursue a uniform course. He ought not to be easily swayed from what he considers right. If he be easily led from his purpose, or induced to vary from established rules, his school must become a scene of disorder. Without decision, the teacher loses the confidence and respect of his pupils. I would not say, that, if convinced of having committed an error, or of having given a wrong judgment, you should persist in the wrong. But I would say, that it should be known as one of your first principles in school-keeping, that what is required must be complied with in every case, unless cause can be shown why the rule ought, in a given instance, to be dispensed with. There should *then* be a frank confession of error. In a word, without decision of purpose in a teacher, his scholars can never be brought under that discipline, which is requisite for his own ease and convenience, or for their improvement in knowledge.

5. A schoolmaster ought to be *affectionate.* The human heart is so constituted, that it cannot resist the influence of kindness. When affectionate intercourse is the offspring of those kind feelings which arise from true benevolence, it will have an influence on all around. It leads to ease in behaviour, and genuine politeness of manners. It is especially desirable in those who are surrounded by the young. Affectionate parents usually see their children exhibit similar feelings. Instructers, who cultivate this state of temper, will generally excite the same in their scholars. No object is more important than to gain the love and good will of those we are to teach. In no way is this more easily accomplished than by a kind interest manifested in their welfare; an interest which is exhibited by actions as well as words. This cannot fail of being attended with desirable results.

6. A just *moral discernment*, is of pre-eminent importance in the character of an instructer. Unless governed by a consideration of his moral obligation, he is but poorly qualified to discharge the duties which devolve upon him, when placed at the head of a school. He is himself a moral agent, and accountable to himself, to his employers, to his country and to his God, for the faithful discharge of duty. If he have no moral sensibility, no fear of disobeying the laws of God, no regard for the institutions of our holy religion, how can he be expected to lead his pupils in the way that they should go? The cultivation of virtuous propensities is more important to children than even their intellectual culture. The *virtuous* man, though illiterate, will be happy, while the learned, if *vicious*, must be miserable in proportion to his attainments. The remark of the ancient philosopher, that " boys ought to be taught that which they will most need to practise when they come to be men," is most true. To cultivate virtuous habits, and awaken virtuous principles ;—to excite a sense of duty to God, and of dependence on Him, should be the first objects of the teacher. If he permit his scholars to indulge in vicious habits—if he regard nothing as sin, but that which is a transgression of the laws of the school, if he suffer lying, profaneness, or other crimes, to pass unnoticed and unpunished, he is doing an injury for which he can in no way make amends. An instructer without moral feeling, not only brings ruin to the children placed under his care, but does injury to their parents, to the neighbourhood, to the town, and, doubtless, to other generations. The moral character of instructers should be considered a subject of very high importance ; and let every one, who knows himself to be immoral, renounce at once the thought of such an employment, while he continues to disregard the laws of God, and the happiness of his fellow men. Genuine piety is highly desirable in every one entrusted with the care and instruction of the young ; but morality, at least, should be *required,* in every candidate for that important trust.

7. Passing over many topics connected with those already mentioned, I shall now remark on the necessary literary qualifications of a schoolmaster. It will at once be apparent that no one is qualified for this business, who

has not a thorough knowledge of the branches required to be taught in common schools. These are Reading, Writing, Grammar, Arithmetic, Geography, and in some cases, the History of the United States. All these branches are necessary, to enable individuals to perform the common business and common duties of life. The three first are requisite in writing a letter on business or to a friend. The fourth is required in the business transactions of every day. The two last are necessary to enable every one to understand what he reads in the common newspapers, or in almost every book which comes within his reach. Of each of these branches, the instructer should certainly have a thorough knowledge; for. he ought to have a full knowledge of what he is to teach. As he is to lay the *foundation* of an education, he should be well acquainted with the first principles of science. Of the letters of the alphabet such disposition is made, as to produce an immense number of words, to each of which a distinct meaning is given, "The nature and power of letters, and just method of spelling words," should be very distinctly understood. If there be defect in knowledge here, there must be a defect in teaching. A man cannot be expected to teach that which he does not know himself. Among all the defects I have witnessed in the literary qualification of instructers, the most common, by far the most common, have been here. Among a great number, both of males and females, I have found *very few* who possessed the requisite knowledge of the nature and power of letters, and rules of spelling. The defect originates in the fact, that these subjects are neglected after childhood, and much that is learned then is subsequently forgotten. Teachers, afterwards, especially of academies, presume that these subjects are familiar, and seldom make the inquiry of such as are qualifying themselves to teach, whether they have sufficient knowledge on these points. As a considerable part of every school is composed of those who are learning to spell and read, much importance is attached to the requisite qualifications of the teacher, to lay a proper foundation for subsequent attainments.

Every one who teaches school ought to be eminently a good reader. The habit of reading, early formed, often continues through life. It is not to be expected that a child will learn to read with correctness and ease, without being well taught. Nor can it be expected that one will teach well, who does not himself know how to read with propriety. Hardly any thing is more difficult than to correct a bad habit of reading, especially where it has been continued for several years.

The value of the art of reading well, is discussed by Dr. Porter, in his Analysis of Delivery. He remarks that " in this country, where literary institutions of every kind are springing up, and where the advantages of education are open to all, no one is qualified to hold a respectable rank, in well-bred society, who is unable to read, in an interesting manner, the works of others. They who regard this exercise as a polite accomplishment, merely, forget to how many purposes of business, of rational entertainment and religious duty, the talent may be applied. Of the multitudes who are not called to speak in public, including the whole of one sex, and all but a few comparatively of the other, there is no one to whom the art of reading in a graceful and impressive manner may not be of great value." To the teacher of children, this is an acquirement of very great importance ; and no one is qualified to engage in teaching, till he is able to read well.

A thorough knowledge of Arithmetic is also indispensable to the schoolmaster. I do not mean that smattering of the science, which so often passes for a knowledge of it ; but a thorough acquaintance with its principles. To be able, by the aid of rules and manuscripts, to solve the question given, is very far from being the knowledge necessary. No one is properly qualified in this branch of science, until able, from his own knowledge of its principles, to originate rules, even if they were not given in his book. He should be able to tell the " why and wherefore" in every operation, else he is not prepared to teach. The pupil will derive but little practical benefit from the study, and every process will be mechanical. As this science is necessary in every condition of life, as it is to be used almost every day in our lives, great importance should be attached to the mode of teaching it. Mr. Parkhurst justly remarks, " It is the practical utility of any branch of knowledge that gives it its chief value. The

difference between the practical utility of the various
branches of knowledge is very great." A knowledge of
the nature, power and combination of numbers, whether
we regard its effect as important to mental discipline, or
its use in the business of life, must be considered among
the most important acquirements.*

The instructer is expected to teach Geography ; and
of course he ought to understand it well himself. This
science is very interesting and useful, and is studied in
nearly all the primary schools. The treatises on the subject, which have been written within a few years, have
done something to facilitate the study, and lighten the labour of the teacher ; but no book can supply the place of
the living instructer. He ought to be able to make the
study more practical than it is possible for any book to make
it, however well written. The scholar may learn many
interesting facts in this science, without the aid of any
instructer; but this will not render it proper, for one to
attempt to teach, without a thorough and connected view
of the whole science, and without being able to explain
what is doubtful, and illustrate what is obscure.

English Grammar is made a study in all our district
schools, and is a very important branch of knowledge. It
is that which teaches how to speak and write, correctly.
If it be an object, then, to be intelligible in conversation
and writing, it is certainly important to be well versed in
this science. But I am obliged, here to remark, that it
has appeared to me, many have overlooked the proper
definition of grammar, and while professedly attending to
it, have neglected nearly every thing but syntax. To
learn to apply the common rules of syntax, to the written
language, which we find in some book, is what is commonly regarded as learning grammar.

But this has certainly little claim to be called the study
of grammar, which should always be explained as the
study of language. There are several things, besides
mere syntax, which are important. One may have ability

* Several valuable treatises on this subject are now before the public. One of
the most useful I consider to be Smith's Mental and Practical Arithmetic. I cannot better express my opinion of the merits of this work, than in the use of the
words of the Editor of the Journal of Education, who says, "it has been compiled,
as all books for school use ought to be compiled, from the results of actual experiment in the school room. It is entirely a practical work, combining the merits of
Colburn's system with copious practice on the slate. '

to parse the words in a sentence,—may be able to apply rules, rather by habit than otherwise, and yet know but very little of language. As in arithmetic, so here, the teacher who is properly qualified, should be able to originate rules, and to illustrate those principles on which they are founded. If he is not able to explain the propriety of the division of language into parts of speech,—if he is not able to exhibit the reason of the means applied, and the divisions which are made, he is not able to benefit those materially, whom he is to instruct. The great deficiency, which has been observed in the qualifications of many in this branch, makes it proper to dwell longer upon it. Owing to this, many scholars have imbibed so strong prejudices against the study as to engage in it with great reluctancy, or neglect it entirely, after having devoted some time to it. Hardly any thing is more common than to hear it denominated a dry study, while it is a fact, that if properly taught, scarcely any study is calculated to excite more interest. Instructers should be well acquainted with their own language, in order to inspire a love for the study of it, in their pupils.*

A requisition, I believe, recently made in some of the states, is, that the civil and political history of the United States should be made a branch of study in common schools. This is certainly very just. Every citizen of a republic, has a deep interest in knowing the history of the country that he calls his own. He ought to know, by what means its civil and religious institutions have been established. He ought to be familiar with the obstacles which his fathers met and overcome, in achieving the blessings of civil and religious freedom which he enjoys. The names of his benefactors ought to be indelibly engraved on his memory. Love of country may thus be inspired. A knowledge of many facts in our country's history must be very limited, after its most interesting times shall have gone by, unless the history of these great events is taught in our primary schools. Very soon all the hoary headed patriots who lived and acted in those

---

* For the use of the younger classes in this subject, in our common schools, I would recommend the Elements of English Grammar, by *Mr. Frost*, one of the Masters in the Boston public schools Its plan is after Murray, but his definitions and language are simplified as far as the nature of the subject will admit, to meet the understanding of children. It also embraces more copious examples and exercises in Parsing, than is usual in elementary treatises.

4

" times that tried men's souls," will have passed away. Instructers, therefore, should be qualified to teach history, and to interest their scholars in it. This they cannot do without a knowledge of it themselves.

History is the " school of politicks," and in a government like ours, it is necessary that every freeman should in some sense be a politician.*

With a knowledge of the above subjects, the teacher may be enabled to answer the *letter* of the law. But it seems plain to me, that some other branches are requisite in order that he may be properly qualified, to engage in directing the studies and disciplining the minds of the young, Among these I shall mention Intellectual Arithmetic, the Constitution of the United States, and of the state in which he lives,† Rhetoric, Natural Philosophy, Chemistry, and Moral Philosophy. By attention to intellectual arithmetick, he will gain a habit of originating rules, by which he will be able to explain the reasons of the operations in written arithmetic, and exhibit to his pupils the process by which an answer is obtained.

He should be familiar with the Constitution of the United States, because, it is necessary frequently to refer the young to the bill of rights, by which their privileges are secured. The earlier children are made acquainted with this, the more likely will they be to respect the law, and yield a cheerful obedience to it. It is important, that every child should be told something of the constitution of his own state. The instructer should be acquainted with it, in order to call the attention of his youthful charge to those subjects in which they have a common interest. If Hannibal was old enough at seven years of age "to take an oath that he would never be at peace with the Romans," our children, at school, are old enough to have their attention turned to the principles of the government which they are to support.‡

* I know of no School History of the United States which may be considered perfect; but the one most deserving of recommendation is probably *Goodrich's*, especially since the appearance of Mr. Emerson's Appendix and book of Questions adapted to this work.

I would here mention a little work which has just made its appearance, entitled, " *Historical and Descriptive Lessons*," embracing sketches of the History, Character and Customs of all Nations, which promises to be a useful companion to the study of Geography. The work is published at Brattleboro'.

† On the subject of Chemistry, *Webster's Elements* may be recommended.

‡ I wish some one in every State would follow the example of *Mr. Jones* of Massachusetts, who has published an edition of the Constitutions of the United States and of Massachusetts, divided into paragraphs, with questions for exercise.

Rhetoric is a subject with which the instructer ought to be acquainted, because he ought to assist his scholars in arranging their thoughts into sentences, and commitiug them to paper. The older scholars in all our schools should be instructed in letter-writing and composition. To be able to write a letter, or to express one's thoughts on any subject, that may claim attention, is highly important. It is what every one will, more or less frequently have occasion to do. If some attention be not given to the subject in school, there will be mortification and regret in after life. Our children ought to be taught *that* at school, which they will most need in the common business and duties of manhood. A knowledge of Rhetoric is necessary to the teacher, to enable him to *correct* the compositions of his scholars, and to give them such rules for the arrangement of sentences, as may be a guide to them in their efforts.

Some acquaintance with Natural Philosophy and the first principles of Chemistry, will enable the instructer to explain to his pupils, many facts which will rouse their curiosity and excite a thirst for more knowledge on these interesting subjects. Many facts are frequently observed by young children, the reason of which they are not able to understand, but which they have capacity to comprehend, if a familiar illustration were given. Those appearances, frequently, which excite no attention on account of their commonness, would awaken very high interest, if explained in a familiar manner. Such are the turning of a wheel, the power of a wedge, or screw, the freezing of water—the formation of clouds, rain, and snow—the transmission of sound, &c. &c. What the young most need, is to learn to think and to investigate. Whatever serves to fix a habit of reflection is of incalculable importance. By some simple illustration the attention of the child may often become interested, and a train of thoughts excited, not less important to himself, than that sublime theory suggested to the mind of Newton by the fall of an apple. The instructer has many opportunities to direct the attention of his scholars to first principles of natural science, without diverting it from other subjects of study. He should certainly then have that knowledge of these branches which will enable him thus to impart instruction and delight.

I mentioned moral philosophy, as one of the branches

with which an instructer should be familiar. I am well
aware that this study is much neglected. But, that it has
been neglected, heretofore, is no reason why it should be
neglected still. If man were guided by instinct alone, to
the attainment of his best good, the subject would be unimportant. Every one knows he may fail of this, either
by inaction, or by ill directed effort. " He finds himself
led astray by his passions, and he looks in vain for a safe
guide, to the example of others. It is then the dictate of
wisdom, to inquire by what means these wayward propensities may be subdued, and the feet be guided in the paths
of peace. Happy are they who are led to make this inquiry in their early years. Happier are they, whom the
hand of instruction, before they are able to make the inquiry for themselves, has been guiding in the path of
knowledge and virtue."* This is the appropriate work
of the parent and the primary school teacher. But alas,
how many parents wholly neglect it! Hence a greater
responsibility devolves on the teacher. " Moral philosophy," says Dr. Paley, " is that science which teaches
men their duty, and the reasons of it." This then is the
knowledge " which the young most need, and which the
friendly instructer should sedulously impart." It is this
which " tends to recall us from low pursuits—to fix our
affections on better objects—to form us to such a character, and direct us to such a course of conduct, as will secure the divine approbation, and be most promotive of our
own happiness, and that of the community of which we
are members. It teaches a knowledge of ourselves, of
human nature in general, of our Creator, and of the rela-
tions we sustain to him, and to our fellow creatures." Can
any one, then, be properly qualified to train the infant
mind, who has not some acquaintance with this science ?

The instructer ought to gain all the knowledge he can
of the nature of his business, in order to be qualified to
commence his important labours. On this subject I shall,
however, remark in another place. I have only to add,
in conclusion of this lecture, that I have not placed the
qualifications necessary for the schoolmaster, any higher
than is requisite, in order to make it safe to trust him with
the care of young immortals, who are forming characters
for this world and the next.

* Parkhurst.

LECTURE IV.

To the subjects mentioned in the preceding Lecture, you have given attention, and have been, I trust, led to make the inquiry whether you possess the requisite qualifications for the important business to which you have turned your attention. I shall now proceed to give you some general directions, which I consider important to your success and usefulness. You will expect me to use great plainness, for the subject requires it.

The first direction which I wish to give is the following :—*Endeavour to become acquainted with the nature of your employment.*

This is important to your *personal enjoyment.* We cannot be happy, when we do not know what to do or how to act. To engage in a business of which you have no adequate idea, must, therefore, subject you to much unhappiness. The situation of an instructer is very responsible. It is exceedingly important that you should be acquainted with the nature and amount of this responsibility, and of the duties which will devolve on you when placed at the head of a school. Without some knowledge of the duties you have to perform, the perplexities and difficulties that may arise, and the constant care that must press upon you, you cannot but experience much inquietude and uneasiness. The very different tempers of those you have to teach and govern, and the wide difference of treatment they have received from their parents at home, will give you much trouble, if you awake to the reality of your situation only when a mountain of care presses upon you.

Form not expectations that cannot be realized, for disappointment will not only make you unhappy at the time, but will unfit you for the duties of the moment. The nature of your business should, as much as possible, be learned beforehand. This is dictated by reason, and experience certainly confirms it. No one engages in any department of manual labour, till he has gained some knowledge of its details. No one commences a journey,

4*

till he has learned the direction he is to go, and the probable character of the road, and of the people he is to find upon the way. No one proposes emigration to a distant part of the country, till he has made diligent inquiry as to the conveniences and privileges, as well as the privations and hardships, which will attend a removal. " Who goeth a warfare, till he has counted the cost, or builds a temple, till he has considered whether he be able to finish it ?" · The reason is obvious. When we expect hardship, we are prepared to endure it with patience ; when we look for trial, we can meet it with comparative composure. If. I foresee that the journey, I am to take, will be attended with extra fatigue, I can bear it without complaint. If I expect the road I am to travel is one of exceeding roughness, I can endure its asperities without a murmur.

But if on the other hand, I reckon upon ten miles and it proves fifteen ; if I expect a good road, and it proves a bad one ; it will appear both longer and worse than it really is ; and what I might have borne with composure, I cannot endure without disquietude and pain. If I expect to arrive home in an hour, and it takes two hours, the last hour will seem longer than two, ordinarily, for I am disappointed, and disappointment makes me unhappy. It gives every thing around me an unpleasant aspect.

In the same way, disappointment in regard to the nature of your business as schoolmasters, will have an important effect on your enjoyment. For, if you form only ideal notions—if you expect, in spite of evidence to the contrary, that every thing will be " perfectly pleasant"— if you suppose the labour to be performed is easy, and without any thing to render it difficult and disagreeable, you will be entirely unprepared to bear the trials invariably attendant upon it. When these trials come, you will experience disappointment, which will make you unhappy at the time, and of course unfit you for the duties of the hour. In a discontented state, you are not prepared to proceed with that, which, at another time, might be perfectly easy. Nor, in this state, are you prepared to enjoy what is pleasant and agreeable. It is generally true, that we bear unexpected difficulties with *far less* composure, than when we had expected them, and of course made up our minds to bear them.

I do not assert, that you can learn any thing perfectly in regard to the nature of your employment, without *experience*. It is not possible in this or other callings. The physician, attorney, and minister, do not expect it. But they still use all the means within their reach, to become acquainted with the nature of their several professions, as far as may be, before entering upon them. This is as necessary for the teacher as for them.

Do you inquire, how this can be done ? I would say, first, read on this subject whatever has been written, to which you can gain access. Several periodical publications have devoted more or less attention to it. The Journal of Education has thrown much light upon it. The School Magazine should be found in the hands of every schoolmaster. But there is, it must be acknowledged, a great deficiency in works on this subject.

Again, you may learn something of your business, by observing the peculiar natures of children. They are men in miniature. Like men they have their prepossessions and aversions. Some, that come under your care, have been governed at home ; others have not. Some are quick of apprehension, others dull. Some will have learning, and desire to make all the improvement of which they are capable ; others will have no taste for learning, and no desire to be improved. Some will be easily governed ; others will require all your wisdom, firmness and prudence, to restrain them from what is wrong, and lead them in a better course. Some have formed habits of application ; and others, have been brought up in idleness. Some will be too bashful ; others, too bold. Some will be benevolent and affectionate ; others, selfish and unsocial. Some will be found very nearly what you desire them to be ; others, the opposite in every thing. Such are the diversities that will be found in every school.

You may be equally benefited, perhaps, in learning the nature of your business, by reflecting on the great variety in the character of parents.

Some will wish you to govern the school, others will wish *to govern you*. One parent wishes you to be very strict, another to be very lenient. Some will wish you to whip your scholars, others dread nothing so much as that their favourite children should feel "the rod of correction." Some will wish you to pursue a certain mode of teaching, others will be strong advocates for a system entirely different. Some will wish you to close early, others will fear that you will not keep your hours. One man will admonish you to show no partiality, and another will solicit very particular attention to *his* children. Mr. A. is willing to trust the school entirely to your management, while Mr. B. is very jealous, lest you assume more than your delegated power. Some will be very anxious to have the school successful, others will be entirely indifferent to the subject. Some will cheerfully furnish all the necessary books, while others will think it enough to send their children without any, or with such as are entirely unfit for use. Some will be ready to listen to every complaint of their children, and others will teach them to "tell no tales out of school." The wealthy may perhaps think *their* children entitled to more attention than those of the poor, and the latter may be ready to imagine such a distinction, even if none really exist. In this enumeration I have not mentioned a single difficulty which I have not had personal opportunity to observe, and in regard to many of them I have noticed the same thing in many different places. This diversity among children and among parents, renders it very necessary for you to reflect much on the manner of securing that influence with both, which will enable you to benefit your scholars in the greatest degree. You must be prepared to govern your scholars at school, and *may* often find it necessary to exert nearly as much influence with *parents* as with them.

You may also learn something of the nature of your business, by frequent conversation with teachers. They will be able to impart to you the results of their own experience. Be not disheartened if they tell you of "strong prejudices against every innovation which you may find it necessary to make; that, with some, reason is but a name, and that every attempt to influence them by it, will be as unsuccessful as that of Canute to rule the sea. There is," they will tell you, "an almost universal disposition to believe, that books for study, methods of learning and teaching, common when we were young, must be as good, at least, as any of the newest in use;

that the spirit of inquiry, awakened within a few years past, is entirely unknown to the great mass of the people; that most men read but little, and have had no opportunity to investigate the character of proposed improvements, or to witness the results of successful experiments." Listen not to such language of your brethren so far as to be discouraged, but only for the purpose of knowing the difficulties in your way, in order that you may rise above them.

After having gained all the knowledge within your reach, on the subjects already mentioned, it is of equal importance for you to understand the nature of your business, as it regards *the mode of teaching*. Without this you can hardly hope for success.

Many have appeared to imbibe the sentiment, that the whole business consists in keeping order in the school-room, and going through a daily round of recitations in reading, spelling and writing, the teacher, meanwhile, furnishing copies, making pens, and performing certain operations in arithmetic, which the students may not be able to perform themselves. But all this has little-better claim to the name of teaching, than the chatter of the magpie has to be dignified with the title of language. Such a course may be entirely destitute of intellectual exercise; and is like the operation of a machine.*

Let it be well fixed in your minds, that *to teach is to communicate ideas*. To teach, then, it is indispensable that you should be *understood*. The words of an experienced teacher† are in point. "Use language that your scholars can understand. Let your illustrations be drawn from topicks within their knowledge. It is entirely out of place in a common elementary school, to use the language of a professor in the University, or to *affect* the use of terms understood only by the more advanced student.

---

* A writer in the Journal of Education, No. 10, has made some remarks on this mode of teaching, which are worthy of particular attention. Speaking of a school conducted in this manner, he says: "There is something so mechanical in the exercises of a school, that I can never contemplate it without disgust. Even the very books with which our children are furnished, instead of being used as a treasury of materials for mental exercise, are regarded as so many little machines, by which all the requisite operations of the school are performed. And in the use of them on the present plan, there is very little, if any, more intellectual exercise than among the children in a cotton manufactory.

† Mr. Rand. Christian Mirror.

If you teach children, use the language of children. Let it be pure and grammatical; but you convey no instruction, if it be above their comprehension. When you compare a thing unknown, with another thing equally unknown, how can the child be the wiser for it? In talking with your scholars, use their own phraseology, and condescend to their capacities." As I shall have occasion, in another lecture, to enlarge on this subject, I shall only add here, that you may learn something of the true system of teaching, by recollecting the manner, in which you have yourselves obtained ideas. The teacher should put himself in the place of the child, and then inquire what course, it would be necessary for him to take, to gain a knowledge of any subject with which he was not familiar.

No means within your reach, for learning the nature of your business, should be left unemployed. If all which are desirable be not accessible, those which are so should be used with the greater fidelity.

A second direction is, *Consider the responsibility of the station you are to occupy.*

If in deciding to devote yourselves to the employment of teaching, you have been excited by the hope that it will be less arduous than other employments in which you have engaged, you have altogether mistaken the nature of its duties and cares. The very first day of your trial will dissipate the delusion. The sight of a company of blooming children and youth, "awed by your presence, waiting for your directions, and turning their inquiring eyes on you, to guide them in acquiring knowledge and forming habits," will tell you at once, in language more forcible than any that I can use, that on you devolves an arduous task—to you, parents are confiding an important trust—to you, your country is assigning a solemn charge.

The responsibility of your situation may be realized in some measure, by considering that these children have minds naturally dark, which are to be enlightened. They are ignorant of that which they most need to know, and must be instructed. They are tender twigs, ready to receive any direction that may be given them. They are miniature men, who are destined to occupy the places of those who are now active on the stage of life. Yes, in the little community with which you are surrounded, there *may* be a Franklin, or a Washington ; or, on the other hand, a Robespierre or a Bonaparte, according to the cast of character which they derive from your efforts. In a country like ours, where character is the passport to the most important stations in society, and where offices are open to every one who shows himself worthy of the confidence of the people, the responsibility of the teacher is even higher, than in those countries where estates and offices are hereditary. He who is selected to educate a prince, even in the first rudiments of science, considers his station as highly responsible. But in a country like our own, every instructer should consider his responsibility equally great.

Again, you may learn your responsibility by considering the *influence which you may exert,* over your youthful charge.

If you succeed in gaining their love, your influence will be greater in some respects than that of parents themselves. It will be in your power, to direct them in almost any path you choose. You may lead them to form habits of application and industry, or by neglecting them, permit them to form those of idleness and indifference. You may win them either to a love of learning and a respect for virtue, or by your negligence and unfaithfulness, you may suffer them to become regardless of both. You have power to lead them to a cultivation of the social affections, to make them kind, benevolent and humane, or, by your neglect, they may become the reverse of every thing that is lovely, amiable and generous. It will be in your power, greatly to assist them in learning to make nice distinctions in the examination of moral conduct ; and to govern their own actions accordingly; or you may, by your unfaithfulness, suffer them to. contract the habit of pursuing, regardless of consequences, every thing they desire, and opposing with temper, every thing that counteracts their wishes. You may teach them the duty of yielding submission to proper authority, and to equitable law, or by suffering them to disregard authority and trample on laws with impunity, teach them to oppose all restraint, and consider all law as unnecessary and oppressive. You may do something towards leading them to cultivate that public spirit, which is so essential to the well being of a

free country, or you may train them in those habits of
selfishness, which will unfit them to be citizens of a republic.

If the consequences of your influence over them were
to cease in *this* world, your responsibility would be less,
far less, than it actually is. But, no. Revelation assures
us, that our future condition will be decided by the character formed in this world,—that man will be rewarded
in the world to come, according to the deeds done in this.
The formation of character is not then a matter important
in relation to *this life only.* The children with whom you
are to be associated, are all the children of one great
Creator. They are a part of His extensive kingdom.
They are the subjects of His government, and are under
the highest obligation to obey His wise and holy laws.
He has given them such laws, and made such require-
ments of them, as are necessary for their happiness. He
has enjoined upon them to "Remember their Creator in
the days of their youth," "to love their neighbors as
themselves"—and to honour their parents. He has prohibited profaneness and falsehood. He has enjoined the
duty of gratitude to the Saviour, and of repentance for
sin ; and each individual committed to your care is liable
every day to be summoned away from this world, and to
render up an account of the "deeds done in the body."
Nor is it impossible, that the influence you will exert over
them by your example and instructions, may deeply affect
them in regard to these solemn considerations. And as
their happiness, present and eternal, depends on the temper they exhibit in regard to the character and laws of
God, your responsibility is indescribably great.· If you are
so happy as to lead them to love Him who has said, "suffer little children to come unto me, and forbid them not,"
how great the benefit you may confer upon them ! But
if by your example and instruction you should lead them
away from the paths of wisdom, how great is the injury !
They will be more likely to listen to counsel and advice,
from a beloved teacher, than from almost any other person. They will generally be more disposed to regard
what you say to them on the subject of their moral obligation, than what is said to them by their parents or their
minister. This talent which you are permitted to occupy,

is one for the improvement of which you are accountable
to God. And how much does it increase the interest of
your calling! Hence I should be guilty of unfaithfulness
if I should neglect to direct your attention to your own
moral obligation. You, as well as the youths committed
to your charge, have an account to render to Him who
gave you your existence. If you are put in possession of
an influence, which, if properly exerted, may greatly aug-
ment individual happiness, as well as that of the nation,
or, on the other hand, if not properly exerted, may, in the
same ratio, increase the amount of human misery; fail
not to ponder well the subject, which is to throw upon you
so important a responsibility.

LECTURE V.

THE next direction which I shall give, is, *Endeavour
to ascertain by what means you are to gain that ascendancy
over your pupils, which is necessary, in order to confer on
them the highest degree of benefit.*

You well know that there is a great diversity in the
influence exerted by different individuals in the same
circumstances. If you investigate the subject, you will
find various degrees of influence exerted by *clergymen.*
While one man's flock are ready to pluck out their eyes
and give him, that of another are hardly willing to render him that which is his due. Both, however, sustain
the character of God's ambassadors. If you look at the
influence of two military commanders, to the orders of
the one, you will see the utmost attention paid, while
to those of the other, very little obedience is shown.
The same will be observed in two schools. To all that
is said by one instructer, the highest deference is paid,
while in another school we witness the reverse. Now
it is certain that there must be some reason for this
difference. In each of these instances, and many more

5

to which I might allude, the same individuals sustain the same office or trust. It does not therefore consist in the office itself.

If you look back to the characters of the different instructers, under whom you were placed, you will probably find that to some of them you listened with great deference, that you were anxious to please them and desirous of gaining their good opinion, while to the esteem of others, you were indifferent, and regardless whether you gained their good will or not. To meet with some of them *now*, affords you pleasure, while to meet with others is a source of no satisfaction. And what is the reason? You will answer, that these different men were of very different characters; that they showed very different degrees of interest in their business; that they possessed very different qualifications and very unequal shares of solicitude for your welfare. Let me ask, farther, which were those traits which pleased you, and which pleased the school generally? Was the master pleasant and obliging, or was he morose and ill-humoured? and with which was the school best pleased? Was he affable and condescending, or was he mute and regardless of every thing but his own ease? and on which account did you like him? Was he punctual to his time, to his promises and to his threats, or regardless of all? and on which of these accounts were you willing to be directed by him? Did he appear affectionate and kind in all his intercourse, or did he seem to delight in giving you pain and fear? and with which of these traits of character were you better pleased? Did he convince you that he was your friend, and that he desired your good, even at the expense of his own ease? 'or did he act as if he were the friend of no one but himself? Was he ever ready to assist you to the extent of his ability, or did he send you away without answering your questions or solving your difficulties? Did he prove to you by his whole conduct that he desired to benefit the school in the greatest degree of which he was capable, or did he appear to regard little else than to obtain the stipulated reward? and on which account do you now remember him with affection and interest?

You are at no loss to decide on these questions. Let these questions then, serve as a directory to you, in making the inquiry, how you can secure that degree of confidence, on the part of your scholars, which will enable you to benefit them in the degree which you desire. If particular directions on the subject are required, I will say,

First, Endeavour to convince the scholars *that you are their friend,*—that you are friendly to their improvement, and desire their best good. It will not take long to convince them of this, if you are so in reality; and if you pursue the course with them, which would, with your own instructer, have excited this belief in you, in regard to him. Remember, however, that merely a declaration of being their friend, will be very far from proving you to be such, or convincing them of it. You would not have been convinced by the mere declaration of your instructer, if this declaration had not been supported by his conduct. Expect not then, that telling your scholars, you are a friend, and greatly desire their good, will gain you their confidence. You must *prove* it to them by showing a greater regard for their welfare than for your own ease.

Secondly, In order to secure a proper degree of their confidence, *you must not be hasty.* Be not hasty to reprove, be not hasty to praise; be not hasty to promise, be not hasty to threaten; be not hasty to punish, and be not hasty to forget a fault. There is somewhere an old proverb, "Haste makes waste, and waste brings want." Haste in schools in any of the particulars specified, will bring want of confidence. Whatever is done in haste is seldom done well. In school it must of necessity subject you frequently to the mortification of countermanding your order, of failing to fulfil your promise, or of exciting the belief in the minds of your scholars that you are forgetful. It is generally true, that in every situation, the deliberate man accomplishes the most; but, in none is deliberation more important, than in him who is to exercise authority over a large community. Loss of time is not, however, the greatest inconvenience of being hasty in school; there must be loss of confidence on the part of the scholars. You are well aware that you place but little confidence in any man who bears the character of being hasty, be his calling or station what it may.

Thirdly, If you wish to secure the confidence of your school, never allow yourself *to speak angrily* or unusually loud, and be sure never to fret or scold. All these things are disagreeable. And surely you cannot expect to secure the confidence of a school, by indulging yourself in those habits which make you disagreeable to every one.

Fourthly, You will secure the confidence of the school by being *punctual* in every thing. Punctuality in business of every kind, gains confidence. It prevents the loss of time, and secures opportunity for every duty. It is no where more important, than in schools. Without it, you can accomplish but little. If, after due deliberation you make a promise, be sure to keep it. If you say that neglect of duty will be followed by punishment, be sure to inflict it. If you require a child to do this or that, see that it is done exactly as you require. To let him go, when he has obeyed you but in part, will be but little better, than not to be obeyed at all. By being punctual in fulfilling every promise, you will not be accused of falsifying your word. Your scholars will not ask a second time for any indulgence which you may once have denied them. They will know what you mean, when you say yes, or no; and thus, you will have their confidence.

By observing these principles, and acting in a manner corresponding to them, you will be able to gain that ascendancy over your youthful charge, which is necessary to enable you to benefit them. You will find it impossible to secure their confidence by the opposite course, for it is opposed to the principles of our nature.

The next general direction which I wish to give, is, *Be willing to devote your whole time, and strive to make the most judicious use of it.* If you have made no reserve of any part of your time, the whole belongs to your employers. I know not that there is any thing morally wrong in making an agreement to reserve a portion of time, to be devoted to your own purposes. But it does seem to me manifestly wrong, if no such agreement have been made with your employers, for you to use any considerable portion of it for your own private benefit, instead of that of the school. This rule ought to be observed, whether the school be large or small ; whether your wages be high or low. If you have made an engagement, for even less than a fair compensation, this apology cannot alter your obligation to the children placed under your care. They are not to be injured, if their parents have misjudged in regard to what ought to be your hire. You had your choice whether to engage or not, and if you have consented to work for a less compensation that you ought to receive, your obligation is still the same as if you were to receive more. If you have engaged to keep the school, without having made any reserve, you are under obligation to give your pupils all the time which you can render useful to them. This direction may seem to you unreasonable, or impracticable. If so, I have only to ask you to examine it attentively, and if you shall then conclude, that you cannot bring yourselves to adopt the spirit of it, I hope you will renounce the idea of teaching, and choose some other business. I do not mean by this, to say that you ought not to take the time necessary for exercise and rest, and for answering the claims of friendship. This would be expected under any engagement whatever. It is expected in all other public employments, and it is equally proper in yours.

But you will inquire, how you can spend the whole of your time profitably for your school, when you are with them ordinarily no more than six hours in a day? I will answer you by giving you some account of my friend Benevolus. On commencing his school, his first object was to learn the state of improvement, the capacity and the disposition of every scholar. His next inquiry was, how shall I benefit each scholar, to the utmost of my power? This inquiry was continued with him, during the whole time he was with them, and excited him to constant effort to do them good. The copy books of the school were all carried to his room, and his first work in the morning was to prepare them for writing during the day. He ruled them himself, and wrote out all the copies. This occupied his time, till it was necessary to repair to the school room, which he did half an hour before the time of opening school, in order that he might be assured that a fire had been properly made, and the house suitably prepared for the scholars when they should arrive. When the morning exercises were finished, he retired to his boarding house, or to some house nearer, as might be most convenient. Two or three of his scholars were expected to hand in letters or compositions each day, in their

5*

turn; and the intermission of the regular exercises was devoted to correcting them, and suggesting such improvements as might be beneficial to the writers. After the hour of dismissal had arrived, he secured the fire, and left the house. In the evening he met a class or more as might be convenient, and devoted his attention usually to a single branch. One evening he requested a meeting of his scholars in arithmetic; the next, he assembled his grammarians, especially those who were beginners. The third evening of the week was devoted to a class in geography; the fourth to a class in reading, and the fifth to spelling. If, at any time, it was not convenient for a class to meet, or for him to have an evening school, his time was occupied with the children of the family where he boarded, or those of some other family, or in preparing some illustration to be used in the school the next day. Thus Benevolus found enough to do duriug the whole day. He was never out of employment. Seeing him so much engaged for them, the *scholars* became as much engaged for themselves. Parents also became awake to the interest of the school, and used every effort to produce an early and a constant attendance of their children. Benevolus taught not only in a single district, but successively in several, and in different states, and the same means were used by him and the same results were experienced. He found but very few who did not become greatly interested in their studies. The spirit of the instructer seemed to be infused into the whole school, and parents were commonly forward to acknowledge that the school made more than double the progress it had usually made before. It seemed to my friend a thing highly ridiculous to hear a schoolmaster say he could not find enough to occupy all his time, when he was surrounded with twenty young persons of various ages.

If then it be true that double the usual improvement might be made in district schools generally, (I speak of schools in the country and not of those in cities and large towns,) the subject is one of no ordinary importance. Let me ask you then to reflect on it a moment longer. Suppose the number of scholars in a school to amount to forty. The time, board, wear of apparel and use of books, cannot be estimated at less for each than $1,50 a week. The wages and board of the master will at least amount to six dollars a week, and probably more, if we include the expense of fuel for the school. The school then costs sixty-six dollars a week, or two hundred and sixty-four dollars a month. If there are six such schools in a town, the expense of them is fifteen hundred and eighty-four dollars a month. Suppose each school is to continue two and a half months, the cost to the town is three thousand nine hundred and sixty dollars, for a single season. Now if there is but half the improvement made, that might be made, we cannot consider the actual loss as less than half this sum.

If any, after looking at the subject in this light, are unwilling to devote their whole time to the work, I would again make the request, that they would turn their attention to some other employment, and not occasion so great a loss to the community. Leave the work to those who will enter upon it with greater spirit, and who are willing to spare no pains.

I have been led to the direction last given from having the conviction forced upon me, that many who have offered their services as teachers, have had no higher motives in so doing, than the attainment of a pecuniary reward. But, while I am firm in the belief that "the labourer is worthy of his hire," and while I am as firmly of the opinion that the ordinary compensation is lower than it ought to be, I cannot conceive that any one ought to engage in this highly responsible business, merely for the purpose of compensation. In business less responsible, it may be justifiable to make that the first object. But where an influence so important is to be exerted— an influence that will probably affect the character and happiness of many, during the rest of their lives ; it does seem to me that *patriotism*, to say nothing of higher inducements, requires that the first object of a teacher should be to do good, and that those only should engage in teaching, who are willing to devote the largest portion of their time, that can be rendered beneficial to the school. How often is it said in our hearing, "that our school has done us no good," that " it has been worse than none"— that " the money might as well have been thrown away." I will not charge every failure on the instructer. It does not always belong to him; but I am persuaded, that a large majority of the instances of failure in the success of schools, is to be attributed to the teacher. Let every teacher engage heartily in his work, and devote his whole time to his business, and instances where the school does more hurt than good, will be very rare.

LECTURE VI.

THE preceding Lectures, have regarded subjects, which ought to claim your attention previous to entering the school-room. This, and several following, will relate to your more immediate duties as teachers. The next direction therefore is, *Govern* your school. This is a direction of great importance. Unless you govern those placed under your care, all your other exertions will be nearly or quite in vain.

"Order is Heaven's first law."

Without subordination on the part of your scholars, without good government on your own, you may as well expect the course of nature to change, as that your school will make any considerable progress. In order to be able to govern your pupils, remember you must *govern yourselves.* If the instructer have little command over his own feelings, if he be angry at one time, fretful at another, easily excited to laughter at another—he cannot exhibit that firmness of purpose which always commands respect. " Correction administered in anger has no effect to humble or reclaim the offender." It shows even to a child that he who administers it, is guilty of a fault as great as his own. Temptations to excitement will undoubtedly occur. A scholar may be impudent ;—from his ignorance of good manners, or in a sudden gust of passion, he may, perhaps, grossly insult you. Hardly any thing is more apt to call forth anger, than an insult from an inferior. But still the indulgence of anger is very unwise. If a pupil commit a fault he ought certainly to be called to account; but if the teacher, by an unmanly indulgence of passion descend to the level of the child, he cannot expect to benefit him materially by any correction administered in such a state of mind.

There is another particular; in which it is very important you should govern yourselves. Be careful to make no contemptuous remarks concerning any of your pupils. Such remarks may excite a smile from the rest of the school, but it will not be the smile of approbation. The affections of that pupil, you have lost; and every effort to benefit him by your instructions will do him very little good. You may, and will often see things that might seem to give occasion for such remarks, but, as your design is to benefit your scholars, use a proper method to correct the fault, and there let it rest. If the pupil make a blunder, he may be reproved calmly for his carelessness, but never should he be made the butt of ridicule.

It is of equal importance that you should govern yourselves in regard to such speeches as may hold up *families* to derision. You may see many things, in family management to excite a smile, and many things which really deserve censure. But such censure does not come well from the instructer of their children. To be ridiculed by the schoolmaster will have very little effect to correct improprieties. If you say any thing at all, let it be simply a remark on what has been the mode or what has been the opinion of others, and leave the school to draw the inference for themselves. I will not blame you for being diverted, sometimes, at what you may observe in family management. I know well that the eccentricity sometimes observable cannot fail to amuse and to vex you. But still, keep your reflections to yourself.

Some of these points may appear of very trifling importance to you, but much of your success, in the important business of teaching, depends on little things.

After having used proper exertions to govern yourselves, you will be prepared to govern those placed under your care. An important object will have been gained, when you have brought yourselves to feel that to govern the school is of primary importance, and that you *can* and *will* have proper discipline and order. When you have imbibed

these feelings, your scholars will read them in your countenance, and will expect nothing else. But the moment
the instructer indulges in the apprehension that he cannot
govern—that it is impossible for him to have proper order,
he may just as well tell his feelings to the whole school;
the scholars will not be slow to read his thoughts, and
will "govern themselves accordingly."

It is not my design to say, that all have an equal ability
to govern, or that the object is accomplished when the
teacher has made the decided *resolve to be master;* but I
wish to be understood to say that no one can exercise a
proper and uniform authority, any longer than he believes
he can do so. This is a natural principle. When we
believe we can obtain a desired object, we try, but when
we think we cannot, our efforts are feeble.

The next direction in regard to government is, *Consider
your scholars as reasonable and intelligent beings.* As
such, they will be influenced by motives, when properly
presented. They may easily be brought to know, that
they are happier when they do right, than when they
do wrong. And when the right and the wrong are
both placed distinctly before them, they will seldom call
the wrong object the right, or the reverse. Right and
wrong may be exhibited to the child of very few years,
and he may be required to decide which he will pursue.
This appeal will usually exert a far better influence upon
him, in leading him to duty, than any that can be effected
by the infliction of stripes.

I shall be better understood in what I wish to say on
this point, by an example.

A complaint is made to the instructer, by George
against John. John is accused of having struck and
otherwise injured his school-fellow. After ascertaining
the fact, and finding that the complaint is not without
foundation, let a course like the following be pursued.

Instructer. John, I am sorry to find a complaint of this
kind brought against you. You have been so unwise as
to make yourself unhappy, and to make others unhappy
also. You may stand up, and answer some questions,
which I wish to ask you. Is it right for one scholar to
beat or abuse another?

John. No, sir.

Inst. Do you think that the school could make any good progress in study, if all the scholars should treat each other, as you have treated George?

John. I think not.

Inst. Would you be willing that one of the larger boys should beat you, or otherwise abuse you?

John. No, sir.

Inst. Well, do you think it is right for you to do to others, as you are unwilling they should do to you?

John. I do not think it is.

[This answer will, almost invariably, be given. Not one child in a thousand would give a different one, where the teacher commences with him in a deliberate and gentle manner. Conscience tells him he has done wrong, and he must be uncommonly hardened, to say that he has done right. If he be inclined to excuse himself, because George said or did something that displeased him, he should be shown that he is accountable for *his own* conduct, and that misbehaviour in another person does not alter the nature of his own offence. That the offence of one, does not justify a far greater errour in another, may be shown by a reference to any judicial proceeding.]

Inst. When one scholar injures another, ought he to make any satisfaction for it?

John. I suppose he ought.

Inst. Well, do you think that you ought to make any satisfaction to George?

John. I don't know but I ought.

Inst. I wish you to give me a definite answer. Is it right or is it wrong for you to make satisfaction?

John. It is right.

Inst. Are you willing to do right when you know what is right?

John. [After some hesitation,] Yes, sir.

Inst. You are willing then to go to George and make satisfaction?

[Here he will probably hesitate again, but after repeating the question several times, he will probably say that he is. In pursuing a mode similar to this, a great many times, I have scarcely found an instance where the culprit has not said he was willing to make satisfaction to the injured party. He may then be sent to George, to ask what satisfaction he shall make. George will probably say, "ask forgiveness," or something similar. If such a course appear reasonable, he should be required to do so, and then to return to the master.]

Inst. You have done what is right, in regard to George, but that does not make satisfaction to others who have been injured. You have set a very bad example,—have broken the rules of the school, and have caused the loss of time, which might have been improved in gaining knowledge. Is it not right, therefore, that I should have satisfaction in behalf of the school?

John. I suppose it is.

Inst. Yes, it is right that every offence should be suit- ably atoned for. And this must be complied with in your case. I have not, however, reflected on the subject suffi- ciently, and shall defer it till two o'clock tomorrow, and shall attend to it precisely at the time I have appointed. I hope you will yourself reflect much on the subject, and be able to tell me what is right for me to require.

It has ever appeared to me, that punishment, if it become necessary in any case, should be deferred for a season. But precisely at the time set, it should be attended to. By deferring the sentence, as in the case above-men- tioned, the pupil has opportunity to reflect. He is induced to reflect on the nature of his offence, that he may form an idea of the punishment he shall probably receive. Such reflection will be of more service to him, than any severity whatever. Indeed, I have seldom been obliged to call a scholar to account more than once, where I have pursued the course here recommended.

I will suppose another case, to illustrate the direction to treat the scholars as moral and intellectual beings.

Laura comes to the master and wishes to be excused from writing a composition, which has been required of her.

Instructer. Why do you wish me to excuse you, Laura?

Laura. I don't know what to write—I cannot write any thing fit to be seen.

Inst. Well, Laura, we will converse about it. Do you wish to be excused from spelling, reading, or writing?

Laura. No, sir.

Inst. Why not from these as well as from writing composition?

Laura. They are easy, and besides we could not do without them.

Inst. Could you always read, Laura?

Laura. No, sir.

Inst. How is it that you can read now?

Laura. By having learned.

Inst. How long were you in trying to read, before you could read with ease?

Laura. I do not know, it was a long time.

Inst. Did you tell the master that you wished to be excused, and that you never could learn and that you could not read in a way fit to be heard?

Laura. No, I did not.

Inst. I saw you knitting and sewing the other day: could you always knit and sew?

Laura. I could not.

Inst. How then, can you now?

Laura. Because I have learned.

Inst. How did you learn?

Laura. By trying.

Inst. Did you tell your mother she must excuse you from knitting and sewing, for you did not know how?

Laura. I did not.

Inst. Why did you not?

Laura. I knew if I did not keep trying I could never learn, and so I kept on.

Inst. Do you think it is necessary to know how to write letters, and to express ourselves properly when writing?

Laura. O yes, sir.

Inst. You expect to have occasion to write letters, do you not?

Laura. I presume I shall, for I have written to my brother and cousin already.

Inst. Then you think if I should help you to learn to write a letter or other piece of composition properly, that I should do you a great benefit?

Laura. I suppose, sir, you would.

Inst. Is it right for me to benefit the school as much as I can, or only in part?

6

Laura. I suppose, sir, you ought to help them all you can.

Inst. Ought I to help you as much as I can, in learning that which will be a benefit to you?

Laura. Yes, sir.

Inst. Now I will answer you. You asked if I would excuse you from writing? I will do so, if you think I could be justified in neglecting to benefit you all that I can. If you can say sincerely, that you believe it is my duty to do wrong to the school by indulging them in neglecting what they ought to learn, then I will comply with your request.

By a course like the above, the scholar is led to see that you act on principle—that you wish the best good of those committed to your care. The child whom you treat in this way will be led to reflection, and will inquire what views the instructer will take on the subject, before he concludes to come to you with it. He will consider himself treated as a reasonable being, and will be far more likely to govern himself afterward. As far as practicable, explain to the school the reason of every thing you do. Let them know that you regard their good in all the regulations you may make. Explain to them the reason why you consider one thing right and another wrong, and they will understand you, and they will be governed far more easily than by the whip and ferule. In no way can you so readily conciliate the willing obedience of your scholars as by pursuing this course, and in no way can you sooner make them your enemies, than by the opposite. Reason should be equally your guide in making laws and in executing them—in granting the requests of your scholars and refusing them. First ask yourself, is the request a reasonable one? and after using proper means to know, and taking time to decide, let the decision be such as duty requires. You may not always be able to decide in a moment; if not, take time, remembering that *no decision at all,* is preferable to a wrong one, and while the scholar is waiting to know the opinion you entertain, he will generally be led to reflect on the principles by which you will be governed, and will commonly be prepared to submit to your decision.

The next direction on the subject of government is, *let it be uniform.* Many fail on this point. I am willing to confess it is very difficult to be so, while the health and spirits of most men fluctuate so much as they do. But still, uniformity is indispensable. I have seen some men very strict one day, and very indulgent the next. I have myself been called to account for doing that which at some previous time had appeared to please the master. To approve to-day, what you punish to-morrow, is certainly very bad management. But to something of this, every teacher is in a greater or less degree exposed, from the different states of temper and spirits in which he finds himself. We can bear fatigue at some times better than at others. When suffering under a head-ache, a school may appear to us very noisy, which at another time would appear very still, so different are the states of the nervous system at different times.

Another fault to which this direction has especial reference, is one that exists in many schools, where the small scholars are strictly governed, while the larger do nearly as they please. I have often seen the child of six years punished severely for a fault, that was hardly noticed when committed by a young man of eighteen. This is unreasonable—it is wicked. If there is to be any difference in the treatment of the two cases, it should be on the other side. But I would still say, govern the large and small scholars alike. The elder ones should never be suffered to transgress laws which you have made for the government of the whole. They will respect you the less, for indulging them in what is improper; and will show a growing disregard for your feelings and for your authority.

Do you say the oldest scholars are to govern themselves, and that your business is only with the younger ones? Presume not on this. Those who have arrived at years of manhood, *ought* to govern themselves; but they must be different from the great mass of youth, not to need much restraint. When it becomes necessary to establish a rule in the school, see that it is regarded by all; and you will find your task much easier, and will gain the confidence of the whole school more, than by the opposite course.

Another direction on the subject of school-government is, let it always be characterized by *firmness*. This is connected with the preceding direction, but it means more than to govern merely with uniformity. The first question to be decided is, whether the rule you have established be a reasonable one. In regard to this, great care should be taken that you do not misjudge. Your rules should not be numerous, and those which are established, should be well understood. When this is done, see that all your requisitions are strictly complied with. Partial obedience is but little better than disobedience. If you direct a scholar to come to you, and he comes half way and stops, your command is not complied with; he has not obeyed you. Now, if you dispense with your order, after a partial obedience, he must either suppose your command an unreasonable one, or that you have not resolution to see it fully obeyed. The impression on his mind will, in either case, be unhappy; and you had better issue no orders, than command and then dispense with a full obedience. Let it be known as your established rule, that every reasonable requisition must be fully complied with, and you will find it far easier to secure implicit obedience, than, in the other case, to have a partial regard paid to your orders. If a scholar ask of you some indulgence, be sure to examine its propriety before you say no or yes, to his request. But when you have said *yes* or *no*, adhere to this one answer. To deny the request of a scholar when it is first made, and then in a few minutes, grant what he desires, because he continues asking, is certainly injudicious. If he give a good reason for repeating his request, you may change your direction. But the reason ought to be known at first, and then the answer given with a reference to it.

I have not unfrequently visited schools, where, if a scholar asked leave to go out—the answer was instantly given, " No; sit down." Within a minute the request was repeated—the answer again was " No." But after the question had been repeated half a dozen times, the patience of the master seemed to be exhausted, and he replied, " Yes, yes, I had rather you would go, than to keep asking all the time." Now the impression was left on the mind of that scholar, that the teacher had less regard to what was right or wrong in the case, than he had to his own convenience. He must have considered his teacher as fickle in mind, and therefore his respect for him must have been diminished.

The schoolmaster, harassed by the many questions asked him during the day, is in danger of forming the habit of answering them without consideration, and merely to be rid of them. But instead of preventing, this greatly adds to his inconvenience. The school ought to be taught, that " *no* means *no*, and *yes* means *yes*, and *must* means *must*." You pronounce a word to a scholar for him to spell, and he says he cannot. You tell him to " try," but he still says he cannot spell it. Now if you put it to the next, and suffer him to disobey your order, the influence is decidedly bad. It is reasonable that he should try, if you have ordered him to do so; and your requirement should not be abandoned. Shew a determination to be exactly obeyed in every reasonable direction, and let this determination be constant, whether the requirement be trifling or important. Hardly any thing can have a worse effect than to command and not be obeyed—to threaten or promise and not to perform—to make laws and not to insist on their execution. Disorder and confusion must be the consequence. Scholars will very soon learn to disregard all that you say—will disbelieve your promises and neglect your commands. If you punish disobedience, this will excite anger, because you had threatened a punishment for the same offence before, but had not inflicted it. When punishment excites anger only, it does no good. I will only add that without firmness of purpose in the government of a school, it will be impossible to make that school pleasant to the teacher, or profitable to the pupil.

6*

LECTURE VII.

The subject of government was commenced in the last lecture, and will be continued in this. The next direction to which I wish to call your attention is—*Let the government of the school be impartial.* In this direction I do not wish to imply that you are to exercise the same feelings towards every individual in the school. The good instructer will love, and he ought to love, the good scholar more than the bad. He cannot, and he will not feel an equal regard for the obedient and the disobedient— for the docile and the perverse. But, notwithstanding this, he should be impartial. The law for one should be the law for all. Though you cannot love an idle, heedless, unmannerly boy, so much as the affectionate, studious, and obedient one, still you should govern them alike. When the good scholar commits a fault, if you neglect to call him to account for it, and punish a less agreeable scholar for a similar offence, the latter will accuse you of injustice, and with good cause. For if you have made a law, it is for the whole school, and should be regarded by all.

No complaint is more frequently heard, than that the instructer is partial—that he treats one better than another, &c. This sometimes proceeds from distrust on the part of parents, occasioned sometimes by listening to the tales of children, told when they have been punished. Without great care on the part of the master, he will be betrayed into a greater or less degree of the fault abovenamed, every day. There may, indeed, be sometimes a propriety in making a difference in the treatment of the same crime under different circumstances. The same law may be broken by two persons, and very different degrees of criminality be attached to each. The man who passes you a counterfeit dollar ignorantly, breaks the letter of the law, as much as the knave who passes it knowingly. But the first is guilty of no intentional fraud. One scholar may transgress a reasonable rule of the school, and may have been led to it by the persuasion of those older or better informed than himself; while another is guilty of the same offence, without any palliating circumstances. There may be a propriety in treating them very differently, and in so doing you need not be guilty of partiality. When the circumstances are the same, the treatment should be uniform.

Partiality, if exhibited in your treatment of scholars, will deprive you of their confidence. Children are not slow to discover it, where it exists, and when they believe that one of their number may do wrong and go unpunished, while another will be treated with severity for the same offence, it is impossible to exert any useful influence over them. There is a loss of improvement to them, and much inconvenience to the master; and not only this, but he is guilty of doing wrong, and must suffer the reproof of his own conscience.

Finally, in the government of the school, consult not only your own convenience and the *present* welfare of the scholars, but pursue such a course as shall produce the most *lasting* results. To do this, the instructer must be *master* in all places and at all hours. It is not enough that you govern and restrain them during school hours; but you must regard their conduct, at all other times when they are not under the care of their parents. I have sometimes been acquainted with instructers, who seemed to care for the behaviour of their pupils only while they were in school. By a proper course the master may as easily direct the amusement and play of his scholars, as their studies, and it is hardly less important that he should do so. For this purpose, he ought to show an interest in their sports, and a willingness that they should amuse themselves during the usual intermissions of study. The difference between different kinds of exercise or amusement should be carefully pointed out, and such as may be injurious should be prohibited. Such as may corrupt the morals or the taste, and such as have a tendency to injure the health or limbs, should be discountenanced. In general, such exercises as tend to excite jealousies and hatred, or to interest the mind so much as to divert it from books and study, together with all the games of hazard and chance, are prejudicial, and should be forbidden. The tendency of all such, is bad. Many of them prevent progress in study, and all of them are injurious to the morals of the scholars. In those districts, where the male and female members continue at the school-room, during intermission, the subject of proper exercise requires much more attention, than in villages where they return to their parents. Every exercise that is immodest or unbecoming should be prohibited, and whatever would give offence to delicate minds, of either sex, cannot be approved.

In order to be able to exercise a full and judicious control, it will be very important that the school should know what you approve and what you disapprove, and the reasons on which your opinion is founded. Exercise or play, proper in one school, may be impracticable or inexpedient in another. There may be circumstances that will have a very important influence in directing your recommendation of exercise. It should be your object to examine what may be attended with the fewest evils and the greatest good.

There is another point on which I wish to make a passing remark. It relates to *the manner of speaking* in the school, proper to be observed both by teacher and pupil.

It will generally be found true, that the mode of address adopted by the teacher in speaking to the scholars, will be copied by them in addressing each other. Every thing dictatorial, lordly and austere should be avoided. A spirit of affection should be infused into the whole school. Ask a scholar to do what you desire, in just such a tone as you would naturally use in asking a favour of a superior. Never command till the pupil has neglected to do as you requested him. It is very ill-judged to display your authority before there is any encroachment upon it, or any disposition shown to disregard it.

Perhaps there is no way, in which the children may be led to speak kindly and affectionately to each other, so easily, as by the example of the teacher in speaking kindly and affectionately to them. And if any suppose that they are adding to their dignity and importance in the estimation of their scholars, by assuming airs of great superiority or lordliness, such persons must have very little knowledge of human nature, and of the art of pleasing. President Monroe lost none of his dignity, when, during his tour to

New England, he cordially took the children by the hand, and spoke kindly and affectionately to them.

If it is ever necessary to call a child to account for improper conduct, the same affectionate manner is recommended. I would much rather say to a child whom I saw breaking some important rule of the school—" John, you may come to me," than to say " Come here, John." The more he sees you benevolent, kind and affectionate, the more plainly will he see the impropriety of breaking those laws, which are designed by you for his own benefit.

In this connexion, it will be expected that I say something on the subject of punishments ; for, after the greatest fidelity and discretion on the part of an instructer, there will be some who will not yield a reasonable and cheerful obedience. Such must be punished both for their own reformation and as a warning to others. It would be doing injustice to those who are well disposed, to suffer the bad, by their frequent misconduct, to prevent them from making the progress they desire.

I have already supposed a case where a scholar was found guilty of doing wrong, and have pointed out the way in which I would proceed in that particular case. To continue the subject of government, I shall now give you a few general directions.

1. *Never be in haste to believe that a pupil has done wrong ;* and be not in haste to accuse him. If not guilty, he feels grieved that you should suppose him to be so. After having been wrongfully accused, he will probably have less dread of doing wrong than before,—for he already feels in some measure degraded, in having been supposed guilty. It is a principle in the civil law, " to suppose every man innocent till he is found guilty." In every case, an inquiry for evidence of the fact, ought to precede our accusation. To make inquiry for evidence to prove the *innocence* of a scholar, may often be attended with happy consequences. If acquitted by the evidence adduced in his favour, he will love his teacher the better for having pursued this course ; and if proved guilty, he will be more likely to be affected by what you may say to him.

2. Be not *in haste to punish* when a fault is committed. Your first object should be, to converse with the scholar,

to show him the nature of his crime, and to convince him that he has done that which, if every one followed his example, would destroy the usefulness of the school. If his crime be that of profaneness, lying, or any thing in direct violation of the laws of God, to those all-wise laws he should be referred. The awful consequences of these vices to himself, should be expressly shown. Their effect on the school, if others should follow his example, and their effect on every community, if all should be guilty of them, ought to be clearly exhibited. After this, he may be required to commit to memory those passages in Scripture, which show with what abhorrence the Supreme Being looks upon these enormities, and, when he has had sufficient time to reflect on the subject, he will be in a state to be profited by the punishment. I would recommend to you never to punish an offence the same day on which it is committed. The scholar will usually endeavour to forget the subject, when the punishment is over, but he cannot, when he knows it is to come. It may, at times, be proper to defer it for two or three days, or a week. Whenever the time arrives, it should be attended to, to the exclusion of every thing else. Before being punished he should be interrogated concerning the degree of punishment, which he thinks his crime deserves, and if he appears to view his offence as more trifling than he ought, it is important to make him sensible, if possible, of his errour. If you *must* punish, do it with seriousness. To exhibit any levity, to laugh while you are inflicting punishment, must always be attended with bad consequences. The sufferer cannot feel otherwise than indignant. He will have good reason to accuse you of a wanton delight in cruelty, rather than to give you the credit of having a desire to do him a benefit.

3. Decide on such a mode as will be most likely to benefit the scholar, and *prevent a repetition* of the crime. Those punishments which have an effect on the body only, usually do little to prevent crime, or reclaim the guilty. As far as possible strive to have it a punishment that will affect the mind, rather than the body. To require the delinquent to ask forgiveness of the master, or of the school—sometimes to require him to read a written confession to the school, or to parents, or guardians, will have

the desired effect. Much must be left to the judgment of the master at the time. Punishment should be varied with the disposition, age, or circumstance of the scholar, or the nature of his offence. It is undoubtedly true, that corporal punishment should be the last resort. When every thing else fails, you may have recourse to that. It is sometimes necessary—it sometimes does good. But yet I am fully persuaded it is seldom necessary. Where a reasonable, calm, and decided course is adopted,— where an instructer makes an appeal to the moral sensibility of the child, and shows him the nature of his fault, experience has satisfied me, that recourse to it will not be necessary, except in a few instances, where the child seems devoid of sensibility, or where he has been neglected till his passions are too strong to be controlled by his reason.

4. Always make the punishment *effectual.* This rule is important, whether the punishment be of one kind or another. If the child deserves the punishment, it should not pass off, till he is brought to feel it as such, and to realize the nature of the crime, which he has committed. It is sometimes true that a child punished but slightly, is only injured, and not benefited by it. He boasts that his chastisement did not hurt him—that he does not care, and sometimes that he loves to be punished. Now if the subject passes off in such a way it would have been better, probably, to have neglected punishment entirely. His chastisement does him no good, if it does not humble him, and cause him to fear being brought again under the censure of his instructer.

Connected with punishments, is the subject of rewards. These may sometimes be beneficial, but, as they are usually bestowed, they probably do as much harm as good. To promise a reward is often an excitement to study, for the sake of the reward; not as a duty, or from a love of learning, or a desire to merit the approbation of the wise and good.

When a prize is offered to a number of competitors, those who hope to gain it, will be excited to emulation and to envy; and those, who have no such hope, will usually be discouraged, and probably make less progress, than if no reward had been offered. I would advise you to *promise* no rewards, and if you ever give them, let such

honours be grounded on the excellence of the scholar, his
industry and faithfulness, rather than the amount of
knowledge he obtains in a given time.   One scholar may
require a week to learn, what another will accomplish in a
day.   If the former perseveres and is faithful in his slow
and toilsome progress, he is to be commended rather than
the other, for he has greater obstacles to encounter, and
has succeeded in overcoming them.   It is not impossible,
but he may be the most benefited of the two.   For it is
commonly true, that those who learn very easily, forget as
easily, while those who learn slowly, remember what they
have acquired.   It is not unusual for the slow gains of the
mechanic, to be eventually more productive than the rapid
and golden streams of the merchant.

If rewards are given at all, let them be "rewards of
merit," and not rewards of intellectual capacity.   The
dull of apprehension are not to be punished for being so,
neither do the more gifted *merit* praise, for what they have
received from the hand of God.

LECTURE VIII.

In connexion with the subject of the last Lecture, I
wish to call your attention to the *general management of
your schools*.   This is a subject of much consequence; for
though you may be able to govern with ease, yet it is possible that you may fail, by ill-directed effort, of accomplishing all that is reasonably expected of you.   Though
you will fail in every thing without good government, yet
government alone will not accomplish all the objects of a
school.

In the general management of a school, it is important
to keep in mind always the great object for which it is
designed.   That object is, to prepare children to be happy;
and to be useful to themselves and others—to teach them
how to acquire knowledge and to apply it.   In a word,
the purpose of education is to teach how to think and how

to act in all the vicissitudes of life. The general management of a school, then, must be guided by a reference to these objects. It should regard both the present enjoyment, and the future good of its members.

1. Endeavour to adopt such a course as shall render the school *pleasant* to those who compose it. If children are brought to associate with the school, a variety of agreeable objects, they will be led to think of study as a pleasure, and delight in it. We are all much affected by the objects around us : if these are pleasant, we are pleased ; if these are gloomy or disgusting, it is hardly possible for us to be cheerful. If we see others smile or weep we are disposed to do the same. Let the teacher of a school wear a smiling countenance,—let him appear happy, and desirous of making others so, and he will hardly fail of seeing smiling faces and contented looks around him.

2. Reduce every thing to system. This will have a great tendency to promote what is required in the previous advice. By means of system much more can be accomplished than is possible without it. Irregularity is the enemy of happiness, and where it extensively prevails, it equally prevents success in business. By having a time for every thing, and doing every thing in season, you will be enabled to avoid confusion, to know what to do, and to take pleasure in doing it. But if you wait for the subjects to present themselves before you think what to do, twenty things may sometimes come up at once, and in your perplexity to choose among them, you are unprepared to attend to any. He who tries to do many things at once, will accomplish nothing. " He that has many irons in the fire must let some of them burn."

In order to introduce system, do only one thing at a time. An instructer called a class to read, and in a moment a scholar wished for a copy ; the master neglected his class and prepared to set one ; while doing that, a boy came with a pen to be mended, and before this was done, another wished to be assisted in his arithmetic. While mending the pen and looking at the slate, another came and wished to be shown some place on his atlas ; the pen and the slate were neglected, and the copy and the class, and two or three minutes were devoted to finding the name on the map. Several other calls were made at once,

7

and the master neglected all the former to scold the latter for making him so much trouble. Here were ten or twelve scholars, all waiting—all doing nothing excepting the *class* which had kept on reading, pronouncing half the words wrong, and neglecting every rule which would have rendered the exercise useful. They were then told they had read enough, and that they might sit down. The other matters were dispatched after a while, another class was called to read, and a similar course was pursued. Now, how, in the name of common sense, can a master endure this?—what benefit can the scholar derive? He had no plan—no system—no order. Hence he could not avoid confusion and perplexity. In all sorts of business, system is of great consequence; in schools, it is indispensable.

In order to have system, it is necessary to do but one thing at a time; to have a time for every thing, and to attend to it at that time. While the class is reading, the entire attention of the teacher should be given to that exercise. He will thus be able to give useful instructions. When a class is called to spell, let this receive the entire attention of both master and scholars. The same should be observed in regard to writing, grammar, arithmetic, geography, &c. In this way, every thing will be done, and done without confusion. But by having no system, much must be neglected, that should receive attention, and what even does receive it, is but poorly done.

3. Another direction, which I wish to give in regard to general management, is, let every thing be done thoroughly, when it is once commenced. It may be said, perhaps, that there is not time; and that the school is so large, it is impossible to go through with the required exercises. Now if this be true, I would still insist on the direction to do every thing thoroughly, when it is commenced. If a subject of study can be attended to but once a day, or but once in two days, the scholar will derive more advantage from one lesson in two days, if well recited and properly explained, than he can from half a dozen, if but half recited and not explained. In teaching, as in other matters, the old adage is true, that "work well done is twice done."

4. Let subjects be classed according to their importance, and receive a proportionate attention. Some instructers have been known to spend a large part of their time, in teaching a small class who were pursuing a favourite branch. In this manner studies vastly important to the majority of scholars have received very little attention. If the master is himself much better pleased with grammar than with arithmetic, and has a class of five in that, while there are fifteen in this, he does great injury to the fifteen, if he spends double the time with the five, that he does with the fifteen. And yet if he happen to be more fond of teaching grammar than arithmetic, he is very prone to do so.

Those subjects which we have occasion most frequently to use, are more important to us, than those which we seldom wish to employ. Reading and spelling are more important than geography, because without a knowledge of the former, we are deprived of more means of knowledge, than by a want of acquaintance with the latter. We have occasion to employ our knowledge of reading much more frequently than a knowledge of geography. So arithmetic is more important than grammar, because we find occasion to use it in the business of life, much oftener, than we do the rules of syntax, to which we attend at school. The instructer should endeavour to divide his time so as to give to each particular subject, that degree of attention which properly belongs to it. It is manifestly wrong for him to give an undue portion of his time to some one subject, merely because he has a greater taste for it than for some other.

The *direction of studies*, will next claim your attention. The best rule I can give you on this point, is to follow the order of nature. Let those subjects receive attention first, which may be most easily understood and comprehended by children—and then follow in the order, which common sense would dictate. The children, placed under your instruction, will ordinarily be such as have received some instruction in reading, and will be able to call the letters of the alphabet by their names, and perhaps pronounce them when united in easy syllables. At least I shall suppose this in the following remarks, and reserve those which I have to make, on instructing chil-

dren at an earlier age, for the lecture, that will be addressed particularly to female teachers.   When the child has
acquired so much knowledge of reading, as to be able to
give a proper pronunciation to syllables and words, his
attention should be directed to the *meaning of words.*
Words are signs of ideas, and it is an object of high importance that a very early habit should be formed, of
knowing the meaning of the words he pronounces.   He
is not able to have recourse to a dictionary, and of course
it must devolve on the teacher to explain them.   This
should, as much as possible, be done by means of sensible
objects.   Some little story, in which the word occurs,
may be related to the child, which will often fix the meaning permanently in his mind ; or the word may be explained by its opposite.   I shall pursue this subject in the
lecture before mentioned, and will only add here, that too
much effort cannot be used to lead the child very early to
an acquaintance with the meaning of words.

Much attention should be given at this time to pronunciation.   This will be learned mostly from the example
of the teacher.   His pronunciation will be theirs.   Great
care is necessary in forming a good pronunciation, because it is as easy to learn right, as wrong at first, and
when one has learned wrong, it requires much time and
care first to unlearn, and then to learn anew.

Children are capable at a very early age, of understanding something of numbers.   They can be taught to enu-
merate and to read figures, much earlier than has been
supposed, as has been fully proved in infant schools.
They should be taught to add, subtract, multiply and
divide, by the aid of corns, and other tangible or visible
objects.   By this process they will be able to form distinct
ideas of the nature and combination of numbers.

I would not be understood to imply, that children at a
very early age will be able to comprehend the more complex operations of arithmetic, but the simple rules, are
easily made intelligible.

Geography may be an early study.   Having a picture
or map before him, the child will be able to understand a
subject, which he could not without such ocular demonstration.   Children are almost always pleased with pictures, and as maps are pictures of places, they are usually

pleased with them. Hence they are interested in this study
at an age when it would be impossible to engage their
attention in the exercise of memory alone.

History is a subject that may be next recommended to
children. They are commonly pleased with stories, and
where the terms made use of in little histories, are such as
they can comprehend, and the facts in the narrative are
prominent, they will be amused and interested. It is
desirable, that the geography and history first used should
be of one's own town, state, or country.

After some attention has been paid to these subjects,
the scholar will be prepared to attend profitably to arithmetic and geography in a more thorough manner, and to
pursue those parts, which would not at first have been
intelligible or interesting.

Grammar may in its most simple parts, be early understood and rendered interesting. But the child requires
judgment, to be able to apply the syntactical rules to language. After some knowledge of these branches has
been gained, it is not so important what others shall follow them. It will be important, however, to have regard
constantly to the probable destination of the child. It
would be improper to direct the preparatory studies of a
merchant or mechanic, in the same manner as those of
him who intends to be a schoolmaster or a physician.

LECTURE IX.

In calling your attention to the *manner of teaching*, a
subject of very great importance is presented to your
notice; and though I may fail of giving you the best directions, I am still confident I shall not fail of suggesting
many valuable thoughts.

In the first place, I would have you guard yourselves
against supposing that your whole duty consists in enabling
your scholars to acquire a knowledge of the books, put
7*

into their hands for the purpose of study. This will be but a part, and sometimes the least part of your duty. It is the subject, not the book, which is more important. The book is the *instrument* which you are to teach them how to use, in order to obtain the knowledge desired. To direct and assist them in this, and to teach them to exercise their own powers, and elicit their own strength, is the pirncipal duty of an instructer.

In teaching, let it be your first object to have every thing understood. In perusing any book, if the language is unintelligible, or even some of the most important words are not understood, we obtain no *distinct* ideas. But let the thoughts be clothed in language with which we are familiar, and our attention is fixed—we are pleased and instructed; we then obtain ideas, and may receive some benefit.

Perhaps, hardly any thing is more common, than for instructers to presume that their scholars understand a subject, when they do not. This error is increased by the decision of the pupil himself. "Do you understand this?" is often asked him, and he answers "yes." No effort is made to know whether he understands it or not. The presumption that he does, satisfies the instructer, and the benefit, which he might derive, is lost to the child. The master should interrogate the scholar, till he knows whether he understands the subject, and if it should be found that he does, there will be an additional benefit to the pupil in this very exercise of his powers in explaining it.

"I know, but cannot tell," is a reply which has been given a thousand times by children, and youth, when I have asked a reason for rules and principles. "Why will it prove, your sum to reject the 9s after performing an operation in one of the simple rules; and how do you know that this is a proper mode of proof?" "I know, but cannot tell." The scholar is *honest*. He supposes he does know, because he finds that the directions of his rule will be proved by the operation. But still he has not a single distinct idea upon the subject.

A willingness to trust to the scholar's own opinion, has led many instructers, qualified to be useful, to fail in doing

the importance of the directions will be illustrated to you by a reference to your own history. You perhaps recollect many efforts to explain a thing to you, which have left you no wiser than before. Fail not then to use such language, as can be understood by the child or by the class. Be very careful lest they associate the idea of study with that of hard unintelligible words, and thus become discouraged in their attempt to learn. It is of great importance, that the objects used to illustrate, should be those, with the properties of which the pupil is acquainted. If you employ, in the way of illustration, any object with the character of which, the scholar is unacquainted, he is not in the least assisted. But if you can seize on something that he can see, or that he can recollect, or something with which he is familiar, and then make a just comparison by which the idea is brought distinctly to his view, he derives not only a lasting benefit, but present pleasure. For example—James came to his teacher and told him he could not understand his map. He had just begun to learn a little of the geography of his own state. The master called him to his desk and took up a slate, and gave him a pencil, and then asked him if he could draw a picture of the school-room floor. James at once made his lines for the boundaries. "Now which is the east end?" James told. "Which is the west?" This he told also. "This is the north, and that is the south." "Now," said the instructer, "we will mark them E. for east," &c. "Now in what part is my desk, James?" "There," said the little fellow. "Where is the fire place?" "There," said James. "Now James, make marks for the boys' seats, aud the girls' seats." He did this. "Now make marks for the doors and windows." This was done. "Now," said the master, "James, do you think you could make a map?" No, sir," he replied." "Why yes you could, you have made one already," said the master. "This is a map of the floor. Now the map you said you could not understand is nothing more than this. There is a line for the east side, and there is another for the west side, and there is one for the north and there is another for the south. Now these lines go round the whole state. This river is put down here, because it is in the northern part, and that river is represented there, because it is in the western. This river is drawn here because it makes the eastern boundary of the state. Now look along here, and see if you can find the name of the town in which we live." "O yes," said James, "here it is." "Why is it put down here?" "Because it is in the east part of the state and touches the river," said the child. The master asked him half a dozen similar questions, and James returned to his seat delighted. The simple illustration made every thing easy. The other scholars were as much pleased as he, and when they were dismissed, were in high spirits, saying they would make a map of their gardens, orchards, &c. when they got home.

3. My next direction is, Let it be your object to make every study as *pleasant* as possible. Nor do I conceive that this direction implies any thing impracticable or even difficult, though the inquiry has been made, how it is possible to create a love of study in the mind of those who have no taste for it. "I feel little hesitation in asserting, that no such scholar ever existed," says Parkhurst, "unless he has been brought to feel this indifference or aversion, by injudicious treatment on the part of parents or instructers. If parents or instructers love knowledge for its own sake, and always *speak* of study as a privilege and a source of pleasure, children will be prepossessed in favour of it before they begin ; and if they at school receive easy lessons, and such as they can understand ; if these lessons are explained to them in language adapted to their capacity, and if such questions are asked as will bring other faculties of the mind as well as memory into exercise, they will find study as pleasant as they anticipated. If teachers expect it to be pleasant to their scholars, they will endeavour to present the subject to them in such a light that they may find it so." This is always an object of importance, and " even in cases where parents counteract the impression which the teacher wishes to make, he may, by well directed efforts, notwithstanding these discouragements, generally meet with such success as will confirm his opinion," that children may be brought to love learning for its own sake, and be pleased with the acquisition of knowledge. " If the scholar is enabled to give new ideas, or to form new combinations of those already gained," he cannot avoid being

pleased. "Hence it is an object of primary importance" to teach them such things as " they can understand either by their own reflections, or aided by the explanations and illustrations given them. What I recommend in this and in several previous directions, appears to have been achieved by Pestalozzi. Madame de Stael, in speaking of his school, says, " It is a remarkable circumstance, that neither punishment nor reward is necessary to excite his pupils in their labours. This is perhaps the first instance where a school of one hundred and fifty children has succeeded without having recourse to the principles of emulation or fear. How many bad feelings are spared, when every emotion of jealousy and disappointed ambition is removed from the heart, and when the scholar sees not in his companions rivals, or in his teacher a judge. Here the object is not to excel, not to succeed in a competition for superiority, but to make a progress, to advance towards an end, at which they all aim with equal integrity and sincerity of intention.

If *one* teacher has succeeded to make every thing so pleasant, that his scholars are interested and delighted with their studies, the same end *may be* and, indeed, it *has been* accomplished in other cases. Let it then be the endeavour of every one employed in teaching to render the lessons of his pupils pleasant. It will be done by exhibiting the importance of the study—showing its usefulness—exhibiting its connexions with business and enjoyment, and, by making the study plain and intelligible, by familiar illustration and explanation. This will not be done without effort, and *persevering* effort; but this is most reasonable, where so much is dependent on it.

After the preceding remarks, it will be my next object to point out to you, such a course in treating the different branches of study, as may be best calculated to benefit those placed under your care. I may not be able perhaps to give you the *best* ideas on this subject, but I shall venture to offer you the best which have occurred to me in the course of my reading and experience.

It will be one of your first objects to teach correct spelling. Spelling is an exercise of so much importance that it should be a part of your daily business to teach it. In order to impress the school with a just sense of its value, you should often speak of its importance, and press it upon their attention. Incorrect spelling is often the source of much mortification, and of real inconvenience. Let your *own* example be such as to excite others to regard the subject properly, and pay that attention to it which its importance demands. If you write copies for your scholars, be very careful to avoid bad orthography in them. They will copy the *spelling* of words, as well as the form of letters. I have not unfrequently found ridiculous errors in copy books, which have been handed me for inspection, and have sometimes found horrible spelling monstrously united with very good penmanship. The following is a specimen of hundreds which have fallen within my observation. "*A goode skoller rites slow.*" Now where there is such carelessness on the part of the teacher, it is not to be expected, that he should pay that attention which is desirable to the blunders of others.

There are many derivative words in very common use, which are not to be found in the spelling-book or dictionary. In order to know how to spell these, the scholar must commit such rules as will apply to them, and by impressing these rules indelibly in his memory, he will not need to hesitate when he wishes to write a word, which may vary in its orthography from the simple word, from which it is derived. There is also a class of words having the same pronunciation, but different in meaning and in spelling. The importance of learning to spell these correctly, should be distinctly explained by every teacher. A moment's reflection will be sufficient to convince every one of the great importance of this branch, and I need not dwell on it, farther than to point out one error which extensively prevails in the habits of country schoolmasters. It is this. In order to make the word easier to be spelled, it is given out with a pronunciation different from that used in reading or conversation. For example—the master puts out the word *immediate*. The *i* in the third syllable, has the sound of *e* in common pronunciation. Instead of sounding it as he ought, he gives the *i* a distinct long sound, in order that the scholar may know that, it is not *e*. Thus, im-me-d*i*-ate. Now this habit is very injurious to the scholar, for when he wishes to write the word, he will

hesitate. The common sound will be on his mind, and
he will be very liable to spell it wrong. Let this be a uniform rule : *Pronounce all words for a class to spell, just as
you would pronounce them in reading or conversation.*
That is, pronounce them right.

Reading is a subject that will claim much of your
attention at school. To read with propriety and elegance
is an interesting and valuable accomplishment. It should
be the object of every instructer, to have his scholars
attend to all the principles there exhibited. By care he
may accustom his scholars to read with a due degree of
loudness, distinctness and slowness; and to regard the
importance of accent, emphasis and cadence. I shall give
but few directions on this subject, as you will find more
books upon it, than upon most others.

1. When a class is called out to read, devote your whole
attention to it. It is a great error to let them read as
they please, and disregard the pauses end sense entirely.
Let it be known as a regulation of the school, that when a
class is reading, no one has leave to ask a question, or to
change his place.

2. Require every scholar to pronounce every syllable
so distinctly, that you can hear and understand the words.
Many instructers fail here, from the fact that they hold a
book, and have their eyes on the word that the scholar is
pronouncing, and understand what it is from reading it,
and not from hearing it read. Hence, it may be well, to
hear a class read at least once every day, without taking
a book. It will then be easily learned how many syllables
are not distinctly sounded by the young scholar. He
should be required to read every sentence till he reads it
right. In this way he will be made to improve more in
reading a single page, than he otherwise would in reading
half his book. It will be advantageous for the master to
question the class on the subjects of distinctness, slowness,
emphasis, &c. before the lesson is commenced.

3. Be careful to show every scholar the importance and
use of the stops or points in reading, and require him to
observe them. The pauses and inflections are of very
great consequence. Without attention to them, no one
can be a good reader. If children form a habit of neglecting them, when young, it will be very hard to correct this

habit afterward. What is more disagreeable than monotony ? What more unpleasant than to hear all the words
of a sentence pronounced alike, or with so rapid an utterance that none are distinct ? Much attention should be
paid to these directions.

4. Be careful to lead the attention of your class to the
character of the lesson to be read ; and to make the manner and tone of voice correspond to it. To this direction,
a degree of attention adequate to its importance, is seldom paid in district schools. To read a pathetic piece in
the same manner as you would read one of Æsop's Fables
—or, to read a prayer in the same tone of voice that you
would one of the humorous essays of Addison, is certainly
unnatural and improper. And yet in many of the schools
which I have had occasion to visit, I have heard pieces
of very different characters read in the same manner, and
I have scarcely ever observed that much attention was
paid to the subject. The fault lies with teachers. The
directions given in books are disregarded, and the same
monotony is permitted which was probably common in
the schools they attended when young. I would not say
that this remark is universally true. There are exceptions, and I believe there is an increasing attention to
this particular, especially in cities and large towns. But
the remark will hold true in relation to a great part of
the instructers of district schools, especially in country
towns.

5. Let it be the object of every teacher, to copy nature
in his own reading, and then he will be sure to read with
ease to himself and pleasure to his hearers. Scholars will
readily copy his tones of voice and manner, and be led to
form a taste for this important acquisition. In reading
on a mournful or playful subject, the manner and tone of
voice will correspond, and the sense of the writer be obtained. As far as possible, we should enter into the feelings of the writer, and utter his words very nearly as we
suppose he would utter them, if he were reading his own
language to us.

8

LECTURE X.

THE study of arithmetic will next claim your attention. It is one which may be very early commenced. Indeed as soon as the child has learned to count twenty, he may be taught to add, subtract, multiply and divide. He may thus at a very early age form distinct ideas of the " ground rules of arithmetic." As far as intellectual arithmetic is concerned, I would recommend the use of Mr. Smith's, or Mr. Colburn's excellent little works. Smith's, perhaps has the advantage, as containing the two systems, intellectual and written arithmetic combined.

I shall confine my remarks to the subject of written arithmetic, as taught to the more advanced scholar.

1. Let it be a first object to lead him to investigate the reasons on which the rules are founded. This is a direction of great importance. If he forms the early habit of inquiring why the direction is given for each step in his operation, he will be likely to proceed understandingly from the beginning. But if he is directed to go to his rule, or to commit it to memory, and then apply it to the performance of his operation, he will probably be led to suppose, that when he has obtained a correct answer, he understands his subject. He may go through with a common treatise on arithmetic in this way, and yet not understand the reasons on which the directions in the " ground rules " are founded. " I have cyphered through," is often said by a young man who in fact would find it very difficult to explain the reasons of the rule given for multiplication or division.

With all the attention such pay to arithmetic, they are but poorly prepared for the common transactions of life. Many persons are aware of this, and therefore provide themselves with a " cyphering book," and write down the operations in that for future use. In this way much more time is spent, than would be necessary for gaining a knowledge of the subject, adequate to the wants of life.

When any engage in this study, whether they are beginners or not, it is proper for you to begin with the simple rules, and question them on all the principles which have led to their formation. If the pupil can give you proper answers, it is well; if not, let him examine and search. Afford him assistance if he cannot find out the meaning for himself. If possible, let that assistance be given in such a way, as shall make him his own teacher. What I mean, is, ask him such questions, as will lead him to the right track, and will make him necessarily come to a just reason, and to a satisfactory conclusion.

I may be better understood, perhaps by an example. A class is called to recite the rule of multiplication.

Inst. What is multiplication?

Class. "Multiplication teaches, having two numbers given, to find a third, which shall contain either of the given numbers, as often as the other contains a unit."

Inst. Well, so your book says, but what does it mean? Can either of you explain it so that John, who has just commenced the rule, can understand it?

Class. [After hesitating some time.] No, sir, we cannot.

Inst. Think: cannot you use some other language which will make it plainer?

Class. May it not be called a short way of adding?

Inst. Yes, and that explains it much better than the long definition which you recited. Can you tell me now why it may be called short addition?

Class. Because it is the same as adding one of the numbers as many times to itself as there are units in the other. If we wish to multiply 3 by 5 it will be the same as writing three 5 times, or five 3 times and adding them together.

Inst. Very well, now tell me why two numbers are given, and not any more, to perform the operation.

Class. If there be more than one multiplicand, there must be two answers, and if there be more than one multiplier, the multipliers will be component parts of each other, and therefore would in reality be but one.

Inst. Why do you place one under the other?

Class. To make the operation more convenient. The work might possibly be done, if the numbers were differently placed.

The instructer may proceed to ask the following questions. Why do you begin at the right hand to multiply? Why do you multiply the whole multiplicand, with the right hand figures of the multiplier, before you multiply with the others? When you begin to multiply with the second figure, why do you put the product one place to the left of the first figure of the line above it? What is the value of the first product figure, in the second line, is it units or tens? When you have taken the third figure of the multiplier, why do you set the first figure of the product still farther to the left, and under the figure by which you multiply? What is the value of the first degree in the third line of the product, is it units, tens, or hundreds? Why do you add all the lines of the product, in order to get your answer?

How do you prove the result? How do you cast out the 9s? Why will this prove it? Will it prove it to cast out the 7s or 8s? Why not? Why do you take 9 rather than another number? Is there any other number that will prove it? Why will 3 answer as well as 9?

If the multiplier be 9, how can the work be shortened? Why will the placing as many cyphers at the right of the multiplicand, as you have 9s in the multiplier, and then subtracting the multiplicand once out, give the same answer as to multiply by the 9s contained in the multiplier?

Answers to all these questions will be necessary, in order to make the rule intelligible. But many of them are those that the scholar will not, perhaps, think of, unless they be asked him by the teacher.

What I wish to inculcate by the direction I have given is, that you proceed in a similar way through every rule. And if any of the answers cannot be given by your scholars, after opportunity is afforded them to try, let your own explanation be as simple as possible.

It is a useful exercise for a pupil to form a set of questions for himself to such rule, before being examined upon it. After he has thus formed all the questions he is able, you may make such additions as you think requisite. In this way he will be led to reflect on the rule, and will strive to understand the principles on which it is founded. He will not only gain more knowledge, but he will gain it in a way that will enable him to retain it longer, and apply it more readily, than by the common method.

Geography is a subject, which will undoubtedly claim considerable attention in your schools. To teach it in the best way is desirable, and though possibly I may not adduce any new thoughts on the subject, I still wish to call your attention to it a moment.

The mode generally pursued is to present a child with a map of the world, teach him its general divisions, how to distinguish them on the map, to bound them, &c. This mode has been approved by most instructers, but I am willing to confess, it has appeared to me the very opposite of the course, that nature would direct. Why should we attempt to teach a child what he cannot comprehend. Why should he learn the names of continents, islands, oceans, seas and lakes, rivers and mountains, many thousands of miles distant, before he is taught the geography of his own town, county, state and country ?

But a want of suitable works on this subject will render it impossible to adopt a course such as I shall recommend, except in a few states.*

Where it is practicable, therefore, let the child be taught something of the geography of his own neighbourhood and especially of his own state, before he commences the study of it, in a more extended manner. Let him be taught the boundaries of his own town ; the names and situation of its mountains, rivers, ponds, and other interesting particulars. Then the same things may be taught him of the adjoining towns, and of the county and state. By this mode, he will be led to form some ideas of distance and the size of places. He will be prepared to learn the same things in regard to other states, and his country and continent. From his own he may pass to other countries and continents, until the features of the world are in succession brought distinctly to his view.

As the above course would be a novelty in many places at the present time, I shall not dwell upon it, but give a few general directions.

1. Endeavour to have the outlines, the more general parts in this study, the first learned and very thoroughly

* Works have been published containing the geography of New Hampshire and of Vermont, designed for the benefit of children in those states.

8*

acquired. These should always be distinguished from the subjects in detail. They will be a guide to other knowledge, and will without doubt be better remembered, than if associated with a multiplicity of facts in detail.

2. Prominent facts in geography may be learned in such a way as to be remembered with greater ease. As far as practicable, let this be done. The mode pursued by Mr. Goodrich and Mr. Woodbridge, may be adopted even if it should not be convenient to use either of their works. By being furnished with the works yourselves, you may use them so as to have them benefit a class furnished with some other.

3. Make it an object to exhibit the facilities of obtaining the necessaries and conveniences of life, furnished by different climates and countries, also the inconveniences and privations peculiar to any section of the world on which the lesson of the class may be. This is recommended for the purpose of comparison with our own happy land, and for showing the general providence of God, which has so constituted things, that one part of the world is dependent on another for some of the conveniences of life ; also, for exhibiting the fact, that no part of the world is unprovided with the means of human happiness. To illustrate : where the soil is of the best quality, we seldom find mines of the rich or useful metals. Where these are found, the soil is often such that agriculture cannot be employed as a source of wealth. The most productive regions of the earth are often visited with dreadful storms and tempests. Troublesome insects, poisonous serpents, and the most ferocious beasts annoy the inhabitants of some parts, where otherwsie a residence might almost be compared to one in the Elysian fields

Scholars will always be interested by remarks on subjects of this kind, and not only so, they will derive lasting benefit from them.

4. Accustom your scholars to drawing maps on slates, from recollection. If they know this will be expected of them, they will examine the situation of places, mountains, rivers, &c. with much more attention than otherwise, and will probably retain the knowledge which they acquire, much better than if not required to attend to this exercise. The instructer, at the close of the recitation,

should examine the slates, and point out the deficiencies or errors. The *outline maps* in the improved Atlas, accompanying Morse's popular Geography, may be used with great advantage.

English Grammar is a study important to all, and is one which you will be expected to teach. The modes pursued by instructers are so various, and the views entertained by writers so different, that we are very far from having arrived at any uniform system. Unquestionably each author supposes his own work complete or nearly so. Some authors have written much better than others, but while there is such a diversity, I shall not select any one on which to apply the few directions for teaching, which I propose to give you.

To say that the mode of teaching grammar, most usual in district schools requires correction, is saying merely what is proved by the fact, that it is usually considered dry and uninteresting by a great majority who attend to it; and of course very little advancement is made in it. The more usual method is to put a book into the hand of the scholar, and require him to commit certain parts of it to memory, and, when this is done, he is called upon to parse sentences and apply the rules of syntax. Parsing is continued year after year, without much attention to any thing but deciding on the parts of speech, and applying rules. When he is able to tell the parts of speech at sight, and refer to rules applicable to the several words, he is often called a good grammarian, and is not unfrequently considered qualified to be an instructer of others. But after all, it may be doubted whether he is better acquainted with grammar, than some have been, who have never studied the rules of syntax. That this mode occupies much time, to little profit, I think must be conceded by all who understand the subject. While I make this remark I wish not to be considered as a convert to the doctrine of those masters who have professed their ability to teach grammar in a month, or even half of that time. But it does appear to me, that time is often, as I have personal experience to prove, misspent and lost, in consequence of not adopting a better system of teaching, than has been usual in primary schools and academies.

If a better mode of teaching than the following can be acquired, I would advise you to pursue it. If you are inclined to judge favourably of the directions I shall give, it will probably be found by you, that the system contains one advantage, at least ; that of making the study pleasing. Among a very large number with whom 1 have pursued it, I have seldom found any, who complained that grammar was unpleasant or dry.

1. Let it be an object to explain to your scholars what grammar is, and the importance of understanding the nature of their own language. This must lead them to see that in attending to this study, they are not learning that which is useless or unnecessary. They will be made acquainted with its usefulness by familiar illustration, and when this is accomplished, they will commence the study with far more interest than otherwise. The exact meaning of the four subjects, on which it treats, should be fully explained. The child often has not the most distant idea, that while he is learning to spell words, he is learning grammar. Etymology is often unintelligible ; but show him how words are derived from each other, and how the part of speech is effected hy varying the word, and he will become interested. To illustrate :—Take the word *man*, and show him how many words come from it, or require him to tell all the words which he can recollect, and then explain the meaning which each has, and why they are classed with different parts of speech ; as, *man*, a noun ; *to man*, a verb ; *manning*, a participle ; *manful*, an adjective ; *manfully*, an adverb ; and *manliness*, another noun. By an exercise of this kind he will be pleased, and will be obtaining the meaning of many words, which he otherwise would not learn. After he has formed the habit of distinguishing the derivative from the primitive, the scholar may be told that this as well as spelling, is a part of grammar.

2. When it becomes proper to have a scholar begin the grammar or text book, let him first learn the definition of the most common parts of speech, as, the noun, pronoun, and verb. Then let him take a sentence and select all the nouns in it, and tell why they are nouns,—all the pronouns and tell why they are pronouns,—and all the verbs, and tell why they are verbs. The next lesson may be to learn the different kinds of nouns, and articles, and what be-

longs to each, and then he should select the nouns in a sentence, and tell why they are nouns ; what kind and why—what number and why—what gender and why—what person and why : also, the articles, and tell why they are articles, what kind, and why of that kind. Let the scholar proceed in this way through the pronoun and through the verb, and then learn the other parts of speech. He should then be taught to parse all the words of a sentence in course, and tell what each word is, and give his reasons for every thing he says about it. In this way he will learn understandingly, and will be able to see why those definitions and rules have been given, which he has been called upon to commit to memory.

After he can demonstrate easily, he may be directed to commit some of the most important rules of syntax, and to apply them to the language which he parses. He should be asked when he says " the nominative case governs a verb," or a " verb agrees with its nominative case," how the rule applies to the phrase in question, and on what principle it is founded ? and, though he may not be able to give an answer, yet, by having been asked the question, he will be more likely to recollect the explanation which you may give, and be able to repeat it when you ask him again.

A mode like the above, pursued through the whole course of grammar, will leave nothing dark to the mind of the scholar. He will understand as fast as he proceeds, and will find nothing hard.

3. When the rules of syntax are acquired and he can apply them with facility, he will be prepared to analyze sentences, and should be taught to distinguish between a sentence and phrase—a simple and compound sentence, and also to know what are the principal parts of a sentence, as, the subject, attribute and object.

The exercise of showing how words are derived one from another should be continued, and the pupil be accustomed to point out the parts of speech, which may come from a single word. He will by this be able to see the dependence of one word upon another, and learn to discriminate the character of each.

In this connexion I would recommend giving him sentences, in which there is some grammatical error, for him to detect, and to give his reason for thinking it an error.

This exercise is very important, as it will lead him to guard against errors in the formation of sentences, and will help him to apply the knowledge which he has acquired, to the practical purpose for which it was designed. In selecting sentences for this purpose, it will be well to take them from the conversation of the scholar himself, or language in common use, which is ungrammatical, as this will lead him to examine his own language by the rules which he has learned.

It will be expected that you should instruct your scholars in Penmanship. This is a very necessary accomplishment, but it would be better if it could be taught in a school, where it should be the only branch. Yet long custom has placed it among the requisitions of a common school. It is not possible, I think, at the present, to obviate this inconvenience, and the only inquiry is, how we may make it the least injurious to other branches of study, and secure the greatest improvement in this.

The result of my own experience has been, that three quarters of an hour, devoted once a day exclusively to this exercise, is better than a longer period, and is the least likely to interfere with other studies.

1. Prepare all the books for writing at your own room, and furnish the copies which will be necessary for the day. If any books are not ruled for writing, I would recommend to the instructer to do it himself, when he prepares the copies. This will save much time to the school, and prevent much disturbance from the noise of borrowing rules, or frequent removals to get them, and using them when obtained. The copies ought to be prepared before you come into school, in order to have your whole time there, to devote to other objects.

When the hour appointed for writing arrives, let every thing else be dropped by those who are to write, let them take their books and pens, and attend to their writing only.

2. While the scholars are writing, devote your whole attention to them. See that every scholar sits in an easy and proper posture. Attend to the manner in which every pen is held, and be careful that every one writes slowly. The master should go from scholar to scholar, and give directions, as he may find them necessary. If the house

is properly constructed, he will be able to go to every scholar in the class once in two or three, or at most, in five minutes. He will be able to direct in regard to the writing of every line—to point out errors and defects to be avoided. The progress of the pupil will depend very much upon the interest he is made to feel in the subject. But without attention, no progress of importance can be made.

3. When the time for writing has expired, let all the pens be cleaned at once, and the books be all returned. If scholars be permitted to continue writing, after the attention of the instructer is turned to other exercises of the school, they will often write carelessly, and make no improvement. When *one* ceases, *all* should cease, and direct their attention to another subject.

By pursuing a course like the above, there will be very little loss of time, and very little danger of the formation of careless habits. But if scholars are permitted to call for copies when they please, and to write as much and as carelessly as they please, they will greatly disturb the course of the school, and probably contract habits which will be broken up with difficulty ; they will waste paper and time, and make very little progress either in writing or in their other studies.

4. In preparing copies, it is important to have a system. The easiest parts of letters should be first made, and a regular course of lessons given. Unless some system is adopted, it will be impossible for the teacher to be uniform with himself. He will be liable to neglect some letters, while others are very frequently used in the copies. Every one who pretends to teach without following some system, will teach but imperfectly.

I shall conclude this lecture, with some remarks on teaching History.* This is a study which ought to be

---

* The following remarks on this point are from the Journal of Education, and better than any that I have seen.

" The teacher's first duty, on this plan, is to make himself familiar with all the details of the history of the city, town, or village in which he teaches, and to take particular notice of every spot or object which is linked with an historical association,—with the occurrence of any remarkable event. The second step in this practical method of teaching, is, to carry the young learners to as many as possible of these places or objects, and to fasten on the youthful mind a correct and abiding impression of them, as connected with the event which gives them their celebrity

pursued in all your schools, at least so far as relates to the history of our own country. Every teacher should speak of it as a necessary study, and as one which will be very pleasant. Though there is no text-book, which seems to me exactly fitted for common schools, yet there are many that contain valuable information, and by selecting subjects from them of the most interest, and making these plain to the understanding of the scholar, by such illustration as the nature of them will admit, the children will be highly interested.

I would recommend to you to commence with a class, by giving them several lectures on the history of their own town or state, or the places where they are most acquainted. Then lessons from books in regard to particular events, which have taken place. Such should be selected as have been connected in an eminent degree with the welfare of the country. When subjects are given them, instead of requiring them to take all the events in their connection, the class will be more likely to engage with interest, and to retain what they learn.—If these lessons are given, following the order of time in which the incidents occurred, a connected history of the most prominent

or interest. Here are several great points gained :—the health of the pupils is benefited by the fresh open air, and the invigorating exercise of walking ;—the corporeal effort and enjoyment produce an active, and excited, and happy state of mind ; —every thing wears the aspect of reality, and of nature, and of life,—curiosity is excited to the highest pitch, and receives the amplest gratification ;—from the living voice of the teacher, the ear drinks in instruction with delight, in the scene of the strange, or romantic, or glorious action which has left its indelible impress on the spot;—the teacher too loses the character of the task-master, and becomes the living and venerated oracle of his young circle of listeners,—he becomes one of their sources of pleasure and is loved accordingly. These results are brilliant ;— but they are not imaginary: they are those which took place in the early lessons received in childhood by the individual who writes this article, and which he has had the happiness of seeing realized in the young listeners to his own words.

"Here a person who is unacquainted with this mode of instruction may start an objection. But what if there is no high, romantic, or kindling interest in the scene where you teach ? The simple answer is, it is not necessary that there should be. The interesting details of humble adventure, the narrative of domestic life, the tale of the early settlers,—all of which have a poetic charm for the young,—will suit the same purpose, will enkindle curiosity, secure attention, and convert the study of history, from a task or a book-dream, into a pleasing reality.— Another objection may be that, with young pupils, this method of instruction is necessarily circumscribed ;—they cannot walk or travel so far as to embrace a very wide circle of classical or historic ground. Granted : still, every village has the little story of its early settlement, and its spots or objects noted for something which took place in days gone by ; and should there be but one such spot or object, it will serve, to begin with to give the study of history the aspect of reality. For every event read in a wider circle of historical narrative, will by association be made to bear a resemblance to this. The young pupil will be made to realise that such things were.

"After such a beginning, the teacher transfers as far as he can, the same method to the study of the history of the county or state in which his pupils reside, and afterwards to that of their native country in general.

events will be obtained, and each general subject will remain firmly fixed in the mind.

To illustrate more fully what I mean.—After a few general subjects, such as may regard the history of the town, neighbourhood or state, I would recommend that the lessons be given out in a manner somewhat like the following.—" You may take your histories and learn, so that you can relate to me, the most important particulars relative to the first discovery of the country. I shall ask you these questions :—Who discovered America? From what country was he? How many ships had he? What happened on the voyage? After his men had grown disaffected how long did Columbus persuade them to sail? What happened during that time? What did Columbus do when he arrived at the shore? What name did he give to the place? Whom did he find there? What was it that interested very much the attention of his men? What did the natives think of Columbus and his crew? What happened when they were on their homeward passage? How were they received? &c." The next subject may be the first settlement of Jamestown; then, that of New-England; the next, the history of the settlement of New-York, and of its being taken by the English. " Now," you may say to them. " I wish you to tell me for your next lesson, about the contest between the Colonies and England, and what was the consequence?—Afterwards, the particulars of the battle of Lexington, then, that of Bunker Hill, &c."

By proceeding in this way, and making the pupil fix his mind on but one subject, for each lesson, he will be able to understand his lesson fully, and will read attentively every thing that regards the subject on which he is to be examined. I am confident that two objects will be secured by this mode, which are not gained as well by putting a book into the hands of a scholar and requiring him to learn the whole : viz. He will be better pleased, and will gain a more distinct knowledge of the most interesting facts. I would not say positively that the mode I have recommended is the best; but it has succeeded better than any I have known in our schools. If the members of a class have different books, it will not be very material, as each author treats of all the most interesting facts in history.

9

LECTURE XI.

In the preceding Lectures, I have remarked on the studies usually required in district schools. But I am not satisfied that these should be the only subjects introduced into these important institutions. In this lecture, I shall speak of some other branches which ought to be pursued, and remark on improving all the opportunities which may occasionally be offered of making salutary impressions on the minds of scholars. Among the subjects that should receive attention beside those already mentioned, *Composition* is pre-eminent. " That which gives to any branch of study its greatest value, is its practical utility." If this sentiment be just, Composition should never be neglected. Every one who can write, has occasion to compose letters of business or friendship, and in some way or other, to express his thoughts on paper more or less frequently. To neglect, while acquiring an education for common business, some things which are as important as others which receive *particular* attention is not the dictate of reason. But this consideration is not the only evidence that this subject claims attention.—Arranging our ideas in sentences, and combining those sentences so as to express a continued train of thought, is one of the best means of making the knowledge, which we gain, practical. Perhaps hardly any exercise is a better discipline of the mind than the writing of Composition. It is the application of knowledge to the business of life. Without such application, much that is acquired will soon be lost, and if not lost of what value can it be to its possessor ? Of what use to the farmer were all the theory that might be obtained, if he never applied his knowledge to his business ?

When Composition is neglected in district schools, it becomes a very burdensome exercise to such as may afterward attend a higher school or an academy. Many have I seen weep, because this was then made a requisition for the first time. " I was never called·upon to write before, and now it seems to me that I cannot," has been said to me by many. " I wish I had been required to write when I attended the district school, and now it would not be such a task."

The following directions may be of service to you on this subject.

1. Labour to impress the minds of the school with a sense of its great importance. This may be done by representing the many situations in which they would highly value the art of expressing their thoughts on paper —the interest they will feel in being able to compose a letter to a friend in handsome style—the inconvenience they must often suffer, if they neglect this study until obliged to write and expose their ignorance, or have to make application to others to do that, which they ought to be able to do for themselves. All this may be impressed upon their minds by means of familiar illustrations.

2. It has been found profitable to commence with young scholars, by giving them a number of words, and requiring them to write a sentence, in which one or more should be used. The first words may be nouns, the next adjectives —the next pronouns, &c. Give the child a slip of paper with the direction and words, as for instance, the following—Write ten sentences and use one of the following words in each. Man, gold, stars, indemnity, gravitation, lines, eagerness, play, home, garden. Compositions should afterwards embrace a variety of other single words or of words compounded.

The object of this course is to make the task easy—to have the invention of the scholar brought into vigorous exercise—and to have him excited to learn the exact meaning of words. It is conceived that by such a mode all these objects are gained, in a more or less important degree.

3. When the scholars are sufficiently exercised in this kind of composition, it may be useful to read a story to them, and then let them relate as much of it as they can in their own words. This enables them to see the importance of paying close attention to what they hear, and of fixing the most prominent ideas, so as to treasure them up. But as they will not be likely to retain any full sentence,

it leads them to the exercise of arranging ideas in sentences, nearly as much as writing an original composition. They will not suffer from not knowing what to write, and will probably be amused and pleased with the exercise.

4. Subjects may afterwards be given them on which to write. These should be those with which they are familiar, or may become so by reading.

It is always better to *give* subjects than to let the pupil *select* for himself; for he will often choose without judgment, and is frequently unable to decide on any one, till he has become exceedingly confused. He will often select the hardest subjects thinking them the easiest. Of this kind are such as the following ; friendship, love, hope, spring, summer, autumn, winter, youth, &c.

In selecting subjects it is very important they should be such as will benefit the scholars in a moral point of view, or in supplying rules and precepts for the transactions of life. If a young person can be excited to a proper course of reflection on the influence which different habits will have upon his happiness and usefulness, he will be much more likely to form correct ones, than he would without such reflections. It is therefore of very great importance to lead the young to such reflections as shall be of the greatest benefit in the formation of correct habits. Such questions as the following, when given, as subjects of composition, have been found very useful. What four things ought the young to seek first, in order to promote their happiness? What six habits may I form while young, that will secure to me the greatest personal enjoyment, and respectability ? By the formation of what five habits can I do the most good to my fellow-creatures ? By what five habits can I most injure society ? Describe the character of such persons or families as you would wish for your neighbours. Must the drunkard be an unhappy man ? if so, why ? Do you believe the thief, liar, &c. can be happy ? if not, why ?

Questions on subjects of this character may be multiplied and varied according to the judgment of the teacher, and may be rendered easier or harder according to the ability of the class. The scholars thus, not only derive satisfaction from the easy accomplishment of their tasks, but are excited to reflect, and to make up their opinions on subjects very important to them, while forming habits and characters for life.

5. Recommend to your pupils to correspond with each other by letters—to ask each other questions to be answered in writing, and also to write down their own reflections for their own private use.

The effect of this course will unquestionably be salutary. They will not only be excited to a cultivation of the social affections, but will undoubtedly be much advanced in the art of composition. This knowledge, however, will not long be retained without practice. Practice, in the way recommended, will be likely to cause them to examine rules, and to correct as far as they can, their own compositions. Every thing, which has a tendency to call forth their own powers of mind, is important and will be productive of good.

After composition, or in connexion with it, it is highly important that you should lead the scholars to become interested in the subject of moral philosophy. It may not indeed be practicable in some, perhaps a majority of schools, to introduce the regular study of this branch, but you may make your scholars acquainted with some of its important principles. You may teach them to examine the reasons of moral distinctions. You may teach them to examine the character of the things they approve, and of those they disapprove ;—why some things please and others displease them. They may be taught that in *all* there is implanted a moral sentiment, and that this has a material influence on human happiness. You may inform them what feelings and what actions are virtuous and what are vicious by referring them to the great rule of duty as presented in the law of God.

It is important for every one to have some acquaintance with some of the *first principles* of Natural Philosophy and Chemistry. With the *results* of these principles every one is daily acquainted. But of the principles which produce these results multitudes are totally ignorant.

They are of course unable to apply these principles to the practical purposes of life. The production of some

9*

of the most common phenomena is often as mysterious to them, as the most abstruse principles of science. Now it certainly would add to their happiness, and often to their success in life, to have many of these phenomena explained to them. Every child knows that water will rise in a pump, but why or how it gets up is a mystery to him—he knows that wood, when put upon the fire will burn, and that a stone will not, but why one should burn rather than the other he cannot tell.—He knows he can raise a weight by a lever, which, without it, would resist his strength, but why he gains power, he does not know. He sees one piece of land productive and another barren, but what should occasion the difference is beyond his power to tell.

Now, what I wish on your part is, that some of these principles should be familiarly explained, for the purpose of correcting wrong ideas and leading scholars to attend to principles of daily interest and occurrence.

In regard to these and other subjects on which you may have opportunity to remark, let it be your undeviating rule to impart all the knowledge within your power.

I wish to add a direction here, for which I have found no better place in these Lectures; viz. study to seize on and improve favourable moments to impart valuable instruction, or important practical knowledge.

There are some seasons when impressions may be made on the minds of the young, much more favourably than at others. The attention is awake, the mind becomes amused and impressions then made will be more lasting, than when the mind is not excited. Such seasons should be regarded as a seed-time, which if improved by the teacher, may be the means of producing very important fruits.

I shall be best understood, by examples. An eclipse occurred during the hours of the school. The darkness occasioned a suspension of labour for a season. After permitting the scholars to go and look at it, and at the objects around shrouded in gloom, the teacher returned with them to the school-room, and addressed them in the following manner.

"You have seen," said he, "a most interesting sight to-day, and one which may lead you to some profitable reflections. The moon is a planet very small when compared with the earth, or the sun, and yet by being near us, and coming between us and the sun, has obscured that light which is so cheerful and necessary. I wish to turn your thoughts for a moment to the interesting nature of the study of astronomy, by which, the motions of the heavenly bodies may be perfectly known, and their size and distance determined with certainty. I wish you to know also, the importance of this science to us. If astronomers had not been able to tell us of this eclipse and had not we expected it to-day, how great must have been our terror! We might have been as much frightened as some of the ancients are said to have been at similar appearances. But now we look upon it with the utmost delight, as a rare exhibition of the effect of planetary motion. Had you seen an astronomer calculating this eclipse five years ago, you might have said he was not surely doing any thing to benefit you; but you now see how much terror and fear he has saved you, by telling you beforehand of the sublime spectacle of to-day. All the art, which *he* had, is what *you* may easily acquire, by attending to the study of astronomy. Who is there that would not delight in a study so sublime and important? He who first learned that this eclipse would happen to-day, was once a little child, and knew no more, than the most ignorant of you. You may, like him, become learned and wise. By resolutely and faithfully pursuing your studies, you may be able to understand all that others know of astronomy, or any other of the sciences which man has acquired. But he, among you, who is unwilling to persevere in obtaining knowledge, must continue to be ignorant of that which others know. Now who of you will choose to be ignorant, and who of you will endeavour to be wise? I shall know your individual determinations, by observing who of you are, hereafter, faithful in improving your time, and who among you choose play and ignorance, in preference to usefulness and wisdom."

Take another example. It was one of actual occurrence. It was a chilly day of winter, and we were all seated in a comfortable school-room. A man of most wretched appearance was seen passing by, drawing a hand-sled, on which were several bundles of woolen rags, the remnants of garments worn till they could be of no further use. He was clad in those but little better, and was ap-

parently so weak as to be scarcely able to draw his sled.
—Some looked out of the window and began to laugh.
The instructer saw him, and remarked, the school may
rise, and all look at that wretched man passing by.—
All did so, and nearly all were diverted to laughter. After
all had seen him, the master told them they might take
their seats, and then remarked : " I was willing you should
look at that man, but possibly my object was very different
from yours, as I see the effect on your feelings was very
different from what was produced on mine. That miserable man, you may at once perceive, is crazy. He has
bundles of rags on his sled, which, perhaps, he values, but
which can be of no service to him.ᐟ You perceived he
looked pale and emaciated ; he was so weak as scarcely
to be able to draw his load. He is very poorly shielded
from the cold of winter, and will very probably perish in
the snow.—Now tell me, my scholars, does this man excite
your laughter ? He was once a school-boy ; he was bright
and active as any of you ; his return from school was wel-
comed by joyful parents, and his presence gave pleasure
to the youthful throng who met each other in a winter
evening for merriment and sport. Look at him now, and
can you sport with him who has lost his reason, and, in
losing that, has lost all ? Should I point to one of you, and
be able by looking down into future years, to say to the
rest, your associate will hereafter be crazy and roam around
a wretched maniac, would you not rather weep than laugh ?
You saw me affected when I began to speak—I will tell
you why.—I once had a friend.—He was dear to me as a
brother ; he was every thing I could wish in a friend.
The character of his mind was such, as raised in his
friends high expectations. I have indeed, seldom, if ever
seen his equal. He could grasp any subject, and what
others found difficult, only served as amusement for him.
I have many of his letters which would not disgrace any
well-educated man, although written by him, when he was
a school-boy. I expected to see him taking a lead in the
affairs of men, and that his opinions would be quoted by
others. I saw him after an absence of two years—where,
do you ask ? it was in a cage, and even then he was chain-
ed ! ! He was a maniac of the most decided character.
The moment he saw me, he seized my hand, and left on

it the impression of his own, for it was divested of the skin, by constantly rubbing it in the other. For years, he has wandered about, when it was safe to liberate him. But he is now, and he always will be insane.

" I have known sorrow—have seen friends die that were as near as friends could be ; but, the hour that I sat by the confined and crazy Bernet, *was an hour of the greatest anguish I ever knew.* Remember, my pupils, from what has passed this hour, to render unfeigned thanks to God for continuing your reason hitherto, and if ever again you are disposed to laugh, when a crazy man passes, remember what *may be* your own condition hereafter."

Many occasions will occur, when you may make salutary and lasting impressions on the minds of those placed under your instruction. Seize these precious occasions, and improve them with a high regard to the best interest of your pupils. I have only to add that in all your intercourse with scholars, it is incumbent on you, to make use of every means not only to promote their present welfare, but to lay the foundation of such habits of thinking and acting, as shall promote their greatest happiness hereafter. By keeping this constantly in mind, you may be the occasion of lasting benefit to them, and have the satisfaction of reflecting that you have done your duty.

LECTURE XII.

I HAVE hitherto said but little to you upon the proper methods of exciting the attention of scholars to their studies. The subject is too important to be passed without remarks.

In the sentiments which will be advanced, you will probably observe a wide difference from those that may have been exhibited to you, by instructers heretofore. I am persuaded however you will give them an attentive examination, before you judge them unworthy of attention.

What are proper inducements to be made use of, in gaining the attention of scholars, and leading them to make a proper improvement of their opportunities for acquiring knowledge ?

In answering this question, it must, I think be conceded, that those inducements should be used, which will lead to the happiest result, and not be attended with particular or general evil : and those methods of excitement are censurable, which are attended with evils greater than the amount of good they are intended to effect. That some of this character are often used, I am convinced by observation. That such are now used is equally certain. The character of the motives in question, will here be presented to your attention.

1. Are emulation and ambition proper to be used for the purpose of excitement ? In order to answer this question, we must examine the character and influence of both. "The meaning of emulation," says Parkhurst,* "*is a desire to excel*, for the sake of the gratification of being superior to others." This gratification includes both the pleasure of reflecting on our own superiority, and also that of seeing and thinking that this superiority is known to our companions and the world. The votary of emulation loves to look down upon others; and the greater the number he sees below him, of those who were once his equals or superiors, the more exquisite is the gratification he feels. He is willing that others should stand high, if he can stand still higher,but, if he must stand low, he wishes others to stand still lower. This principle of action seems sometimes to become so strong, as to swallow up all others. Of this a striking instance is offered in the language which Milton ascribes to Satan :

" Better to reign in Hell, than serve in Heaven."

" He who is actuated by a principle of emulation chooses to obtain a superiority to others, rather by elevating himself, than by depressing them : First, because he will in this way not only become superior to his competitors, but also to others at a greater distance, and will thus hold a more elevated station in the view of the world ; and, secondly, because he will give more applause and admiration, if he

* Moral Philosophy, p. 149.

raises himself by fair means, than if he retards or sinks others, in order to get above them."

2. "The word *ambition* is frequently synonymous with emulation ; but it is also used in a sense in which emulation is not. The latter term is confined chiefly in its application to children and youth, while ambition is used chiefly to denote the operation of the same principles in men, especially those who signalize themselves in a military and political capacity. Emulation has respect chiefly to rivals near at hand ; ambition seeks a superiority which has no limits. Emulation seeks to excel in things, chiefly, which are of a personal nature; as in bodily strength and agility, or in mental attainments and powers. Ambition, besides seeking to excel others in the same endowments, exercised on a larger scale, also seeks to exceed them in grandeur, wealth, and fame. The *principle* in all these cases is the same. It is a desire of superiority for the sake of the gratification and personal advantage it affords."

I know that the word emulation is not always used in the sense given to it by the author quoted ; but, still I am not able to disprove the general correctness of his definition. We sometimes hear the expressions, "virtuous ambition," "just ambition," "proper ambition," &c. The word is sometimes used to express an ardent desire after an object, without reference to the means, or to rivalship and competition. "Thus a child who studies alone is said to be ambitious to learn, meaning merely that he is very anxious to learn and to acquire knowledge. Thus a man sometimes says it is his ' highest ambition,' to please another, meaning that he has a *very strong desire* to please another and to gain his approbation. In this case ambition is totally distinct from emulation. I am not certain, however, that this use of the word is found in any good writer."

You will understand me as using the words "emulation and ambition, as denoting the same principle." In order more fully to answer the question, whether it is proper to use emulation in exciting attention to study, it will be necessary to consider with what it is connected ; and also, from what it is distinct.

1. It is very evident that it is intimately associated with both pride and vanity. Here the author before

quoted, speaks my own sentiments. "Pride is the thinking of ourselves more highly than we ought to think." Emulation, by leading a person to think frequently of his own attainments and excellences, cherishes pride. Vanity is a desire of admiration, and this is an essential ingredient of emulation. The votary of emulation usually receives his chief pleasure from being admired and commended. Here and there an individual may not be satisfied with a proud consciousness of a superiority; but there are few who would desire any great superiority to others, unless their superiority were known and noticed.

2. "Emulation is intimately connected with hatred and envy." "Plato makes emulation the daughter of envy;" but I would rather say, she is the mother of envy, since it appears to be a desire to possess the superiority and advantages which we see another possess, that leads us to envy him of these advantages. Envy appears not to be a simple principle, but compounded of a desire to deprive some other of a good which he possesses, because we do not possess the same ourselves, and hatred of that other, because he enjoys something which we do not. The connexion between emulation and envy is, therefore, that of cause and effect. Emulation if unsuccessful always produces envy; and of course hatred, that being an essential ingredient of envy. Sometimes the envy that is produced by unsuccessful competition, is small in degree and transient in duration, being overcome by other principles; and sometimes it rises into anger and revenge, or settles into inveterate hatred and malice. And any one who has made use of emulation in the education of children, must have had opportunity to notice these unhappy effects."

Emulation is entirely distinct from some other principles, which are virtuous, or at least innocent, with which it is sometimes compounded.

1. "It is distinct from a desire to make great attainments in virtue and knowledge. A person may desire knowledge and make great efforts to attain it, because he loves it; because every new idea which the mind acquires is a source of pleasure; and because he derives a satisfaction from the exercise of his mental faculties in acquiring ideas, and in afterwards recollecting and compar-

ing them. Again, he may desire knowledge for the sake of becoming more useful in the world, of promoting the happiness of others in a greater degree. This is a virtuous motive. In the same manner he may desire any virtuous endowment whatever of body or mind, not because it will render him superior to others, but because it is valuable in itself, and may promote his own good or that of the public.

2. " Emulation is also distinct from a comparison of our-selves with others, for the sake of judging more correctly what progress we have made in knowledge and improve-ment. If emulation exists, a comparison of ourselves with others is sure to fan the flame, and if it does not yet exist, such a comparison is likely to enkindle it. But this comparison is not emulation itself, and may be made without exciting it. Suppose that a youth is pursuing his studies, actuated by a desire to do good. He observes that he makes greater progress than his fellows. This gives him pleasure, not because he excels, but because his prospect of being useful in the world is brightened. If, however, he believes their object the same as his own, and reflects that their inferiority in talents and learning will render them less useful than they might otherwise be, this reflec-tion will give him more pain than he will derive pleasure, from the prospect of his own superior usefulness. But after all, a frequent comparison of our own talents and attainments with those of others, is a dangerous experi-ment ; and a disposition, frequently to make it, is almost a sure sign of a spirit of emulation.

3. Emulation is distinct from a desire to do much good in the world. Distinguished activity to do good, let it proceed from one in a station ever so high, may spring from the purest benevolence, and is therefore no evidence of a spirit of emulation, or an ambitious principle. A man who thus distinguishes himself is not to be called ambi-tious, unless he appears fond of being known to be emi-nently useful, and gives evidence of love of fame and applause.

4. Emulation is distinct from a desire to imitate the virtuous deeds of another, or *resemble* him in virtuous character. Virtue appears more amiable, when it is ex-hibited in a living character, and when its happy fruits

10

are actually seen, than it can appear, when viewed in the
abstract. Whoever loves virtue, therefore, will feel a
stronger desire to possess and practise it, in proportion as
his perceptions of its excellence are more distinct and
lively.* A desire to imitate the wise and good is easily
distinguished from emulation, because it involves no desire
of superiority. There is an instance in scripture where
this desire to imitate the virtues of another, is spoken of
under the name of emulation. But in this place, Rom.
xi. 14. the term is evidently used in a good sense, for
it was Paul's object to persuade the Jews to imitate
the Gentiles by believing in Christ. The appropriate use
of the word may be seen in Gal. v. 20. where it is classed
with " hatred, variance, wrath, strife, envyings, murders,"
&c.

5. " Emulation is distinct from the desire of having a
good name and enjoying the approbation of the wise and
good. A good name is to be desired for the sake of increasing our influence and usefulness in the world. The
approbation of the wise and virtuous is to be desired for
the same reason, and also because it assures us of the
friendly regard of those whose approbation we enjoy.
There is an innocent and lively pleasure in being beloved
by those we love; and some degree of this pleasure is felt,
when we learn that we have gained the approbation of good
men, even though we have no personal acquaintance with
them. This is totally distinct from the love of praise and
the desire of admiration and applause."

Such being the character of emulation, the conclusion
must be obvious, that its tendency is injurious. " The
encouragement of emulation, cannot fail to strengthen
the selfish principles of our nature. That all selfish and
malevolent principles have a hurtful tendency is evident.

" Instead of having a good effect, emulation has an injurious one, on the acquisition of knowledge, and the
improvement of the mind. In order to have a scholar
understand and remember what he learns, it is necessary
for him to love learning for its own sake. And he who
studies diligently, because he derives pleasure from it,
will not while studying think of any other motive. The

---

* See Kame's Elements of Criticism, vol. i. p. 55.

constant pleasure he derives from the exercise of his mental faculties and the acquisition of new ideas, is a stimulus that makes him diligent and persevering, and impresses on his memory, that which he learns. But emulation affords a motive entirely different from this. This pleasure is the *reward* to which he looks forward as the fruit of his application. Just so far then as the mind dwells on this subject, it is withdrawn from its present employment.—And just so far as the desire of excelling others has a place in the breast, it excludes the love of study for its own sake. If the scholar, while studying is constantly calculating how far he has got, and how far he can get, and anticipating a triumph over his rivals, or fearing that they will triumph over him, it is next to impossible that he should get his lesson *well*, or remember it *long*. He exercises his memory while studying, in order to recite as much as possible, but does not bring his judgment or discrimination into exercise. When his lesson is recited, he thinks of it but little, and applies himself as before." This is an evil much worse in common schools, than in seminaries where there are various examinations afterwards, for which the scholar is required to be prepared. But it is undoubtedly, on the whole, an evil wherever it is made the exciting principle in schools of any description. "This will be very apparent when we bear in mind that the successful votaries of emulation must be few." There is but one head to a class, and after trial, all but one or two will be liable to feel a discouragement, which will dampen the ardour of study, and diminish the amount of knowledge gained.

Again, the use of emulation as a stimulus in schools lays the foundation for ambition in the pursuits of life. "I wish to beat"—"I'll try to beat "—"I can beat," is language you will hear from children and youth as common as any language, where emulation is the instrument of excitement in any institution of learning. It is introduced into amusements, and leads to all those games where the trial of agility or strength is, to see, who will *beat.* A foundation is thus laid for what we so often see in after life, of the race of popularity, office-seeking management and manœuvres, and efforts to elevate one's self by the downfall of others. And "let it be remembered that

emulation, but he may be told he has done *well*—has done better than *usual*, or that he has not done as well as he ought, when he has been negligent. For the most part, however, the countenance of the instructer will express sufficient approbation or censure, without the aid of words. If he loves to teach, and to see the improvement of his scholars, they will readily perceive his feelings, and the liveliest emotions will be excited in their breasts. The pleasure which the good scholar feels, when he sees the smile of approbation, is innocent, so long as the principle of emulation is excluded.

3. A love of learning for its own sake is a very powerful stimulus. This is a motive which will not only draw the pupil from amusements or other employments to his studies, but will operate powerfully while he is studying to produce intense application and perseverance. The scholar who derives a pleasure from the acquisition of new ideas, and the exercise of his mental powers, will be far more likely to understand thoroughly what he learns; will find the new ideas he has gained frequently revolving in his mind afterwards from day to day, and will retain them in his memory, ready for use, whenever occasion may require.

4. Present to your scholars their obligations to study as a duty, which if properly regarded will add to their happiness, but if disregarded will subject them to the reprehension of their own consciences.

It is a duty which they owe to themselves. They are under obligation to regard their own happiness, and to make all reasonable preparation for it. They have an opportunity to add to their enjoyment by increasing their knowledge. To disregard it and to misimprove the opportunity afforded them, will be to lay the foundation for subsequent sorrow and regret.

It is a duty, they owe to their teacher, to make the best use of his instructions. His time is devoted to them. He is anxious to help them, and affords every reasonable assistance in the acquisition of knowledge.

It is a duty they owe their parents, to make the best improvement of the facilities furnished them for gaining knowledge. They have furnished the means for making improvement in that which will be useful to them in after

10*

life, and it is an abuse of paternal solicitude and anxiety, not to make all the advances in knowledge of which they are capable.

It is a duty they owe to their country, to qualify themselves to be useful citizens ; and this cannot be done, if they remain ignorant and uncultivated. The country has a claim on all to be as useful as they have the means to be ; this claim reaches children, as well as those of maturer years.

Lastly, it is a duty they owe Him who made them. He requires them to make a due improvement of their time, and promises his favour to those who obey, and threatens his displeasure against those who disregard his command.

" Take fast hold of instruction, let her not go; keep her for she is thy life. Get wisdom, get understanding and forget it not. Wisdom is better than riches, and all the things that may be desired are not to be compared to it." Such are the declarations of the book of God, and they require serious attention from the youthful scholar.

To conclude : Make use of every proper motive to lead the scholar to just views of the value of knowledge, the best means of gaining it, and the proper use to be made of it when acquired. Point out plainly the consequences which must result to himself and others, from indifference and inattention to the opportunity he has of gaining knowledge.

It is believed that such inducements as have been mentioned, will be found abundantly sufficient to excite all the attention and application necessary to insure success in acquiring knowledge, except in such instances, as those, where there is an entire want or perversion of every common principle. There may be instances where every thing will fail, but extreme severity. But such are very uncommon and owe their existence to the neglect or imprudence of parents or teachers. In such instances when they occur, it may be necessary to resort to unusual means, and these must be left to the judgment of the instructer to apply as the exigencies of the case may require.

I wish here to add one remark, not perhaps belonging to the previous subjects, but still important. It will be of

tion to the pliant twig, the first bias to the infant intellect.
Your station is one of great responsibility. You have it
in your power either to promote the welfare of the little
group around you, or to do them the greatest injury. Next
to mothers, the character of children will depend on you.
If you are judicious and faithful, you may be benefactors
to the community,—if you are negligent of duty, or misjudge on important points, the best of parents, and the
best of teachers can never repair the mischief, you may
do to the infant charge committed to your trust.

You have it in your power to create in the minds of
the children a taste for the school—for its exercises and
amusements ; and from you they may derive such an aversion to these pursuits as will not be overcome by the labours of your successors in many years. But these subjects will claim attention in their order, and I need only
advert to them here.

The first remarks I shall make, will regard the youngest children, placed under your care. These are usually
from three to seven years old, though sometimes younger.
The first object at which you should aim, is *to please them*
—to make the school as pleasant to them as possible. In
order to do this, you must consider what they are, and how
their attention can be excited ; how they are pleased, and
in what manner they may, most easily be governed. But
before the remarks I shall have occasion to make on these
points, I wish to bear a decided testimony against the
common course pursued by most female teachers in the
country. The children, of the age I have mentioned, are
sent to school in the morning, and after they arrive at the
school-room, are required to take their seats, and there sit
till noon, with the exception of being called up to read
once or twice, and perhaps, of being permitted to go out
once. They have an hour at noon for play, and then are
confined again till the close of the school. They become
restless, tired and cross ; and no wonder that they should.
To confine a volatile child for six hours in a day to one
place, without employment and with no change of scenery
—with nothing but a dull round of exercises in which it
takes little or no delight, is not only unreasonable and
cruel, but is a sure way to make the school an unpleasant
place, and to make dolts of the scholars themselves. I

have long ago ceased wondering at the lines of the poet, describing the infant school-boy

> " With his satchel and his shining morning face,
> Creeping like snail unwillingly to school."

It is indeed, rather a matter of wonder that more children do not form an aversion to school, so great, that it is never overcome in subsequent years. They will often, indeed, attend school with pleasure, from no other motive than the opportunity it affords them to play with their little associates while going and returning, and during the intermission. Aside from the facilities for play, the school would be an object of aversion. By so much confinement, they suffer in their healths, and more in their spirits.

Where there is nothing of more interest before the child, while in the school-room, than simply his letters in a spelling-book, it is no wonder that it should take him a great while to learn them, for curiosity is not awakened, and he sees nothing to attract attention.

In studying to please children, it is important to unite amusement with instruction. This is the object sought in the management of infant shools. Mr. Wilderspin tells us that a whole day sometimes elapses in his school, of three hundred children, from eighteen months to six years old, without a single tear or serious complaint. They are treated as children, but still as if old enough to be moral and intelligent. They have an almost continual change of exercises, but every exercise is designed for their improvement.

It may be proper to pursue a course like the following, with such as are not enough advanced to study lessons. They should be formed into a class, and taught to count. The children should all speak together, distinctly, and very slowly. The teacher or a monitor should count with them ; thus, one ; two ; three ; four ; five ; six, &c. to a hundred. Such as are already able to count, will serve as guides to the rest. When they have counted fifty or one hundred, the exercise should be changed. The class may be shown a picture of some animal, as of a horse, and the following course pursued.

Teacher. Children, I have a picture here, do you wish to see it ?

Children. Yes, yes, we do.

T. Can any of you tell me what it is?

C. Yes, a horse, a horse. [The whole should speak together.]

T. What is a horse good for? is he of any use? can you tell me, little children?

C. Yes, a horse is useful to carry people on his back.

T. Can you think of any thing else he is useful for?

C. Yes, to draw wagons, carriages and sleighs.

T. Any thing else?

C. Yes, people use horses to plough and harrow.

T. Can you think of any thing else?

C. No, ma'am.

T. Is the flesh of a horse good to eat?

C. No, people don't eat it.

T. Is the skin good for any thing?

C. Yes, ma'am, to make leather.

T. Can you think of any thing else?

C. No, we can't.

T. Then I will tell you. The hair is sometimes used to put into mortar. The hair of the mane and tail is used to make sieves and sometimes brushes. Are the bones of any use?

C. We don't know.

T. They are used sometimes for handles to knives, but not so often as the bones of some other animals.

The teacher may next hold up a Bible and ask, What book is this?

C. A Bible.

T. Who is the Author of the Bible, or who gave us this precious book?

C. God gave it to us.

T. Ought we all to know what it contains?

C. Yes.

T. Can you read it?

C. No, we cannot.

T. Do you wish you could?

C. Yes, we do.

T. Well, if you will try to learn, I will teach you to read.

The teacher may then proceed with the lesson, and extend it as far as she may judge proper. If the class read in the alphabet, it is important to have large letters, such as those on the infant school cards, or, if these cannot be obtained, you may cut them out of an old newspaper. Hold up the letter, so that all can see it distinctly, and then ask, What letter is this, little children? Let them all answer together, and if but a part speak, it is better to ask a second or third time.

An exercise to succeed that of reading, may be the making of letters on a slate. Every child should be furnished with a slate, black board, or black paper, which may be used for this purpose. Let a monitor hold up a letter, so that all can see it, and then let the class try to imitate it. Then another, and another, till the children have made half or the whole alphabet. While this exercise is going on, you may be engaged in hearing lessons, or in other departments of the school.

The children should not be too long confined, but, should be permitted to go out and march, or play under the care of the monitor whom you may place over them. While they are out of the school-room, they may be taught to count, add, subtract, multiply or divide, and this will not tire, when they are at the same time engaged in play.

When you have time to attend to the smallest children again, let them count by two, or by five, as two and two are four, four and two are six, six and two are eight, &c. After this exercise, you may again question the children on a picture of a cow, sheep, or some other animal, or a picture of some object as of a house, boat, tree, carriage or tool, and ask such questions as will lead them to an acquaintance with the nature and uses of the animal or object. The teacher may then tell them some short story from the bible, or some other book, and question them again, about learning to read, preparatory to reading. As you have opportunity, you may always please and greatly benefit the children by conversing with them on such subjects as they can comprehend, and can answer questions about, without much assistance. Arithmetic should unquestionably be the leading subject, because this can be more readily comprehended, than almost any thing else. In repeating numbers to young children, I think it important usually to call the name of some sensible object.— If you wish to teach them to add, it is useful to hold balls or something which the children can see, as two apples

and three apples, are how many apples? Four cents and
three cents, are how many cents? Five pins and three
pins, are how many pins? Six sticks and four sticks, are
how many sticks?

In subtraction, multiplication and division, the same
course may be pursued. When the objects are seen before them, they can comprehend the operation, even if
very young.

It will be attended with much benefit to children to
converse much with them about the nature of things, and
call forth their own thoughts as much as possible. What
I mean may be illustrated by an example. The teacher
held up a nail and asked, What is this, little children?

Children. A nail.

Teacher. What is it made of?

C. Iron.

T. Can you tell me where iron comes from, does it
grow as trees do?

C. No, it is obtained from the ground.

T. Can you think of any thing else that is made out
of iron?

C. Yes, a knife, a chain, an axe, a crane, a hoe, a part
of ploughs and harrows.

T Can you think of any thing else?

C. Yes, the stove is made of iron.

T. Can any of you think of any thing else?

C. Yes, a horse shoe.

T. Any thing else? This question may be repeated ten
or twenty times, or as long as the children can recollect
any thing to mention. When the teacher has elicited
every answer that can be given by the children, she may
vary her questions, and inquire whether it is very useful—
whether people could live in civilized society without it—
or whether iron or copper is more useful? This may be
done by comparing the uses, to which each is appropri-
ated. The conclusions they will be able to form will be
very generally found correct. The chief benefit of this
course, is the exercise of mind it gives to the children.
They are led to think—to examine and to inquire, and
will thus be led to form habits of reflection.

It is to be hoped that every district in our country, will
soon be disposed to furnish some parts of the infant school

apparatus. This is desirable, if *economy* is consulted, as well as when the benefit of the children is regarded. The cards, containing reading and spelling lessons, and pictures, are durable, and as a whole class read from the same card, which they are never allowed to handle, it is much cheaper to furnish them, than to furnish books. Every female teacher ought to have the little work, entitled, " Hints to Mothers and Infant School Teachers," also " An Essay on Infant Cultivation ;" and a work entitled " Infant Education." From either of these books, some very important suggestions may be received, and important instructions obtained in regard to the best mode of teaching the youngest children of the school.

2. I would recommend *to spend a part of each day in questioning the children on the meaning of words.* This may be done by giving a word and requiring them to tell its opposite. The teacher may ask, What is the opposite to cold ? The children will at once say, heat. What is the opposite of great, good, pretty, virtue, knowledge, &c. ? I think this is one of the best means of leading children to distinct ideas of the knowledge of words, and it is always pleasing to them. Many other means may be employed, for making them acquainted with words. One that is well calculated to interest the attention, is that of giving them a word to explain, and then reading a little story, which will explain it. Let the word *cruelty* be given ; then to explain it, read the account of the treatment of Joseph by his brethren, and tell them that their conduct was cruel. The story of Absalom's usurping the throne of his father, and going to war with him, after his father had treated him with great kindness, will be a proper illustration. The story of the trial and scourging of the Saviour, by the wicked Jews, will be a better illustration than either.

3. The next direction I wish to give you is, *Keep the children fully occupied.* This is important for children of every age. In order to attain this object with the youngest, you will be obliged to employ the assistance of some of the older pupils, while you are attending to the other exercises of the school. Such as may be employed as monitors, will be benefited by it, as much as by giving the whole of their time to their books ; for while they are

11

teaching others they are learning more thoroughly themselves. In no way, perhaps, will they be more benefited
than by being thus employed a portion of time each week;
for they are not only fixing the knowledge they have acquired in their own minds, but are learning how to teach.

When the school is properly arranged, and every scholar
has constant employment, there is no time left for mischief,
or for that "busy idleness," which is so often observable
in our schools. System and order are every thing in
school, and these cannot be gained, where the scholars
have not constant employment.

In many districts it may be expected that you will instruct the female part of your school in "needle-work."
All I have to say on this subject is, that the practice of
sending children to school, to learn to work, is not consistent with the best interest of the school. If this must
be attended to, it will be better to assign some portion of
time each day to it, and while instructing in that, let it be
the only thing at the time, to receive attention. It would,
unquestionably be better, both for the scholars and parents,
to have a school for work only, when children cannot con-
veniently be taught at home. It would also make the
labours of the teacher much more pleasant.

4. I should be glad to avoid the following remarks, on
the subject of *neatness*, did I not believe they are *sometimes* needed. I have not always observed that attention
to it, which is important. Children should always be led
to associate order, comfort, neatness and regularity, with
the school which they attend. This cannot be, where
the floor is left covered with leaves and litter, from week
to week; and where there is no effort to make use of the
means at hand for ornamenting the room with evergreens,
&c. Every school-room should have as many attractions
for the young as possible. Every degree of negligence
on the subject of neatness, must have a bad effect on the
school, and should be carefully avoided.

5. Another part of your duty will be to teach the children propriety of conduct. The remark is often made
to an unmannerly child, "You must go to school to
learn manners." But with what propriety is it made,
when so little attention is generally given to the subject
in schools? Still it is important, and should receive atten-

tion. Children should be instructed how to go into a room, and how to speak, when they have entered. They should be told what is proper when leaving the house of a neighbour, or when spoken to by persons in the street, or addressed by a visitant at home. Propriety of address and manners should be inculcated, in regard to every situation in which they may be placed. Every species of rudeness and clownishness should be carefully corrected, lest it grow to a habit when they become older. If children are early taught to treat each other with politeness, the habit will be likely to show itself in their treatment of every body else. The truly polite person will never say or do that unnecessarily, which will make any one around him unhappy. Every mode of speaking or allusion to things which will injure the feelings of others is therefore to be discountenanced, and reproved. All vulgar joking, blackguarding, or desire to accuse others of things of which they are not guilty, must be considered as the opposite of politeness and good manners. It is the duty of the teacher to keep a watchful eye on every thing connected with this subject.

To conclude : Let it be your endeavour, and spare no pains, to make the children fond of their studies, and desirous of doing right. Strive to have them early accustomed to vigorous mental exertion, and to do right, whether at home or abroad, at school, or at play. Go daily to Him, for guidance and direction, at whose tribunal you must account for the manner you teach the youthful charge entrusted to your care. His assistance alone will enable you to succeed in your efforts to do them good. His approbation and that of your own conscience, will be an abundant reward for every exertion you can make, to promote the best interest of those who look to you for guidance and instruction.

QUESTIONS ON LECTURE I.

1. Is a person properly qualified to become a teacher by the acquisition of science ?

2. What else ought he to study ?

3. What has been the practice of many who have tried to teach?

4. What ought every one to obtain, who means to teach school ? *Why ?*

5. Of what is there a general conviction ?

6. Is the value of common schools sufficiently realized ?

7. What shows the importance of district schools ?

8. Who exhibit a high degree of interest in the character and usefulness of schools ?

9. What is one way in which *indifference* is exhibited ?

10. *Do you think that every parent ought to attend the district school-meeting* in his neighbourhood ?

11. What vote is sometimes passed by a district ?

12. How is indifference shown by parents, after a school has commenced ?

13. Is the indifference universal, of which the author speaks ?

14. From what may indifference to the character, and usefulness of schools originate ?

15. Is that person a real friend to his country, who has but little regard to the character of the schools, which his children attend ?

16. What would be the effect of ignorance on the welfare of our country ?

17. How do parents endanger their own happiness?

18. What is the duty of every parent ?

19. How is it sometimes shown that parents do not have a proper affection for their children ?

20. What do such seem to think most important ?

21. Are there exceptions to what is said ?

22. Is any part of the indifference to common schools, the result of not realizing moral obligation ?

23. Is it to be considered strange, that schools are not more useful, when so many things exist that are injurious to them ?

QUESTIONS ON LECTURE II.

1. What are many parents backward to furnish ?

2. Would some cheap apparatus be highly useful in every school ?

3. Why are some parents unwilling to furnish new books for their children ?

4. How do both parents and children suffer loss?

5. From what two things, does the unwillingness of parents to furnish proper means to their children, for making progress in acquiring knowledge arise ?

6. Are parents sometimes more willing to spend money for things useless or even hurtful, than for furnishing their children with the means of making their studies pleasant and profitable ?

7. What stories are told to illustrate this ? 1st ? 2d ?

8. What is the next thing mentioned, that has operated extensively to prevent the usefulness of schools?

9. How do " district parties" sometimes originate ?

10. *Have you ever known any such, which have been unfavourable to the schools in your neighbourhood ?*

11. *If you find parties in the districts where you may be employed, what will be their effect on the usefulness of your labours ?*

12. *Will it be your duty to strive to unite such parties, in efforts to benefit the schools ?*

13. By what means do parents sometimes injure the usefulness of common schools ?

14. Are academies ever injurious to district schools ?

15. What observations are made in the note on the subject ?

16. Would united Christian effort be productive of good, and is it just to attribute a part of the failure in the usefulness of schools to a want of it ?

17. What is the fifth reason mentioned why schools are not more useful ?

18. What is said of the qualifications of the first class of teachers?

19. What is said of the next class ?

20. What is said of the third class of those who engage in instructing ?

11*

21. Why are many of this class deficient in qualifications?

22. What is the sixth obstacle, to the usefulness of schools?

23. What is the seventh thing mentioned?

24. Are school-houses badly constructed, and frequently badly located?

QUESTIONS ON LECTURE III.

1. What is the first requisite in the qualifications of a good schoolmaster?

2. What does the author mean by common sense?

3. What is the second requisite?

4. Why is this important?

5. What is the third qualification?

6. Why is this necessary?

7. What is the next requisite trait in a teacher?

8. Is decision of character important to persons in every situation in life?

9. Why ought a schoolmaster to be affectionate?

10. Is it important that teachers should have a just moral discernment?

11. What is of even more importance to children than intellectual culture?

12. What studies does the law require to be taught in common schools?

13. What is said of the four first?—of the fifth?—of the two last?

14. In a proper knowledge of what are most teachers deficient?

15. What remarks are made on the subject of reading?—of arithmetic?—of geography?—of English grammar?—of the history of the United States?

16. With what other studies ought the instructer to be familiar? What is said of each?

17. *Do you believe that all these studies are requisite, to qualify you to teach with success?*

18. *Have you evidence of possessing the necessary qualifications?*

QUESTIONS ON LECTURE IV.

1. What is the first practical direction to teachers?

2. Is this important to the personal enjoyment of the master?

3. Can the nature of your employment be fully learned without experience?

4. From what publications may something of the nature of teaching be learned?

5. Will you learn something of the nature of your business, by reflecting on the common nature of children?

6. What varieties may you expect to find among them?

7. What is said of parents?

8. Will it be a benefit to converse with experienced teachers?

9. Should you be discouraged by what they may tell you?

10. What have some considered the business of teaching?

11. What remarks are made in the note, on this subject?

12. What is teaching?

13. What language should the teacher use?

14. For the purpose of knowing how to teach, what should you recollect?

15. What is the second general direction?

16. How may you learn your responsibility as a teacher?

17. What is said of the influence a teacher may exert?

18. What consideration shows the importance of this influence?

19. What has God enjoined upon the young?

20. What is the last suggestion to show the responsibility of the instructer?

QUESTIONS ON LECTURE V.

1. What is the next general direction?

2. Is there a wide difference in the amount of influence exerted by individuals sustaining the same office?

3. With what particular trait of character, in a teacher, is it natural to suppose the scholars will be pleased?

4. What is the first requisite for gaining the confidence of a school?

5. What should you remember?

6. What is the second direction for gaining the confidence of scholars?

7. What is the third direction on this subject?

8. *Will you endeavour to remember this?*

9. What, fourthly, is necessary?

10. What is the fourth general direction?

11. Why should you be willing to devote your whole time to your school?

12. What account is given of the course pursued by Benevolus?

13. What seemed to him highly ridiculous?

14. How is the importance of this direction further illustrated?

15. What request is made of such as are unwilling to devote their whole time?

16. What is said of the compensation allowed to teachers?

QUESTIONS ON LECTURE VI.

1. What is the next general direction?

2. In order to be able to govern others, what is first necessary?

3. Against what must the teacher be well guarded?

4. Is it injurious to make contemptuous speeches about scholars?—about parents?

5. After being able to govern himself, what is of great importance to the teacher, as a first step towards governing the school?

6. What will be the effect on the school, if the master believes he cannot govern the scholars?

7. How ought the teacher to consider and treat his scholars?

8. How is the mode recommended illustrated?

9. What is said of being uniform in the government of a school?

10. What is the first species of irregularity, to which this direction has reference?—the second?

11. Ought the large and small scholars to be required to obey the same laws in school?

12. What is the next direction on school government?

13. What is said of the practice of some teachers?

14. What must this course lead the scholar to suppose?

15. Of what is the master in great danger?

16. Is it proper to excuse the scholar from doing what the teacher directs, because he says he don't know how?

QUESTIONS ON LECTURE VII.

1. What is the next direction on government?

2. Can a master have the same feelings towards a good and a bad scholar?

3. Ought this to effect his government?

4. Is a complaint of partiality in school very common?

5. Is it often too well founded?

6. What will be the effect of partiality if it exist?

7. What is the last direction on governing a school?

8. Ought the teacher to direct the amusements and play of a school?

9. What amusements ought to be prohibited?

10. What other subject is mentioned?

11. Is it commendable for the teacher to assume a lordly or commanding mode in addressing his scholars?

12. What effect does this mode of speaking to scholars have upon them in their intercourse with each other?

13. What general rule, for speaking to a scholar, is given?

14. How may scholars most easily be led to speak kindly to each other?

15. Is the dignity of a person lessened by adopting a kind and affectionate mode of speaking to inferiors?

16. Is the same mode recommended, even when a scholar is to be called to an account for improper conduct?

17. Is it wrong to be hasty in believing a scholar has done wrong, or in accusing him?

18. What is a principle in law?

19. Is it a proper mode to make inquiry for evidence to prove the scholar innocent, when a complaint is brought against him?

20. What is the second direction?

21. What ought to be the first object with the master, when the scholar has done wrong ?

22. Why is it considered better to defer punishing a fault for a season ?

23. What is the third direction on the subject of punishment ?

24. *Do you think this is a reasonable direction ?*

25. What modes of punishment are recommended?

26. What should be the last resort in choosing a mode of punishing ?

27. What is the fourth direction in regard to punishment ?

28. May rewards ever be serviceable ?

29. Should they be promised ?

30. For what ought they to be given, if ever given ?

QUESTIONS ON LECTURE VIII.

1. Is the general management of schools highly important ?

2. What is the first direction on the subject ?

3. What is the second ?

4. Can much be accomplished without system ?

5. What must be observed in order to have system ?

6. What story is told to illustrate the importance of attempting to do but one thing at a time ?

7. What is the third direction ?

8. What is the fourth direction ?

9. What has been the practice of some instructers ?

10. Can a teacher be justified in pursuing this course ?

11. What subject ought to receive the greatest share of attention ?

12. What does the author consider to be the best rule in directing the studies of scholars ?

13. What is recommended as soon as a child can read ?

14. How should a child be taught the meaning of words ?

15. To what should great attention be paid ?

16. Can children very early understand the first principles of arithmetic ?

17. What is said of geography ?

18. What study may next claim attention ?

19. What remarks are made on the study of grammar ?

QUESTIONS ON LECTURE IX.

1. Is the manner of teaching of very great importance ?
2. Against what should the teacher guard ?
3. What should be the first object in teaching ?
4. Why is this necessary ?
5. What is a common fault with teachers ?
6. What is the second direction in regard to teaching ?
7. What story is told to illustrate the importance of this direction ?
8. Against what should the instructer guard ?
9. What objects should be used for the purposes of illustration ?
10. *Was the teacher judicious in the mode taken to assist James to understand his map ?*
11. What is the third direction given ?
12. If the scholars are not pleased with their studies, what is the reason ?
13. How should teachers and parents speak of study before children ?
14. What is said of the school of Pestalozzi ?
15. How can studies be rendered interesting and pleasant ?
16. What remarks are made on teaching how to spell ?
17. What error is mentioned on the part of the instructer ?
18. How do many teachers pronounce words to a class ?
19. What rule is given for pronouncing words to be spelled by a class ?
20. What is the first direction on teaching scholars to read ?
21. What is the second ?
22. Do you consider this important ?
23. What mode is recommended to insure distinctness in reading ?
24. What is the third direction ?
25. To what should particular attention be paid ?
26. What is the fourth direction ?
27. What is the fifth ?
28. *Are these important ?*

QUESTIONS ON LECTURE X.

1. When may the child begin to learn arithmetic?

2. In teaching written arithmetic, what should be the first object?

3. May a scholar perform all the given operations in arithmetic, and yet not understand it?

4. How is it best to commence with scholars whether they are beginners or not?

5. What mode should be adopted in assisting a scholar?

6. By what example is this illustrated?

7. Is it important to go over every rule, as in the instance given?

8. What course should the teacher adopt with a class before calling on them to recite a rule?

9. What benefit will result from it to the scholar?

10. What is the common mode of teaching geography?

11. Is this a natural mode?

12. What is the first direction for teaching geography?

13. What is the first direction, where such a mode is not practicable?

14. What is the second?

15. What is the third?

16. Will scholars be interested in this mode?

17. What exercise is recommended in the fourth place?

18. What proves that the common mode of teaching grammar is not a good one?

19, What is that mode?

20. To what parts of grammar is the chief attention usually paid?

21. What is the first direction given?

22. What is the second?

23. What is the third?

24. What exercise should be continued?

25. What is recommended?

26. Does the author consider writing as properly belonging to the subjects of attention at a district school?

27. What is the first direction?

28. What is the second?

29. What is the third?

30. What will be prevented by pursuing this mode?

31. What is the fourth direction?

32. How is it recommended to begin with a class in teaching history?

33. After these lessons, how is it proposed to proceed?

34. How may a connected historical view be obtained in this way?

35. What may be a first lesson?

36. What questions may be asked upon it?

37. What other lessons in their course are mentioned?

38. What will be the result of pursuing such a course in teaching history?

QUESTIONS ON LECTURE XI.

1. What is a subject of great importance, to be introduced into district schools?

2. Why is composition necessary?

3. Does writing composition, have a good effect in disciplining the mind?

4. What is sometimes the effect of neglecting it in common schools?

5. What is the first direction on teaching composition?

6. What has been found a useful mode of commencing with a class?

7. What is next recommended?

8. What will be one benefit of this mode?

9. Is it better to give subjects than to let scholars select for themselves?

10. What subjects are commonly selected by scholars?

11. Are these easy to write upon?

12. What should be kept in view in selecting subjects for composition?

13. What should the teacher recommend to scholars?

14. What benefit will result from this?

15. Besides composition, what is important?

16. Why ought they to be taught something of moral philosophy?

17. Ought every one to have some acquaintance with natural philosophy and chemistry?

18. What is the next direction given?

19. Why should opportunities, which occur, that pro-

12

duce considerable excitement of mind, be improved for making lasting impressions on the minds of scholars?

20. What is the first illustration?

21. What is the second story designed to illustrate what the author means?

QUESTIONS ON LECTURE XII.

1. What inducements should be made use of, to excite the attention and promote application to study?

2. What does emulation mean?

3. What does ambition mean?

4. Is ambition ever used in a different sense?

5. How will the author use the terms?

6. With what is emulation connected?

7. With what secondly connected?

8. What does Plato call emulation?

9. What is it better to call it?

10. From what, first, is emulation distinct? second? third?

11. What is the conclusion on emulation as an inducement to study? For what does it lay the foundation?

12. What is a proper subject to be made use of as an inducement to study? second? third? fourth?

13. Are scholars under obligation to themselves to make a proper improvement of their time? to their teachers? to their parents? to their country? to their Maker?

14. What is recommended to teachers?

QUESTIONS ON LECTURE XIII.

1. Will the Lectures to schoolmasters furnish important instruction to female teachers?

2. Mention the particulars, in which directions should be the same to both classes of teachers?

3. What will devolve on instructresses?

4. What have they power to do?

5. What may they become?

6. What will be the consequence of pursuing a wrong course with young children?

7. What should be the teacher's first endeavour in regard to the youngest scholars?

8. How is this done?

9. Against what does the author protest?

10. What is the natural effect on children, of confining them to sit in the school-room through the day, when they are not old enough to study?

11. Why are children so long in learning the alphabet?

12. What should be united with efforts to please?

13. What does Mr. Wilderspin say in regard to his infant school?

14. How are children treated in his school?

15. What is the course recommended to be pursued with such as are not old enough to commit lessons?

16. What is the second exercise recommended?

17. Mention the third thing recommended.

18. What is the course recommended in teaching the alphabet?

19. What exercise is to succeed that of reading?

20. What is next recommended?

21. Mention the course recommended, when the teacher can devote attention to the smallest scholars a second time?

22. Why should arithmetic be a leading subject?

23. Repeat the directions given upon it.

24. What will be a great means of benefiting children?

25. Mention the example.

26. What ought to be provided for every district school?

27. From what books may the teacher derive great benefit?

28. What is the second general direction?

29. What is the third direction?

30. What observations are made on having work carried into school?

31. What is the fourth subject mentioned?

32. Why is great attention to neatness, on the part of the teacher requisite?

33. What ought children to associate with school?

34. What is the fifth subject mentioned?

35. Is it true that a proper degree of attention is paid to this subject?

36. What is the concluding advice?

37. What is the teacher's best reward?

LECTURES ON SCHOOL-KEEPING.

LECTURES

TO

FEMALE TEACHERS

ON

SCHOOL-KEEPING.

BY S. R. HALL.

BOSTON:
PUBLISHED BY RICHARDSON, LORD & HOLBROOK.
No. 133, Washington-Street.
1832.

PREFACE.

THE success of a course of Lectures, addressed to SCHOOL-MASTERS, has encouraged the Author to hope that the present volume will be found both useful and acceptable to those for whom it is designed.

The circumstances of *summer schools* are, in so many particulars, different from *winter schools*, that it was impracticable to furnish all the directions in the former Lectures, which are important to the FEMALE TEACHER.

From all who are intrusted with the care and government of children, the subjects embraced in the following pages, require consideration. If the Author has succeeded in presenting them to INSTRUCTRESSES in their proper light, he hopes his labour will be productive of good to them, and, also, to their juvenile charge. He has aimed to render all the directions *practical*, and make the volume a general directory,

1*

for properly discharging the responsible duties involved in the office of the PRIMARY TEACHER.

The work is designed, not merely to be *read*, but to be STUDIED ; it may also be made a daily manual, during the time devoted to teaching.

Teacher's Seminary;
Andover, Mass. April, 1832.

CONTENTS.

_____

QUESTIONS.

LECTURES

LECTURES

ON

SCHOOL KEEPING.

LECTURE I.

YOUNG LADIES,

I ENGAGE in my present duty with pleasure. Experience and observation justify the remark, that suggestions made to females, on subjects of importance, are always secure of attention. I am led to expect, that all which is necessary, to induce them to effort in achieving an object, is to present its claims, and prove its practicability. While I call your attention to the nature of the employment in which you are to engage, and to the requisite qualifications for discharging its duties, I shall be confident of your attention, even though I fail of making suggestions, which are *new*, or those which are fraught with uncommon interest. I plead the cause of children ; and in behalf of them, your sympathies are already excited.

The *age* of those to whom instruction is to be given, by the female teacher, adds importance to her labours. Infancy and childhood are the periods in the life of man, when he is

2

most open to impressions ; and when these produce the most important results.

You are to become the cultivators of a soil, on which, as yet, little seed has been thrown ; and which, if preoccupied before the fowls of heaven have scattered that which is noxious, we may hope will yield desirable fruits. You are to watch and water and nourish plants, which are not to remain always in the nursery ; they must soon be removed to other fields, where their growth and expansion will very nearly correspond to the early culture they have received.

You will therefore indulge me in directing your attention to the high importance of the labours, you are to perform, and to the results which must unavoidably follow.*

* " A child, like a plant, grows up, and expands, and blossoms, and bears fruit, accordingly as it shall be guided, and nourished, and pruned, and guarded, by those to whose care it is submitted. Its little eye is ever open to behold, and its ear quick to hear, and its heart ready to receive impressions, which every act and word of those who are around, cannot fail to make, in all that they perform or say in its observing presence. I venture to assert, that there is not one in this assembly, who if he will reflect but a little upon his past existence, cannot recur to habits which may have cost him many a tear, and which originated in some casual circumstance of childhood. Some thoughtless act, sanctioned by the praise and example of a parent or guardian or instructer, may lay the foundation of future happiness or misery, in the mind of the child who is beholding him ; and when that parent or guardian, or instructer shall have ceased to exist, there may be immortal minds still on the earth, for whose actions

Let me first introduce to you the group of children, which are to become your charge. Contemplate them ; and though the warriour might say, what are these to me?—though the miser may view them with less emotion than he feels, when he fastens his eager gaze on yellow dust ;—though the politician may hardly deign to glance his eye towards them, while he hastens on in the race of ambition ;—though the votaries of pleasure may not pause for a moment, in their pursuit of fancied good,—still *you will not, cannot* behold them with indifference.

They are *young* it is true ; but each revolving sun adds to their age. They are ignorant I know ; but they have noble powers and capacities for developement. They see every object around them ; and they notice whatever is uttered in their hearing. They are *babes,* —but so was Alexander once ; so were Bonaparte and Washington. The "mad boy," whom the monarch of Persia sent his satraps to seize and bind and scourge," was, twenty years before, in his cradle, or on his mother's knee. The conqueror of Italy had hardly numbered the years of manhood, when the trump of fame announced " him the hero of the age," and crowned heads trembled before

he shall be at least partly accountable, because they proceed from principles which were instilled by his example, and perhaps nourished by his care."

Rev. Mr. Blagden's Address at Brighton.

him.   A very *few years* were sufficient to mature their gigantic minds.

The group of children before *you* are both *young* and *ignorant*.   And who of all the busy multitude around you were not equally so, a little time since?   The Hottentot and the Savage may, in manhood and in age, continue *children* in knowledge, but for those, who have commenced their existence in a republick, renowned for knowledge and patriotism, there *ought* to be, there *will* be another destiny.   These infants must acquire knowedge, either proper, or improper, beneficial, or injurious.

Instead therefore, of presenting a reason why your attention to the children before you is unimportant, their *age** presents one of the strong-

---

* In the following sentiments of able advocates for early education I cheerfully concur.

" If the influence of our primary schools is but too often ineffectual for moral and religious culture, may it not be attributed, in part, to the long preoccupation of the field of contest?   The correction of bad habits is proverbially more difficult than the formation of good ones ; the eradication of vicious propensities infinitely more arduous than the implanting of right dispositions. But the power of evil has for years been gathering strength, before the ordinary means af public education are directed against it.   Yet, surely the Serpents that invade the cradle of infancy are as formidable as the Hydra that attacks the manhood of life.   Let charity commence its Herculean toils at an earlier period ; then will its first victories be its best omens of future triumphs.   Benevolence has long appreciated the value of that field, which the *childhood* of the poor has opened to its cultivation ; *infancy* is a rich but unclaimed waste ;

est reasons, why you should feel a lively interest in them, and bestow on them your most assiduous attention.

It would not be surprising if, when a company of *aged persons*, just ready to drop into the grave, were placed before you, you should find other assemblages more attracting. *They* have accomplished their work, and spent the days of their manhood and vigour. For them,

it is a soil, capable, when watered by the dews of heaven as well as cultivated by the hand of man, of producing the fairest blossoms, and bearing the richest fruit. If he that causes two blades of grass to grow, where only one has grown before, has been thought worthy the patriot name, with what title shall he be honoured, under whose hand, not unblest, the wilderness of the infant mind is made to blossom as the rose ; and these the waste places of human life to bloom with moral beauty, and teem with moral fragrance. The Christian philanthropist has no need to lament that his predecessors have left him no room for triumph ; here opens to him a fair and fertile world, and a crown that fadeth not away is the guerdon of the fight."   Rev. Dr. Mayo.

"There is a general conviction extending, of the importance of greater activity in the education of infants. It has been till recently, neglected in a most deplorable manner, and especially among the poorer classes. Parents are too generally accustomed to think they have little to do with the education of their children at an early age. But while they delay what they suppose to be the work of education, each child is in fact educating himself; for the infant left to himself is by no means inactive. Every thing he sees for the first time, whether good or bad, makes an impression upon him. That unceasing activity which we admire in a very young child, always finds the elements upon which to exercise itself; and urges on his developement."

M. Monod.

2*

the objects of general excitement have few attractions. They will

> " Want but little here in time,
> Nor want that little, long."

This *may* be true of *some* of your infant
charge. Death may diminish their numbers,
before their sun arrives at its meridian. Some,
however, perhaps many, are destined to act a
part, on the busy stage of life. they will be
occupied with the affairs, charmed with the
pleasures, or active in the pursuits of the
world. Exposed as they must be to ten thousand snares and evils as they traverse life's
rough paths, the foundation must be laid in
childhood to avoid them. With the nature of
the dangers, which will beset them, they are
unacquainted, and must depend on others to
assist in understanding, and guide in escaping
them. Adequate attention to the results of
experiments daily made by themselves, can
hardly be expected, without assistance from
those, to whom they look as guides and instructers.

The effect of habits formed in early childhood, will be as lasting as life. If these are
such as it is desirable they should be, numerous evils will be averted, and important good
secured ; but if a wrong bias is given in infancy or childhood, obliquity must be expected
in every subsequent period. *Experience, de-
monstratively proves that " a child left to himself bringeth his mother to shame." Children

are often more ready to form wrong habits
than right ones. The experience of this fact
led the Psalmist to say that they " go astray
as soon as they are born."

Will you tell me, these are things which belong to parents, and have no claims on you ?—
That you are to teach them the first principles
of science but have no farther duty to perform?

Before suffering yourselves to rest on this
ground, let me ask you to reflect seriously on
several things.

First, what is the character and situation of
many parents? They *ought* certainly to be
most tenderly alive to the best interests of their
offspring. They ought to be well acquainted
with the dangers, to which children are exposed, and the best means of averting them.

It ought to be their daily and hourly care to
" train" the beloved beings, of whose existence
they have been instrumental, in " the way they
should go." But what *are* the facts? Is it
true, that even a majority of parents, especially
of those, whose children attend the free schools
of the state, understand much of the nature of
parental responsibility? How many parents
seem to have no thought beyond the necessary
provision for the temporal wants of their children. How many send their children " to
school to learn manners" and *morals*, as well as
letters! How many others furnish their offspring with constant examples of every thing,
that is unlovely and revolting !

Look at that mother, surrounded by her numerous offspring. Her husband is perhaps intemperate, or engaged in labours which require his constant absence from home. The mother must therefore control them when in health, and attend to their incessant calls,—must administer to them in sickness, and in fine, perform all that is done for them. Is it not nearly impossible for her to govern, train and instruct them in the best way? But if it were possible, what does she know or realize of the nature and importance of her duty? She was either a servant, before marriage, or belonged to a family situated like her own; or, perhaps, was deprived of the opportunity for instruction on the nature of parental duties, before she became a parent. And could she be expected to make those advances in knowledge afterwards, which are necessary for the station she occupies?

Do you say I have presented a case which is strongly marked? I know it. But I know also, that there are many such instances, and some in almost every district where a school is kept. Many mothers are dependent on their daily labour for subsistence. Others are found, whose thirst for gain is so great, that their children are secondary objects of solicitude.

These children will soon arrive at manhood, and become active in the community. They will be freemen, and must exert an influence on others. Many of them, in turn, will become parents. All of them have commenced an existence never to terminate. And let me beg you to remember that all the salutary influence which will be exerted upon many of them, will be limited to that, which they will feel in the district school. Let them grow up unrestrained in their passions, unintelligent and immoral, and their influence must be destructive to the peace, morals and happiness of society.

Another consideration, which adds interest and responsibility to the office sustained by you, is the *unbounded influence*, which you can exert over your pupils.

The kind and affectionate teacher is, in the estimation of the child, the standard of truth and excellence. If the instructer approves any thing it must be right ; and every thing disapproved must be wrong. Here then, a power is put into your hands, which renders your office one of peculiar interest and importance. You are responsible for the use you make of it. If you cultivate a habit of discrimination, the same habit may be easily formed in those who are under your instruction ; and, on this habit in them, will depend the justness of their conclusions, on many subjects connected with their present and future welfare.

The child, that reasons correctly on *one* subject, will be led more easily to reason correctly on others. Teach him to entertain just views of his duty to his instructers, and you will easily lead his mind to perceive the na-

ture of the duties he owes to his parents.
Lead him to reason rightly with regard to the
treatment of his school-fellows, and he will at
once be prepared to perceive the higher claims,
his brothers and sisters have upon him. The
teacher, who leads young pupils to cultivate
kind and affectionate feelings towards each
other, not only sends a happy influence into
every family, from which the school is collected, but also transmits this influence to future
generations. *Young* children are capable of
conviction on things where their happiness is
affected ; and this conviction is not easily destroyed when they advance to maturer age.

The confidence, which your juvenile charge
repose in you, puts their destiny in an important degree, into your hands ; and must tend,
I think, to excite in your bosoms feelings of
deep interest towards them. So far as you
desire to promote happiness, and prevent misery,—to remove ignorance, and disseminate
knowledge,—to purify society and elevate human character,—so far, you must be interested
in your employment, and in the charge, waiting to drink in instruction from your lips.

I may be permitted to advert here to one
fact, which I have had occasion to observe to
some extent : some female teachers have appeared to think, that the children usually committed to them are too young to receive instruction in any thing, but the first princsples of science ; and that to impart knowledge, on sub-

jects connected with the early studies of children is all, which devolves on them. " It will do them no good," some have said, " to teach them any thing else, for they are *too young* to remember it." In reply, I would say, pray what good will it do to teach them any thing? Are children inclined to remember how to spell and pronounce words, and to forget every thing else? Can they retain a knowledge of facts in geography, history and arithmetick, and forget what makes them *happy* or *unhappy* ?

Is it more difficult to remember why they are to love each other, and to be obedient to instructers and parents, than to retain the names of rivers, lakes, mountains and cities? May the little oak be left, while it is small, to grow oblique, because it will, bye and bye, feel the hand of culture more sensibly? Is good seed to be withheld, while there are no noxious weeds to retard its vegetating, and to be scattered, when the field has become preoccupied with brambles and thistles ?

This reasoning is very unlike that, which we adopt in relation to other subjects. It is easy to bend the pliant twig. So it is the *early* impression, made on the mind and heart of childhood, which usually remains the longest, and shapes the character of manhood. The *age* of your pupils, therefore, presents one of the strongest inducements to great faithfulness in cultivating every thing lovely, and checking the growth of every thing noxious and unlovely in

LECTURE II.

I commence this lecture with the inquiry ; What are the *duties* involved in the office of primary instructers ?

Some of these were *implied* in the former remarks. But it may be important to present them more explicitly.

1. It becomes necessary to have consistent views of all the objects to be obtained by your labours. These are many ; but they may be summarily comprehended in one sentence : *To qualify children for happiness and usefulness.* The great purpose of education is to cultivate all the powers of body and mind, and lead the young to choose that course of conduct, which will save them from vice, and conduct them in the paths of virtue. Hence the whole field of labour is to be surveyed, and the character of all its parts understood, before one can be properly prepared to enter it.

Perhaps no single point, requires so much attention, as that of accustoming the members of your schools *to submit constantly to salutary discipline.* Every child wishes to be his own master, and makes the effort to establish his independence, long before he is sent to a place of instruction. With how much success, such efforts have often been attended, you will

3

have sufficient opportunity to judge. If this
propensity cannot be resisted, what must be the
result to children in later periods of life? Laws
are indispensable to the maintenance of society; but the child who breaks away from all the
wholesome restrictions, imposed on him at
home and at school, will hardly be restrained
in manhood, even by those laws, which the
congregated wisdom of the country has established, for the welfare and protection of its citizens.

Habits of submission to laws, requisite in the
nursery, family and school, lay a foundation for
submission to the usages of society, or common law; and of course to the enactments of
legislative bodies.

The *earlier*, children are brought to submit
to wholesome authority, and are made to *know*,
that they must yield to the decisions of those
who are qualified, better than themselves, to
know what will best promote their *own*, and
the general good, the more certainly *their* happiness is secured.*   Submission is not irksome

* The following remarks so exactly express the sentiments, I wish to inculcate, that I give them in this
place.

" The idea of obedience ought to be early and firmly
associated with the ideas of security and happiness.
And here again the imbecility and helplessness of infancy afford us the means of effecting our salutary purpose. Entirely dependent on the wisdom and experience of others, to guard them from the danger to which
they are hourly exposed, children might be easily made
to learn the advantages of obedience; and they infalli-

to him, in whom it has become habitual.—
Should your labours result in accomplishing

bly would learn it, if obedience were properly enforced.
Were all prohibitions *made absolute,* and the necessity of
issuing them, guarded against as much as possible, so that
they should not often occur, it would go far towards
rendering obedience natural and easy ; for it would then
appear a matter of necessity, and as such be submitted
to without reluctance.

" I was some years ago intimately acquainted with a
respectable and happy family, where the behaviour of
the children excited my admiration. One morning, on
entering the drawing-room, I found the little group of
laughing cherubs at high play round their fond mother, who was encouraging their sportive vivacity, which
at that time was noisy enough, but which on my en-
trance she hushed into silence by a single word. No
bad humour followed ; but as the spirits which had been
elevated by the preceding amusement could not at
once sink into a state of quiescence, the judicious mother did not require what she knew could not, without
difficulty, be complied with ; but calmly addressing
them, gave the choice of remaining in the room without any noise, or of going to their own apartment where
they might make what noise they pleased. The eldest
and youngest of the four preferred the former, while the
two others went away to the nursery. Those who stay-
ed with us amused themselves by cutting paper in a
corner, without giving any interruption to our conversation. I could not refrain from expressing my admiration at their behaviour, and begged to know by what
art she had attained such a perfect government of her
children's wills and actions. " By no art," returned
this excellent parent, " but that of teaching them from
the very cradle an *implicit submission.* Having never
once been permitted to disobey me, they have no idea
of attempting it ; but you see, I always give them a
choice, when it can be done with propriety ; if it cannot, whatever I say they know to be a law, like that of
the Medes and Persians, which altereth not."

Journal of Education.

nothing more than a cheerful submission to reasonable law, you will certainly obtain a most
important and beneficial end. It is an object
second to no other in importance ; and should
be primary in your estimation. Neglect this,
and though you may gain some others, your labours will accomplish but little of permanent
value. For how can the mind be highly cultivated, and especially, how can a just *moral
sense* be created, without it ?

To prevent misapprehension, let me say,
that to control children, merely for the sake of
showing our power over them is entirely unjus-
tifiable. To say to a child, you shall obey me,
because I have the power to enforce subjection,
shows ignorance of the great object of government, and a want of correct moral feelings, in
the teacher. *Reason* must therefore be the
constant guide in establishing requisitions and
withholding indulgences.

2. Another duty devolving on the instructer
is to lead children to cultivate habits of *self-
government*. Most young persons are sometimes placed in situations, where self-control is
all, on which they can depend. Neither parents nor teachers can always be present to
counsel and assist them ; and if no other habit
is formed, but that of yielding obedience to
their requisitions when they are present, a child
is but poorly prepared to profit by habits of general submission. *Self-government* can be exercised in the presence of governors, as well as

in their absence. If the young can be persuaded to establish habits of self-control, a permanent foundation is laid for their security, in any situation of subsequent life.

But no one can be expected to cultivate this habit successfully, till he has some knowledge of its nature and importance. You will therefore inquire, whether it is possible to make *young* children understand it. Without pretending to have certain evidence of the correctness of my opinions, I wish merely to say, I have seldom found any instances of *more apparent* self-control, than in children from four to ten years old. They are generally capable of understanding the importance of this habit at an early age, if a judicious mode of inculcating it is adopted by the instructer. The advice I wish to give on the best manner of inculcating it, will be more appropriate in another place.

3. Another department of your business is to form in your scholars, *the habit of thinking*. No one can have had much acquaintance with children, without observing a disinclination to exercise their own powers of mind in investigating new truths. Nor is this trait confined to them. To think originally and independently is not common, even among men. But what is more important than this? What can give us so much control over our own thoughts? By what means can the mind be more thoroughly disciplined? If this habit can be cultivated in children when young, its results will

3*

be most important during every subsequent period of life.   Children may be led to cultivate
it by engaging their attention, with subjects of
easy apprehension at first, and afterwards, leading them gradually to those points which are
difficult.

The reverse of this is too generally practis-
ed.   A child not unfrequently meets with a
difficulty too great for him to remove, and finding his own resources insufficient, he adopts the
easier expedient of employing others to think
for him.   The habit soon becomes fixed, and
upon the occurrence of every new difficulty he
has recourse to his teacher.   His opinions, of
course, borrow the complexion of those, of his
tutors.   These being frequently changed, it is
not wonderful, that children have so few distinct
and clear conceptions.

These results may all be avoided by cultivating the habit in young children, of thinking for
themselves; of surmounting, by their *own efforts*, the obstacles which they meet.   The
wisdom of the instructer must be constantly put
in requisition, to keep them from falling on difficulties, which will dishearten and discourage
them.   In adopting the *right mode* here, your
skill, as teachers, will be tested more readily than in any other department of your duty.
It is easy to lead your scholars to excercise
their powers of memory, but not so easy to induce them to think profoundly and reason correctly.   The *memory* should be cultivated;

but all the other powers should be made to
proceed with it.   Otherwise, what is the
capacity of the pupil better than a book
containing a full enumeration of facts?   Let
me say again, it is a very important part of
your duty to teach your scholars to *think for
themselves*, on all subjects, which they are able
to comprehend.

4. Another part of your duty is to lay the
foundation for habits of ORDER and SYSTEM.

This subject, so important with regard to the
future success of the child in *any* department
of business, is usually, I am obliged to believe,
almost wholly overlooked by a large majority
of primary teachers.   The accomplishment of
a task, by manual labour, may secure its prominent results, let it be performed in what manner you please : but the amount of time requisite, and the ease and pleasure of doing it
in one way, may be as dissimilar, to affecting it
in another, as the operation of weaving threads
by a steam-loom, is unlike their slow and laborious combination by the unaided machinery of
the fingers.   To do a thing may be important ;
but to do it in the *right way*,—in the best manner, is, under some circumstances, vastly more
important.   The husbandman can till his field,
by the aid of a mattock,—he may make a
small portion of the land, equally productive ;
but how wide is the difference between the
amount of labour he can accomplish with this,
or with the plough.

Children early lay the foundation for the successful, or unsuccessful efforts, which they make in after life. Washington took his first lessons in military tacticks, while commanding a company of his school-fellows, armed with corn-stock guns. West's first lesson in painting, was the pretty face of a little relative, sleeping in the cradle. The approbation, his mother bestowed on this effort, decided his future course. These instances, I know, are decidedly marked, but something similar might be observed in the life of almost every individual. The attention, which you may give to the subject, MAY be the means of shaping the whole future course of many a promising child. Order in thinking, and order in acting, if cultivated in childhood, and continued through life, would give to one of only common capacity, a superiority over both genius and talent, as they are usually cultivated. If you rightly direct a child in his early efforts at reasoning,— if you show him the difference between commencing at one point, or at another,—and if you can make him perceive that there is one place only, where the key to a difficulty can be applied, you will do more for him, than if you store his mind with many individual facts, connected with the study he pursues.

Do you reply, it must be the business of those, who succeed you, to cultivate habits of system and order, and that you can do nothing with children so young? In reply, I must say,

you are labouring under a mistake. It devolves on *you* to lay the *foundation*. All,
who succeed you are builders on it.   By neglecting to place the first stone of your edifice
right, you subject every one of your successors to inconvenience and unnecessary toil.
They must either demolish what you have
done, or see the superstructure disproportion-
·ed, inelegant and insecure in all its future ele-
vation.

It is quite as easy to acquire correct habits
of thinking at *first,* as it is to learn in an opposite manner ; but it requires painful effort to
unlearn what has been before taught in a
wrong way.   Of this fact, I am obliged to have
daily illustration, while employed in teaching.

Do you say, again, children are so volatile,
that they will not recollect and apply the instructions given, and that you must be constantly employed in repeating them ?

True, children are volatile and need a constant repetition of instruction.   But you still
expect to teach them *something*, which they
will retain.   And is it not as easy to cause
them to remember that, which is important, as
to remember what is afterwards to be unlearn-
ed ?   In pruning your rose tree, or cultivating
your flower garden, do you expect success,
without repeating your efforts day after day ?

We know children are volatile,—but we
know also, that they are constantly becoming

acquainted with new facts, some of which they will always remember. If children are volatile, there is need of increased effort, but no ground for discouragement. If we could terminate our efforts, by a single remark, or a single explanation, or direction, the labour of teaching would cease to involve the high responsibility, which it now assumes.

5. Your office involves the duty of teaching those subjects of science, which are at the foundation of education.   Spelling, reading, arithmetick, geography, history and grammar are required to be taught in the primary schools of this, and most other states, where schools are established by law.   All these branches are important; but I am not disposposed to believe that they are all, which you are required to qualify yourselves to teach. But as I shall have occasion *hereafter* to direct your thoughts to this subject, in particular, I shall dismiss it in this place.

Whatever you may teach, the *manner* is highly important, and the results must materially depend upon it.

6. Another duty, devolving on you, is to benefit parents.

It is not saying more than facts will justify, when I assert, that very many parents are destitute of right feelings on the subject of their duty and responsibility to children.   To both of these your attention is unavoidably given, in connexion with learning your own duty.

of maturer age, are called away from time.
Without a heart to love and obey the gospel,

mind resembles a piece of ground which will by no
means lie wholly bare, but will either bring forth weeds
or fruits, according as it is cultivated or neglected.
And according as the habits of vice and irreligion, or
the contrary, get the first possession of the mind, such
is the future man like to be. We do not think it proper to leave our children to themselves to find out the
sciences of grammar, or numbers, or the knowledge of
languages, or the art of writing, or of a profession to
live by; and shall we leave them to settle the boundaries of right and wrong by their own sagacity, or to
neglect or to misunderstand a religion which God himself has condescended to give us as the rule of our faith
and practice? What can it signify to a youth that he
go through all the liberal sciences, if he be ignorant of
the rules by which he ought to live, and by which he is
to be judged at last. Will Greek or Latin alone gain
him the esteem of the wise and virtuous? Or will philosophy and mathematics save his soul?

But it is to be feared that parents in some cases,
through a mistaken notion of the true method of giving
youth a religious turn, often run into the extreme of
surfeiting them with religious exercises, instead of labouring chiefly to enlighten and convince their understandings, and to form their tempers to obedience. The
former, though noble and valuable helps appointed by
divine wisdom for promoting virtue and goodness, may
yet be so managed as to disgust a young mind and prejudice it against religion for life ; but the latter, properly conducted, will prove an endlessly various entertainment. There is not a duty of morality, you can have
occasion to inculcate, but what may give an opportuni-
of raising some entertaining observation or introducing
some amusing history. And though it may sometimes
happen that a youth well brought up may, by the force
of temptation, run into fatal errors in after life, yet such
a one, it must be owned, has a much better chance of
recovering the right way than one who never was put
in it. I am ashamed to add any more upon this head,
it being a kind of affront to the understandings of man-

they are unprepared for the enjoyment of devotion here, or the exercises of the heavenly world hereafter. They have commenced an immortal existence. It cannot be too early impressed upon their minds, that they are accountable for their actions, both to their earthly parents, and their Heavenly Father. And, let me add, you will find, that, in proportion as you are able to fasten this conviction, your labours will be rendered more pleasant and successful in every other department.

If you faithfully discharge this part of your duty, you will be able to look back with pleasure, on such labours, long after you have finished them ; and may I not add, from the closing hour of life ?

kind to labour to convince them of a truth as evident as that the sun shines at noonday.

A parent, in any station of life whatever, may and ought to bestow half an hour or an hour every day in instructing his children in the most useful of all knowledge ; nor is there any thing to hinder a master of a private seminary of education to bestow generally an hour every day, and more on Sundays, in instructing the youth under his care in the principles of prudence, morality, and religion. This may be digested into a scheme of twenty or thirty lectures beginning from the foundation and going through all the principal particulars of our duty to God, our neighbour, and ourselves, and from thence proceeding to a view of the fundamental doctrines, evidences, and laws of revealed religion. In all which there is nothing but what may be brought down to the apprehension of very young minds, by proceeding gently and suiting one's expressions to the weak capacities of the learners."

Jour. Ed. No. 21, *pp.* 543—4.

4

LECTURE III.

PERMIT me now to direct attention to some of the qualifications most essential in the primary instructer. What are these?

I shall, perhaps, be justified in stating, in the ·first place, some of the things, which must *unfit* you for this important work.

1. *Ignorance of its responsibilities, must present an insuperable barrier to desirable usefulness and success.*

The station of any one, intrusted with the care of children, is immeasurably important. No one can have intercourse with them for an hour, without making an impression on them, which may last during life. This is particularly true of those, who are required to control, govern and instruct young minds, for a considerable period of time. The taste, the temper, the disposition, the thoughts and habits may all be influenced, and made to incline in any direction, the teacher may choose. And if one, occupying a station, so important, has not an impressive sense of her responsibility, I know not how she can be expected to secure those results, which are most desirable.

But there is another important view of this subject. Where responsibility is not realized, *effort is generally feeble.* Who will long attend the instructions of that moral teacher, who contemplates the work of the ministry, as light and unimportant? Who expects to witness valuable results, from the labors of such an "Ambassador?" Who will contir e to employ the physician, that considers the station *he* occupies as unimportant, or its duties as demanding but little attention?

It is generally, I believe, true, that he, who realizes *most fully*, the responsibility attached to his calling, will be found the most untiring and efficient in his labours. It is certainly natural to anticipate faithful effort, in any one, whose views of the character of his achievement are distinct and elevated. And I must believe, that any one who contemplates the duties of a female teacher, as devoid of high responsibility, and of peculiar solemnity, has no right to hope for success in her employment.

2. *A want of interest in the society of children, will inevitably unfit one, for the labours of teaching, governing and interesting them.* There are those, who apparently contemplate a company of children, with about the same feelings, that they would a company of *apes*, whose mischievous pranks are to be the source of constant vexation and complaint. There are others, who would consider life as most highly fraught with ills, if it is to be spent in the presence of those, whose elasticity and buoyancy are such as prevent them from being classed with mutes and dolts. And how can

persons of this character gain the confidence, or secure the love of children? But without the possession of both, you have an uninviting company to guide and control. A child will ascertain in an hour, the character of your feelings towards him, and whenever you betray a disrelish for his society, you cannot, readily induce him to obey you with cheerfulness and exactness.

You may have all the various knowledge of a learned professor;—may be profoundly versed in the mysteries of science—may drink deeply from the fountains of literature—but if you do not *love children*, you are unfit to be their teacher, for they will not,—they cannot, and I may say, they ought not, to love you.

3. *Ignorance of the manner in which children imbibe ideas, must prevent success in teaching them.*

Here, I am disposed to believe, is one of the prominent reasons, why so many fail in their attempts to communicate instruction. To those accustomed to trace the operations of their own minds only, there is a strong inclination to suppose, that what is intelligible to them, is intelligible to children. I have not unfrequently heard teachers, when giving instruction to a class of young scholars, use language far better adapted to the college lecture-room, than to the place of primary education. " It is so perfectly plain, that any one can understand it,"— yes, it *may be very plain to you*, but very far from it to your scholars. Would you not believe a person designing to insult you, who should show you the various parts of a complicated machine, and explain them only in the technical language of his profession, and then should say you have an equally intimate acquaintance with it, as he has, after years of labour and study?

Teachers, who presuppose that the young are able to think in the same way, and acquire ideas in the same manner that they do, after a long course of mental discipline, have yet to take the very first steps in a course of preparation for their work. Children learn by induction; and it is not to be expected of them, that they can analyze, till the mind has been trained to such an exercise. If you are to teach children, *you must know how children think.* To know this, you have to look back and remember how *you* thought—how *you* reasoned and formed conclusions when you were children. If you are unable to do this by the aid of your own memory, you must learn it from your intercourse with children, and by watching the operations of their minds, while instruction is imparted to them, in such a way as to make it intelligible. Many opportunities of this kind will occur, which should be improved with the highest care. Let me press this point still more closely. To say nothing of the loss of time, consequent from your ignorance of its importance, the disrelish which your scholars

4*

will form for study, must be very injurious. The difficulties, which arise from rendering studies unintelligible, become associated with the *study itself*, and not unfrequently, the little learner sits down in despair of ever being able to accomplish his task. The repugnance which many show to the study of arithmetick and grammar, is generally the result of an unskilful course of instruction pursued by teachers. A professional gentleman of high respectability remarked, not long since, he never understood arithmetick, till he heard his little son repeat and explain his exercises in Colburn's "First Lessons." And he added, that this was owing to the manner in which he was directed to study it when a school-boy; at which time, he acquired so strong a distaste for it, that he could never overcome it in his subsequent course of study.

Hundreds of similar instances have passed before my observation, and I have no doubt others may be furnished by your own recollection. But I forbear to enlarge.

4. *Ignorance of human nature, especially of the peculiar characteristics of children, unfits any one for becoming their instructer.*

There are cords which if touched will vibrate in harmonious unison, and others which never fail of producing discord. If it is manifest, that there is ignorance of this fact, it cannot be expected, harmony and improvement can be secured, by the labours of such an instructer.

Children are not all alike. They have been governed differently and are diverse in their dispositions and tempers. One is amiable and another the reverse; one has learned submission to necessary laws and another must be made to learn subjection. One can understand you, while another is seemingly incapable of it. If you are unacquainted with these facts in detail, or are so unfortunate as to suppose that the same manner is to be adopted with all, you can hardly fail of injuring some. Almost the same variety of character is to be met with, in primary schools, which is found in a more extensive community. The only difference is, here the *bud* or *early blossom* is seen; in older communities, the fruit has grown and ripened.

It is not only important to understand *these* different and various shades of character, but also, to know those principles of human nature, which are nearly uniform in all. There is a way to reach the sympathies of every individual. Acquaintance with this, throws the person almost completely in your power. If actuated by a benevolent desire to do good to your interesting charge, you may, by this key, enter the arena of every heart, and establish your empire over every mind. Without possessing yourselves of this, it is impossible for you to succeed to the satisfaction of yourselves or others. You must know how to influence children, if you wish to benefit them to the extent of your power.

5. *Those to whom the labour of teaching is irksome, and who can enjoy no pleasure in observing the opening powers of juvenile minds,* I would never advise to assume the responsibilities *of teachers.*

Before that person, who is engaged in any business in which he is uninterested, there can be only a dreary path. His task is a heavy and painful one. His exertions will be feeble, and his hopes of success must be limited. To one of high moral feeling, the sense of duty *may* be sufficient to induce *constancy and faithfulness* in labour. But I am unable to believe, that in any case, under these circumstances, the *same* success is realized, which may be rationally expected, where the employment itself is a source of constant enjoyment. It is unreasonable to expect it.

It may be asked, do not all take pleasure in the exhibition of opening intellect, and can *any one* fail of being pleased with a situation favourable for observing it? Admit the truth of this: still there is a wide difference between merely witnessing results, and being actively employed in producing them. It gratifies me when I see the operations of some .interesting machinery, but it does not follow, that I must be pleased with the employment of making it. Nor does it follow of course, that because I am delighted with observing the progress of some grand design, I should be found in possession of those traits, which would give me a pleasure in executing it.

There are those, who appear to take pleasure in many things, which cost *them* no effort, but who are the last to be gratified, by the same things, when obliged to be the agents in their accomplishment. Many are ready to declaim in favour of the interesting business of the instructer, who would be the last to delight in the labour of performing it themselves. But if there is not pleasure in the labours involved in the office, success must, to say the least, be doubtful.

6. *Impatience must be a barrier to success in teaching and governing children.*

In training the young mind, "line upon line" and "precept upon precept" are indispensable. The frowardness of one, and the ignorance of another; the forward confidence of some, and the diffidence of others, must be met. If the thousand little unpleasant occurrences of the day are sufficient to prevent you from preserving that evenness of temper, which is desirable, you are not prepared to make your labours pleasant to yourselves, or agreeable to your scholars. Impatience throws a shade over every object. It discolours every thing with its own reflection. When under its influence, time drags heavily in its flight. Obliged to wait an hour longer than you expected, to meet a friend, and no other society can make amends for the disappointment.

For those who instruct children, a large share of patience is indispensable. Unless *scholars*

can be preserved from impatience, there must
be an end to quiet submission, and cheerful attention to instruction. Impatience is a conta-
gious disease; it can never be the disorder of
one, without exposing others to its direful influence. If you are impatient, you must expect
others to contract the distemper. No one can
envy your situation, if impatient yourself and
surrounded with others equally so.

7. It is hardly necessary, perhaps, to say,
that ignorance of any of the branches of study,
which are to be taught to the children placed
under your care, will prevent the possibility of
desirable success.

No one can be expected to teach what he
does not know. Without the required amount
of literary attainments, you must fail of cultivating in others a taste for study, and also must
fail of communicating valuable ideas.

It will not be out of place to remark also,
that ignorance of the mode, *the best mode* of
imparting that knowledge, of which you may
be possessed, must materially reduce the amount
of your usefulness to your young charge. But
as I am to state definitely some qualifications,
which are important, I need not enlarge on this
topick here.

LECTURE IV.

I have made the inquiry, What are the qualifications essential to the success of the female teacher? and have noticed several things which must operate to diminish, or destroy her usefulness. It will readily be inferred, that the opposite of these things are among those qualifications, which are deemed essentially requisite to success.

1. A deep conviction of the responsibility attached to the office of instructers.

2. Pleasure in the society of children.

3. A knowledge of the manner in which mental operations are performed, or the manner in which children think.

4. A general acquaintance with human nature.

5. Patience in overcoming the obtuseness and perverseness of childhood.

6. A knowledge of the studies, it is important children should pursue.

7. Every teacher of young children ought to be intimately acquainted with the different modes, by which they may be made happy.

I think it must be acknowledged by every one, that it is an object of great importance to make them *happy at school,* for by this they will be led to associate every thing that is pleasant, with the attainment of knowledge. But there are various means of making children pleased with school, and the results of these, may produce very different effects upon their future character. It is by no means difficult to please children. They may be gratified with those things which will exert an influence both on character and happiness, highly undesirable : nor is it more difficult to present other subjects to them, equally interesting and attractive, which shall result in the most salutary and lasting effects. The importance of being able to discriminate, between the effects of these different impressions and of presenting the right objects, is no less than the importance of exerting the most salutary influence on the character of your pupils,—an influence to be felt by them, so long as they may live.

If I *flatter* a child into obedience, or attempt to secure his love by bestowing unmerited commendations I may gain one point —that of exciting in him a love to attend school; but at the same time, I may do him an injury, which the wisest instructers can never afterwards fully repair. But, if I can convince him, that obedience to necessary laws, is the most certain means of permanent enjoyment to himself, and can show him the inseparable connexion between his duty and his happiness, it is. thus, that I throw the deepest interest around all the subjects of study, to which his attention may be given. Then I may hope for equal success in making him delighted with his situation, and at the same time confer a permanent benefit on him.

If the happiness or enjoyment of children at *school* were all, the subject would be of far less consequence. It does not terminate here, but extends very much farther. If study can be made to have charms which few other things possess, it will not cease to be attractive, when the scholar retires from the school room. He has entered a field, in which he will delight to linger,—whose beauties he will be happy in surveying, long after he has once passed over it. Children are sometimes averse* to study, when

* Mr. Parkhurst gives some of the reasons why this is true. He says,

"The aversion of some children to learning is derived, by *sympathy*, from their parents, and others with whom they daily associate. The child imbibes, very early, the feelings and sentiments of the parent. Whatever feelings are manifested by a parent or a domestic, the child catches them by instant sympathy. In this way, many things become objects of desire to a child, which would have been to him objects of aversion, if they had been so to the rest of the family ; and many become objects of aversion, which would otherwise have been objects of desire. Hence, there is little hope, that a child will be fond of learning, who belongs to a family, which, from whatever cause, has a disrelish for literary and scientific pursuits. It is extremely difficult for the most skilful instructer, in such a case, to counteract, entirely, the unhappy influence, to which the child is daily exposed in the domestic abode.

Some children become averse to learning, in consequence of being required to get *longer lessons* than they are well *able* to get. The body, especially of a child, becomes weary and uneasy, by being long confined to

5

they enter the school, and hence the great importance of knowing how to overcome this, and
to make study interesting to them.

the same posture ; neither will the mind of a child patiently bear a long continued application to the same
subject. It is evident, that an aversion to learning
must be the consequence of assigning tasks so hard as
to require a painful effort to perform them.

Some children become averse to learning, in consequence of the *unfavourable light* in which the subject
is represented to them by their parents and others. All
those by whom the young child is surrounded, *expect*
that he will find learning an irksome task ; and this
expectation becomes well known to the child. Though
they may have long since overcome the aversion which
they felt to learning in their early years; yet they remember their former feelings, and take it for granted
that the path must be equally thorny and toilsome to
all children. Hence, whenever they mention the subject, they speak in such a way, as infallibly gives the
child a prepossession against the very name of a book.
And when he actually begins to learn—or rather to repeat, like a parrot, the sounds that fall from the lips of
his instructer—the most effectual means are employed
to strengthen the unhappy impression that has been
made.

One of these means is, to *drive* him to school, to *com-
pel* him to study, and to *punish* him for not learning.
The natural consequence of this mode of procedure is,
to raise the incipient aversion of the child to the highest pitch ; for even if he now loved learning, such a
course might be expected to change his love into hatred. One kind of punishment, frequently inflicted on
children for negligence or for other crimes, consists in
giving them an *additional lesson*, to be learned, perhaps,
after the other scholars are dismissed. How extremely
unwise this is, it is difficult to make those see, who
know nothing of the philosophy of the mind ;—and yet,
it seems as if they might see, that to do such a thing is
as much as to tell the child that a lesson is an *evil* thing,
and that it is of the same nature as a whipping, and
equally to be dreaded.

8. *It is very important that a teacher should be able to enter into the sympathies of children.* When a child comes to tell you of his

Another means employed to make children learn, is to *hire* them. We forbear to make any enumeration of the good things, which are given to children beforehand to induce them to study, or which are proposed as the future reward of application. We are aware, that in condemning the practice of bribing children to study, or rewarding them for studying, we are treading on ground where we shall be likely to encounter opposition. We readily admit, that this *alluring* process is much less objectionable, than the *compulsory* one on which we have just animadverted. We are sensible, too, that the hurtful tendency of this method is not so obvious as that of the other. But we do, nevertheless, believe, that the tendency is hurtful ;—that the effect is, to make on the mind of the child an impression, that study is, in *itself* an *evil.* Yes, paying a child for learning evidently implies, that a lesson is an unpleasant task, which the child would not perform of his own accord. Parents never reward their children for eating such food as is pleasant to their palate; but they do sometimes hire them to swallow a potion of bitter medicine. And the child cannot but see what is so clearly implied. He cannot but perceive, that the parent, though he considers learning a necessary thing, and looks forward to beneficial consequences to result from the possession of it, yet considers the acquisition of it a disagreeable employment.

In objecting to the practice of rewarding children for learning, we would by no means debar the parent or teacher from manifesting to his pupils the *pleasure* which their proficiency gives him. It is important that the child should see and feel that his teacher and others are pleased with his efforts and his success. The only caution necessary in this case is, that the learner should be guarded against feelings of vanity and pride. The attention of parents, as well as instructers, is respectfully solicited to the above remarks.

" Many children become averse to learning in conse-

his troubles, or acquaint you with his little joys, there are few means by which a more direct avenue to his heart can be opened, than by exhibiting a tender interest in his feelings, and by sympathizing in his joys and sorrows.   To the child, the subject is of absorbing importance. It is, for the time, the *world* to him.   Turn away from him with coldness, and you lock up his heart in the frost of winter ;—*listen* to him, and sympathize with him, and you open a channel for his affections, which will flow forth towards you with all the warmth of filial love.   It is, when he is in this state of feeling, that you may make deep and permanent the impressions which you wish to create.   Now, when you have gained his confidence and secured his attachments, will he cheerfully receive instruction and remember it.   But let him think his confidence misplaced, and his love slighted, or entirely neglected at this interesting moment, and when you *would* fain call forth his sympathies, your task is difficult, and your success doubtful.   He knows you have little regard

quence of not *understanding* the lessons that are assigned them.   Probably few, even among instructers, are aware how *small a part* of their lessons children in general understand.   It is natural to imagine, that what is familiar to ourselves, is so to every body.   Hence the parent or instructer, when he hears children utter words whose meaning is familiar to himself, readily concludes that they suggest the same ideas to the mind of the child that they do to his own.   This mistake commences as soon as the child begins to talk , and it continues in a greater or less degree, through the whole course of his education."

for him, and of course receives your attentions with suspicion and dissatisfaction.

Rarely does any moment occur in the whole period of childhood, when the guiding hand of judicious instruction is so important, and so efficacious, as when with burdened bosom the infant seeks to make others the partakers of his emotions. Be watchful to seize on these favourable opportunities, nor let them pass unimproved. Now address to the confiding heart of your charge, those important truths which you wish to inculcate. Press them upon him with affectionate earnestness,—with that manifest solicitude for his happiness in your look and tone and manner, which shall convince him of your desire to promote his highest enjoyment, and you have reason to hope for triumphant success.

9. *Every teacher ought to have a deep acquaintance with the character of all those obstacles which may be expected to oppose her success.*

It is not sufficient merely to know that there *are* obstacles; but the *peculiar nature* of these obstructions must be known, and the best means of surmounting them distinctly understood. She must certainly be a very superficial observer, who does not perceive in the state of things around her, many causes, which are exerting a very hurtful influence on the character and usefulness of summer schools. To some of these, it may be important to advert in this place.

5*

A very prominent reason why schools so frequently fail of usefulness, is the manifest want
of interest in them, on the part of *the most influential families* in the neighborhood.   Many
of this class are found in almost every town,
respectable for its wealth or intelligence.   For
their children *another* school must be provided.
Though their wealth is the means chiefly
of sustaining the *free schools*, they deem the
manner of its appropriation quite foreign to
them.   It will follow of course that interest
in the success of the school is small.   The multitude are usually ready to follow the example of
men of commanding influence.   Consequently
the means, by which the great majority of children, are to be educated receives a degree of
attention far below its importance.

How is this obstacle to be surmounted by
the teacher?   Can you adopt any course, which
promises *so much success* as that of pursuing
such a judicious and interesting mode of teaching and governing, that the character of the
school shall secure the confidence of all, especially of the intelligent?   *Other* means are to
be employed ; and can be employed by *yourselves* to a limited extent.   But convince the
families in question, that you are masters of the
business in which you are engaged,—that you
deserve their confidence and patronage ; and
that they can entrust their children to your
guidance, with a prospect of the most desirable
results ; and you will not fail to obtain their ef-

ficient co-operation.   When this is secured,
you will have little difficulty in accomplishing
any thing, which you desire.

Another obstacle to the success of your labours, will be found, in the *very general* feeling among parents, that a *summer school* has
little value, except as it relieves parents from
the care of their children, during several months
of the year.   That this impression is universal,
I do not assert.   But if I may judge from facts,
which have come under my own observation,
I fear you will find it prevailing to a greater or
less extent in every place.

It seems to be supposed by many parents,
that their children are too young to derive much
advantage from an attendance at school, and of
course, their primary object in sending them
there, is to avoid for a time the trouble and inconvenience which they occasion at home.   If
such opinions obtain in any considerable degree, they must unavoidably exert an unfriendly influence on the success of your labours.

You will ask, How may such erroneous views
be corrected—their embarrassing and pernicious consequences averted?   Endeavor to
convince parents that, in entertaining these ideas,
they labour under a great mistake as to the
powers and capabilities of their children.   Prove
to them that the impressions they receive in
their tenderest years, are, if possible, *more* important, than those which are made on them at
any later period.   Follow out the influence of

early habits, trace the operations of first causes
through all the vicissitudes of subsequent life.
Take a child, and ask him, in their presence,
such questions as will be presented in some of
the following Lectures,—let them see that
young children have minds, and can use them.
An hour spent in any well regulated Infant
School, would be worth more to this class of
parents than all the logick and rhetorick, you
can call to your aid. The prejudices of parents will inevitably yield to the testimony of
their senses. But in the absence of this source
of conviction, the hints above given may aid
you to remove the difficulty under consideration.

Ignorance, on the part of parents, of what a
school should be, is a very serious obstacle to
the success of your efforts.

You will probably observe many, in the districts where you may be employed, who will
make no more inquiry, with regard to the character of the school, than they might be expected to make with regard to the character of
operations in a workshop or manufactory.
The solicitude of others will cease, when they
learn that their children are not punished with
severity. And others still will be very well
satisfied, when it is ascertained, that they will
not be called upon to make any additional ap-
propriations for books or apparatus.

As I have before suggested, the great objects
to be gained by education are, to many, almost

entirely unthought of; and in many instances
all your plans and efforts must be carefully explained, in order to be understood.   This will
render your labours far more unpleasant than
they would otherwise be; but ought not to
operate as a discouragement to exertion.   Dis-
heartening as this indifference may be, it has
been made to yield to the judicious efforts of
other teachers, and may disappear before yours.
But if it should not, you cannot be justified in
remitting your diligence, or neglecting any
probable means, by which success may be secured.

Though these are the *prominent* difficulties
you may have to encounter, there are many
others of secondary importance.   Inconvenient
school-rooms, want of suitable furniture, books
and apparatus; and the disposition often manifested by th girls and their good mothers, to
introduce sewing and other work into school,
are very common.

It may be, also, that you are deficient in
capacity, or in the acquirements necessary
to discharge the duties of your stations with
success.   If this is true in any instance, the
remedy lies entirely with yourselves.   It is not
a question, whether the absence of suitable
qualifications, on the part of teachers *has* con-
tributed materially, to prevent the success of
schools.   This is a point universally conceded.
And it will not be asking too much, if I request
that you will give particular attention to the in-

quiry—Am I really qualified for the work before me?—If the result of the inquiry is, a persuasion that you do *not* possess suitable qualifications, I pray you to abandon the employment without delay, and leave the work to abler
hands.

10. *Ability to govern children is an indispensable qualification.*

If you fail on this point, every endowment of nature,—every attainment of study or
experience will be unavailing. An ungoverned, disorderly school, is a sad spectacle to every friend of youthful improvement. Without
an ability to govern well, it is impossible to
teach well. If the stubbornness of one and the
waywardness of another, cannot be subdued;—
if children cannot be reduced to order and submission, you can do nothing for them which
will materially conduce to their benefit. Fail
not to remember this remark from day to day.

By ability to govern, I do not mean simply
a capacity to awe children into submission to
your wishes, by fear of punishment. This may
secure attention to your orders, while the scholars are seated before you, but cannot produce
that regularity and uniformity which are essential to their improvement. By ability to govern, I wish not to be understood to approve of
that power which some possess, of making every one fear being in your presence. It is said
of the Gothic invaders of Italy, that the glance
of their eye was sufficient to dishearten the

boldest Roman soldiers.   A haughty sternness
may terrify,—will repel, but cannot soothe, attract, and charm.   A severe and angry look
may excite fear and aversion; it cannot secure
confidence and affection.

Firmness, discretion, and kindness combined are the principal requisites in forming the
character of a good disciplinarian.   Firmness
in pursuing a proper object,—discretion in
granting or denying favors, and kind feelings
towards the subjects of government, must always be united in those who exercise authority,
if they would render their superiority pleasant
to themselves, or salutary to others.   Visit the
school of Miss G——, and you will find she
maintains the strictest order and quiet without
apparent effort.   Every pupil is under the influence of an irresistible charm, and seems to
have no inclination to do wrong.   Visit the
school of Miss X——, and you will think every child is a savage.   The latter teacher scolds,
complains, and punishes from day to day, and
lives in bedlam still.—The former merely waves
her hand, or casts a look upon the school, and
all is peace.   The whole secret of the difference in the two cases is this, one knows how
to govern, the other how *to punish.*

LECTURE V.

I HAVE before stated, that ignorance of the studies to be taught must prevent the possibility of success in the business of instructing. Perhaps it is now important to answer the inquiry ;—What are the requisite literary qualifications?

In the various departments of business, it is necessary to have, not only a knowledge of the labour to be performed, but to understand its connexion with other things, and often, its dependance on them for the means of accomplishment. He must be very imperfectly prepared for success, whose knowledge extends no farther than to the mere outlines of his employment. Nor is he much better qualified for successful effort, who is skilful only in the practical details of his occupation, while he is deficient in acquaintance with every thing else. Practice without theory, and theory without practice, will alike fail to fit a man for the ordinary business of life.

These general remarks apply in their full force to the primary teacher. You can read, but it does not follow that you are prepared to *teach* reading with success. You can write, or perform arithmetical operations, or apply a rule in syntax. But this is not satisfactory evidence, that you will be a skilful teacher of writing, arithmetick, or grammar.

The literary qualifications requisite for the primary teacher, are *first*, those which will enable her to understand the nature of the human mind, and the mode of presenting knowledge to it in a way to render instructions adapted to its capacity.

The teacher, who depends on acquiring the mere outlines of the few studies which the law specifies, must have narrow views of the results to be obtained by her labours.   She, who knows the letters of the alphabet may repeat them and teach others to do the same.   And she, who knows how to unite the letters, which compose a word, may direct others to repeat and unite them in the same order.   But is this teaching? Are any ideas communicated by such a course? Let me say on this subject,—

1. *You ought to be well acquainted with some parts of natural history.* I say *some* parts, because it is unreasonable to expect you to explore the whole field embraced by this science ; it is limited only by the boundaries of the world.

No subject presents greater attractions to the young mind, or is better calculated to cultivate habits of thought and investigation.   Such an acquaintance with those parts of this science, as will enable you to present its most interesting features, will prepare you to converse with your pupils on a variety of interesting and important

6

topicks.   By this they may be led to examine,
compare and think for themselves, and take
lessons from almost every object around them.

A *picture* has charms for children found in
few other things.   They usually listen to simple and intelligible descriptions of the objects, of
which they have any knowledge, with great
satisfaction.   Seldom will a child be found, who
is not willing to leave his *play*, to hear you tell
a story about an animal, or even an insect.   I
have often seen children two or three years old,
listen to a story on some subject in natural history, with an eagerness of attention not surpas-
sed by those of any age.   All of you have observed in children, the pleasure with which
they hear the stories of the nursery.   If this
childish curiosity,—this passion for novelty thus
early developed, receive a right direction from
the teacher, it may be made a powerful instrument in her hands, for the good of her charge.
But if there is a deficiency of the requisite
knowledge,—if the teacher has not materials in
her mind, by the aid of which, she may make
her communications instructive as well as interesting, she cannot avail herself of this principle in the infant mind.

It is highly important that every teacher of
children should devote considerable time to this
kind of instruction ; but ignorance of natural
history disqualifies her for doing it.

2. *It is very important that the instructers of
young children should be able to sing.*   All,

who have ever seen the operations of a well
conducted Infant School, will need no argument on this point.   But it may be proper to
refer others to the interest, which even infants
universally manifest in hearing musick.   The
" lullaby" of the mother or nurse, is one of the
most grateful sounds, that falls on the young
child's ear.   It calms his agitated feelings, and
lulls him to repose, or causes him still to slum-
ber after the demands of nature have been satisfied.

If the child is quieted and pleased, by merely *hearing* the notes of musick from others ;
will he not be much more delighted, when he
can tune his own voice to sound these strains ?
I stand not alone in the opinion, that there are
very few who may not acquire the art of singing.   In the Infant Schools, which I have visited, a very large proportion of all the children
become very sweet singers.   This is what
might be expected, and certainly ought to induce all who have the charge of children, to
make the experiment with them.   Mr. Woodbridge, who has spent several years in visiting
the schools of Europe, makes the following remarks, to which I invite particular attention.
" Many, who are ready to admit the pleasure
and the profit to be derived from vocal musick,
suppose that they can never be extended to
the mass of the community.   We are met on
the threshold with the objection, that this branch
of education must be reserved for those who

have what is termed a 'natural ear' and a 'natural voice,' and that only a few persons can distinguish musical sounds, and imitate them accurately.

If the grounds of this opinion are demanded, we are presented with a greater or less number of individuals in society, who tell us they cannot distinguish one sound or one tune from another—that they know not whether notes are high or low; accordant or discordant; and that they cannot imitate any of them.

The first difficulty sometimes arises from not understanding the terms employed. Sounds, like colours, cannot be described in words. They must be taught by examples, patiently repeated and carefully attended to, until the ear is familiar with them; and gradually extended, as its powers of discrimination are increased. I have known cases in which persons who said they could not distinguish one note from another, have found no difficulty in doing it, as soon as a few notes had been sounded before them, and the use of the appropriate terms had been illustrated.

But, in addition to this, the examples taken are not fair ones. They are of persons whose ear and vocal organs have been formed to certain habits so long, that they cannot be supposed to be so susceptible or flexible as they once were. Read a portion of French or German to the same individuals, and see if they can distinguish the similar words and sounds at once.

Call upon them to pronounce the nasal and guttural sounds of these languages; or require a foreigner to pronounce our own language, and it requires no second sight to determine that they would not succeed better than in musick. Is this an evidencee that they have not a natural ear or a natural voice for German, or French, or English? Surely not. Why then apply this reasoning to musick? Indeed, the argument would be more applicable to language, so far as experience extends. Who ever heard of an individual who spent whole days, for several years together, in singing, who did not find an ear for it? But we have few examples of men who pronounce a foreign language without obvious errors, even after years of study or of residence in a country where they speak it incessantly. Until we are presented with individuals who were taught musick as they were taught language, from their childhood, and who still cannot distinguish or imitate musical sounds, there is no good reason for admitting that any considerable number of persons are naturally destitute of an ear for musick.

I do not mean to deny that there are defects of hearing of every degree, from absolute deafness, to mere dulness of hearing, which renders it difficult to perceive nice distinctions, and so on to a perfect state of the organ; nor that some individuals may have a natural rigidness or other defect of the muscles and cartil-

6*

ages of the mouth and throat, as others have in
their limbs.   Nor have I any doubt that great
natural differences exist as to the degree of ac-
curacy in imitating musical sounds, as they do
in the distinctness of articulation and the correctness of reading, in those whose organs are
not obviously defective.   But I am satisfied
from the testimony of those who have had extensive means of observation and experiment,
both in this country and in Europe, as teachers
of musick, as well as by an obvious course of
reasoning, that these cases are almost as few in
number as those of the lame, and the deaf and
dumb.   Vehrli, the remarkable teacher of the
agricultural school in the institution of Fellen-
berg, assured me that among several hundred
poor neglected children confided to his care,
he had found only two whom he could not teach
to sing.

Pfeiffer, the author of the Pestalozzian system of instruction in musick, informed me, that
he had found not more than one or two in ten,
who could not be taught to sing.   The same
opinion was expressed by most of the practical
teachers I met with in Europe.   The few I
found of another opinion, were men whose exquisite sensibility of ear and of nerves, rendered the discord of a learner's notes a species of
torture, and who therefore could not exercise
the patience necessary to go through an elementary course, except with very apt scholars.
The same difficulty would probably have aris-

en, if they had attempted to teach their own
language to a foreigner.   Several of the most
experienced teachers of musick in our own country have assured me that the result of their experience was the same.   One who has taught
four thousand pupils, and enjoys much reputa-
tion as an instructer, assured me, that although
he found the same variety in these organs as in
others, he never found an individual who could
not be taught to sing.

But we shall find substantial reasons for believing this true, arising from the nature of vocal musick.   It consists of a succession of vocal
sounds, some of which are long and others short,
some slow and others quick, some high and
others low.   Now what else is speech? Speech
also has high and low sounds, slow and quick,
and long and short; and these variations have
been reduced to a system of surprising accura-
cy.   Chapman, in his Rhythmical Grammar,
and Rush and Barber, in their works, have
pointed out very clearly the musical intervals,
which are necessary in order to speak and read
correctly and intelligibly.   They have shown
that in order to ask a question, the voice usually rises a third, or three tones; that when the
question is more earnest, or asked with surprise,
the tone is a fifth higher than usual; and that
when the earnestness is still greater, the voice
rises eight tones; and that these intervals are
to a considerable extent uniform.   The answer
falls in the same manner.   The rapidity and

force with which we speak, obviously vary with
the state of our feelings. In short, a very little examination will show us that our speaking
is in effect a kind of singing. This, indeed, is
the great obstacle which a foreigner has to encounter in learning our language—and the want
of it is that which we term a foreign accent. It
is evident, then, that every man who understands the difference between the mode of pronouncing a question and an answer, and between a common question and an earnest one,
can distinguish a high note from a low, and can
even tell the difference between a third and a
fifth. He must, therefore, so far, have a musical ear.

The ordinary tones of voice are in the major
key. The tones of distress, or the whine of a
beggar, are in the minor key. If he can *distinguish* these, he proves that he has, to this
extent at least, a musical ear. If he can *imitate* all these various sounds, I know not how
we can deny him a musical voice. In short,
he who can discriminate the variations of speech,
can distinguish musical sounds. He who has
learned to *speak correctly*, may learn to *sing*.

We cannot omit noticing a topick which properly belongs to another lecture,—that practice
in musick will be the best preparation and aid
for the formation of good readers and good
speakers, and that he who does not understand
something of musical tones, and has not habit-
uated his organs to the sudden and precise va-

riations which they require, cannot understand
perfectly the modern rules of elocution, nor enjoy the full benefit of the excellent instructions
we now have in this art.

In regard to all the efforts yet made among
us, to ascertain how large a portion of the community can be taught vocal musick, the experiments have been desultory in their character,
short in their duration, and generally conducted by unskilful hands. Nothing then can be
inferred from them against a new experiment,
at a period when the habits of the body and
mind are not fixed.   But the complete answer
to all doubts on this point is furnished by the
fact, that wherever the experiment has been
made at the proper age, and in the proper manner, it has been successful.

I have already stated that it forms a part of
common school education throughout Germany
and Switzerland.   In the improved schools, it
is deemed no more difficult, and no more remarkable to read and write musick, than language.   I have also quoted the opinion of Lu-
ther, as to its importance.   Allow me to add
the opinion of distinguished men of the same
countries, both in regard to the importance,
and the practicability of teaching it to all.

Niemeyer, one of the most celebrated writers on education in Prussia, observes;—'The
organs of speech are improved by singing ; the
ear is formed and rendered more acute, and
the well known power of musick, even upon sav-

ages, proves that we should least of all neglect a branch of instruction, which exerts so important an influence in softening the passions, in elevating the social and finer feelings, in aiding the moral cultivation, and cherishing the spirit of devotion.'

Schwartz, one of the surviving fathers of education in Germany, remarks ;—' In the cultivation of the ear, we have a means of cultivating the harmony of the soul and the purity of the heart, and of promoting heavenly love and spiritual life, which will probably not be fully appreciated for a long time to come.'

Denzel, a veteran of this cause, who has been employed in organizing the school system of two of the German States, observes ;—' The formation of the voice is too important, and the influence of vocal musick on the mind and heart too great, to permit us to dispense with it in common schools.　It is no longer doubted that it ought to constitute a branch of study, in every institution for elementary education.' "

As this subject has not hitherto claimed an adequate degree of attention in this country, I shall be justified in presenting the remarks of another writer in the Annals of Education, on *Musical Talent.*

He remarks :—" If those who are interested in the dissemination of correct principles on any subject would labor diligently to collect all the *facts* which could throw light upon it, there is good reason to believe, that increased knowledge would so far change the grounds of a disputed question, as to induce both parties to engage in *investigation*, rather than debate. This I believe to be especially true in regard to musick; and when musical science shall be placed on the same basis with all other sciences, that of experiment and patient research, instead of sweeping and vague theories, *then* we may hope to see it take that dignified rank among the branches of study esteemed necessary in the course of education, to which its eminent adaptation to increase the happiness of man, and assist in preparation for a future existence, seem to entitle it. But while it is made the mere instrument of gratifying the senses, and is but slightly connected with the other studies which are thought to be necessary in the course of intellectual discipline, in fine, whilst those who love musick, and those who love philosophical research, are believed to be characters of so different a nature that it is impossible to find the two united in one person, we cannot expect to find musick in its legitimate station, purifying and elevating the young mind. It will be perverted to the ignoble purpose of a transient gratification to those who are not able to estimate its best qualities and purposes; and those who cultivate it, must still be looked upon as an inferior class of beings, to the cultivated and well educated portion of the community. This day is, however, fast passing away, and men are opening their eyes to the probability that an

3. *Primary teachers ought to be well acquainted with the principles of good reading.*

I am inclined to believe, there is generally a

and who has within a few years been a teacher in various kinds of vocal and instrumental musick and of thorough base. The principle then, upon which the above mentioned very simple plan is grounded, is this :—teach a child to sing a tune with his *own* mouth, and to give the accurate and constant attention of his *own* ear to the sounds which compose that tune, before you tell him of Clefs, Resolutions, Cesuras, &c. He will not proceed far in the love and practice of musick, before he will perceive the necessity of these things, and learn them with reference to an understanding application of them ; whereas, if he learn them without seeing their use and application, he will be in a fair way for imbibing a natural disgust for the whole business. Indeed one is almost forcibly led to the conclusion by what may be seen in society, that there must be something peculiarly repulsive in what are usually called the rules of musick, which prevents that general diffusion of musical taste and knowledge we might expect to find on so entertaining a subject. " I know of nothing," said the President of one of our Colleges, " which I so much regret, as not having learned to sing or play on some musical instrument in the proper season of my life ; *I consider every man who can do so, as a benefactor to society ;* but the *rules of* musick seemed to bear nothing of the perspicuity of demonstration about them, and I could make *nothing of them.*" This was logical, it was natural, and what we might expect from a great mind, accustomed only to a language of definite ideas, attempting to glean from that language information concerning that language of the soul which expresses no definite ideas. . . Now if this gentleman had been led in the early part of his life to exercise his ear and voice in such a way as to learn several tunes, we have no doubt he would have been sufficiently acquainted with the rules of musick in after life : for be it observed, he belonged to that class of mankind who are said to have musical ears.

Notwithstanding what has been said, I am ready to

greater deficiency, in their knowledge of the
art of reading, among the female instructers of
New England, than in their acquaintance with

believe, that there are some, nay perhaps very many,
in society, whose peculiar habits of mind, occupations,
attainments, &c. might render it rather a matter of indifference whether they first acquired a tolerable degree of skill in practice, or the rules; and perhaps as
far as they are individually concerned, from their habit of making every acquirement in its first stages, a
process of committing to memory or by rote, it would
be preferable to teach rules and practice together; but
it will be remembered that I am considering the case of
some sixty to a hundred children, and am endeavoring
to answer the question, how shall instruction be adapted to the whole. But I recur to the principle laid down
in the first part of this article; there should be a special adaptation of methods in teaching to the results,
&c. I have been considering how, in this case, my
proposed simple plan provides this adaptation; I will
now turn attention for a few moments to the results,
the actual results of this plan as tried.

1. The greater part of the children learned to sing
from twelve to twenty popular tunes, with a very tolerable share of correctness and taste. Now this is as
great an acquirement, as many persons of mature minds
make in the course of a winter's laborious drilling in
so much of the theory and practice of musick as may be
found in the singing books. And in a large majority
of cases, these latter have gained another " *unappre-
ciable*" acquirement, viz—an almost invincible disgust
at any thing that looks like extending the study of musick, a careful review and understanding application of
the rules, &c. &c. As confirmation of what I say, we
need only for a moment to consider the fact, that any
one who can make an understanding application of the
common rules laid down in the singing books, is a suitable person to instruct in sacred musick.

2. A musical spirit has been diffused among the children as another result of the plan. Their social meetings, the Sabbath schools, the daily school, their fire-

read a page, and render every word intelligible
to the hearer. When faulty habits of reading
are once formed, it will be found extremely
difficult to correct them afterwards. The first
objects of reading, that of understanding the
meaning themselves, and making themselves
understood by others, receives too little attention from our teachers, in all our schools and
academies. I know but few exceptions to this
remark in schools, whether taught by males or
females. I hope that to you at least this subject will appear with its just importance.

4. Another necessary qualification is a thorough knowledge of the English language. Perhaps it is not always expected that the teachers
of summer schools will find it necessary to instruct in Grammar. But if not a single scholar, should be prepared to commence it as a
regular study, it is not less important that
there should be adequate qualifications on the
part of the instructer. Children take their first
lessons on language, from the lips of their parents and teachers. Every expression, uttered
by them, and especially by the latter, will be
considered according to the most approved
standard. If improprieties in language are
sanctioned by your practice, your scholars will
naturally copy them. Habits formed in childhood are afterwards forsaken with difficulty.
From this arise the incorrect modes of speech
so frequently heard from persons who have
enjoyed eligible opportunities for education.

From the *pulpit* and the *bar* even, are uttered sentences, which a school-boy might correct.

5. Arithmetick should be familiar to primary instructers. Intellectual arithmetick is a proper, and highly important study for children. Though it is by no means the *first* to which they should attend; still, it ought to be taught in every summer school. Most children, who have learned to read, are able, under proper instruction, to make use of Emerson's Arithmetick or some other work of similar character. And certainly no one is prepared to act as a successful instructress, without a thorough acquaintance, with the science of numbers, at least, so far as taught in Mr. Colburn's "First Lessons." It is not sufficient to be able to ascertain the answer, in a given instance; but the whole process of reasoning on every sum, should be as familiar as a rule in syntax, or a definition in geography. Without this, it is difficult to interest yourselves in the science, or secure the attention of the children placed under your care. It is true, that written arithmetick is not always required in primary schools; it is necessary however, that you should be *able* to teach it if necessary.

6. Geography and History are demanded in all primary schools. With both you are expected to be familiarly acquainted. To the former, children may attend as soon as able to read the lesson, and the latter immediately follows it in a judicious course of study.

I wish here to say, that the kind of knowledge usually acquired of these studies, does not fit one to teach them in the most interesting manner. Attention to definitions, and the position of places on maps, is too often considered all that is necessary. How little this kind of knowledge prepares an individual to teach geography intelligibly, may be learned fully by visiting some of our schools. A child taught by an instructer of this character, was asked, "Where is Europe?" "In my atlas," he replied. "Can you point towards London?" "Yes, Sir," answered the young geographer, smartly; "it is there on my map." "Can you tell where the West Indies are?" "Yes, I just saw them; there they are." "What are they?" "O they are a parcel of little dots all about here," he replied, at the same time spreading out his fingers on the map. These questions were answered with as much confidence of their perfect correctness as if the boy had been a pedagogue for ten years. How many such geographers, our schools might furnish, I will not undertake to decide. That they are not numerous, certainly does not result from the mode, too often pursued in teaching them.

History is generally taught with little more regard to its real object, and teachers generally are not so well prepared to instruct in this as in geography.

7. Primary instructers ought to have so much

knowledge of Rhetorick, as to enable them to give proper instruction to children, in their primary attempts to clothe their thoughts with language, and form words into sentences. Whenever children become able to write, they ought to be required to attend to this exercise, and every one, under whose care they are placed, should be able to assist them in doing it properly,

Some knowledge of Moral and Intellectual philosophy, is important to every teacher. No duty is more incumbent on you, than that of teaching the young how to secure happiness, and avoid misery.

And can any one be qualified to train and discipline the young *mind*, without some acquaintance with the principles of intellectual philosophy?—without some knowledge of the operations of the mind and the means by which it may be improved?

With the qualifications above stated, and a willingness to devote yourselves assiduously to your work, you may hope for success in the important labour in which you are about to engage. But with less than these, it must be unsafe to entrust to your hands those precious plants, which require the hand of faithful and skilful cultivation.

It may be asked shall the employment be renounced by those who are deficient in some, while they are eminently qualified in other departments of knowledge?

No answer can be given, which will be ap-

LECTURE VI.

On entering your school-room, one of the first questions you will ask, is, How ought these children to be governed ?—and another will follow, How can *I* govern them ?—To suggestions on these subjects, I now invite your attention.

1. How ought children to be governed in school ?

They are intelligent beings, and of course, are to be governed as such. They are able to distinguish, in many cases, between right and wrong ;—or if not, when *first* placed under your care, they may soon be made capable of doing it. They have sensibilities ; they can easily distinguish between a smile and a frown, —between a friend and an enemy. They may be moved by kindness or unkindness,—they are capable of being influenced by various kinds of motives.

They ought then to be governed as rational, and not as irrational beings. The brutes must be controled as brutes. The whip and the goad may be the most necessary instruments with them, as they are incapable of appreciating your reasons, or of understanding the ground, of the requisitions you make. Not so with those whom you are to control and govern. They are intelligent, and can comprehend principles, and draw inferences from them.

The following directions present the general
course I wish to recommend.

1. *Require nothing of your pupils which is
unreasonable.* Some demands must be made
if you would have the school a source of enjoyment to them or of pleasure to yourselves.
But in all these you are to consult both their
good, and your moral obligations. Whatever will lay a foundation for their highest improvement, cannot be neglected with impunity.
And whatever is not necessary to this, you cannot justly demand.

Do you ask what requisitions may reasonably be made of them? The answer must be
varied with circumstances. But in general
terms, they ought always to attend to the objects, for which they are furnished with the
means of instruction. If able to study, they
must be required to do it. If able to learn a
lesson, they must be obliged to accomplish it in
a reasonable time. They must be made sensible of their duty to obey all the necessary laws
of the school. They may properly be expected and required to treat their teacher with respect, and each other with kindness. It is important that they become accustomed to realize
that all the regulations of the school are made
for *them,* and the wishes of the instructer must
be their law. It is reasonable that they be required to obey cheerfully, exactly and constantly. No rule made for them can be disregarded, without present and future injury. Par-

tial and imperfect obedience, is little better than disobedience. The direction just given implies that nothing *un*reasonable can, with propriety, be demanded of them. The teacher must be just to herself and to those she instructs. She cannot make unjust laws without tarnishing her character, and proving herself unworthy of the confidence of children. She must guard against errors in judging what scholars ought to do, and what they ought to avoid. In this decision, it is not sufficient to regard their present welfare only. Every thing which tends to lay the foundation for future excellence of character, is equally important with that, which regards their present good. Indeed, many of the rules given them ought to regard the future, even more than the present.

2. *Make every rule intelligible, so that it shall be understood by your scholars.*

It is possible, you may think this a direction with which it is difficult to comply. But such an opinion is erroneous. Young children can be easily convinced on those subjects of duty, which they are able to comprehend. They readily perceive the reason why they are furnished with books and instructers. They easily see the impossibility of making any progress in study, while they are idle, or engaged in play. They know that noise and confusion are not consistent with the rapid acquisition of knowledge ; and of course, they will readily understand the necessity of submitting to such

8

laws, as may be requisite, for securing order in
the exercises and success in their studies.

A person, who has never made an appeal to
the common sense of children, will be surpris-
ed to find how correctly they decide on the
principles by which their conduct ought to be
governed. I should feel very little unwillingness
to obligate myself to abide by their own decision, when proper questions are fairly submitted
to their good sense. I will endeavor to make
myself intelligible by the subsequent example.

The teacher enters the school-room, and is
soon surrounded by a group of children, varying in age from three to twelve years.

Teacher. Good morning, children. Have
you all come to *school*, this morning?

Children. Yes ma'am.

T. Well, I am very happy to see you. I
love little children, and delight to be with them.
And now can you tell me why you came to
school ?

C. (All together.) We have come to learn.

T. But do you not know enough already ?

C. (All speaking.) No : if we did, there
would be no need of coming to school.

T. Don't you know how to play ?

C. (Laughing.) Yes ; but we came here
to learn.

T. But will it not be pleasanter to spend
your time in play ? Perhaps I can tell you a-
bout plays you never heard of. Will it not be
your choice to have me assist you in your plays,
rather than in your studies ?

C. (Confused and hesitating.) No ; we can play at home.

T. Yes, so you can ; but may not children come to school for the purpose of learning how to play better when at home ?

C. No ; we think not.

T. Perhaps there are *some* who wish to spend the summer in play. If there are any, who would like to have me spend my time in teaching them how to play, they may raise their hands.

[The children look at each other, and at the teacher, but not a hand is raised.]

I do not see any one who wishes to be taught how to play better than is known already. Now all those, who wish to acquire as much knowledge, as possible during the summer, may raise their hands.

[Every hand is raised.]

I notice every hand is raised ; and of course all of you wish to be instructed in those things which will be useful. But to be more certain, I will write the name of every one who thinks it is better to spend every day in acquiring knowledge, than it would be to waste it in idleness and play.

[The question is put to every child, and the answer is uniformly the same. The teacher proceeds.]

I am glad all the children present wish to gain knowledge. It is very pleasant to teach

those, who desire to receive instruction.   I am
never happier than when assisting children to
acquire a useful education.   Another question
may now be proposed.   You know that it is necessary to have some regulations in a school.
Who shall make these, you, or I ?

C. You must make them.   You know better than we do, what rules are necessary.

T. How many wish me to make them ?
All, who think that I ought to do it, may raise
their hands.

[Every hand is again raised.]

Are laws to be made for me to obey, or for
the school to regard ?

C. They ought to be made for the school.

T. If any think they ought to obey the rules
given by the instructer, they may raise their
hands.

[The children raise their hands.]

I will write this down then, so that I may
know who think it is right that my orders be
obeyed.   But, *I* prefer to have *you* make *some*
of the rules for the school.   If you make those
which I disapprove, I shall consider it right to
alter them, though I think there will be no necessity for this, as I have found those children,
who wish to learn, generally able tell what is
essentially necessary, for their improvement.

Will it be right for the children who attend
school to strike each other, or to quarrel with
each other ?

C. We think not.

T. I will write this opinion in a book.   *The children of this school think there ought to be no quarrelling, or ill nature among the scholars.*

Will you establish this as one rule of your school ?

C. Yes, we will.

T. Will it be right for scholars to leave their places, and go out of their seats, just when they please ?

C. It will not.   We must not do it without leave.

T. I will write this also.   *The children of this school agree, that it will be wrong to leave their places without permission from the teacher.*

What do you think about interrupting each other ?

C. We ought certainly to be still, and not disturb each other.

T. I will write this opinion also.—

The teacher may thus proceed till every important subject has been presented to the children, and their opinion has been expressed upon it.   The necessary regulations will be *understood* by every one, and there is, to say the least, stronger reason to expect children will regard these, formed in a measure by themselves and fully comprehended, than that they will be obedient to laws, the reason and importance of which they do not appreciate.   It is not within the limits of probability, that, at this age, they

8*

will appreciate the importance of all the necessary regulations, without exercising their minds
in relation to them.

By pursuing a course like the one marked
out, it will be easy to comply with the direction,
to make every thing intelligible. But without
something of the kind, you must repeat laws or
rules from day to day, and still the reasons on
which they are founded will not be comprehended by all. Experiments like the above have
been attended with the happiest results. I
proceed now to the next direction, which is,

3. *Uniformly proceed, on the same principles of government.*

The importance of this direction appears
from two considerations. First, there is considerable variety in the feelings of the instructers, at different times; and secondly, the feelings of children are equally variable. It will
require but half the effort to hold the reins of
government to day, that it may require tomorrow. With a healthy flow of spirits at one
time, you can meet a lion unmoved ; but at
another, while affected by some slight disease—
while your nerves are in a state of irritation, a
shadow may annoy you or drive you from
your path. A child will be brought to cheerful submission at one moment, by very little effort ; but at another, it may demand all your
wisdom and firmness to ensure obedience.

Whether the difference exist in the instructer or pupil, the importance of maintaining uni-

formly, the same *principles* of government,
must be obvious. If strict in discipline to day,
and lax tomorrow,—if you punish an offence
at one time, which you have disregarded at
another,—or if you suffer an irregularity to pass
unnoticed now, and censure it tomorrow ; how
can your scholars have confidence in your
judgment? How can you convince them that
your motives are correct? They are very
quick to observe any irregularity in your mode
of teaching them, or in your general system of
government. I hope, therefore, the direction
will receive careful attention from all who are
intrusted with the management of schools.
Let no one suffer herself to be deceived by
thinking, that irregularity will pass without exerting an unhappy influence.

4. *Govern with impartiality.*

I do not give this direction without a knowledge of the difficulty of complying with it. No
teacher can entertain the same feelings towards
the scholar who is always making mischief and
giving occasion to reprove or punish him, and
another who constantly strives to do right, or
commits an errour unfrequently. Suppose both
of these have been, in a given instance, chargeable with the same fault, under the same circumstances ; it is difficult to feel that they are
to be treated alike. But still, impartiality requires this, and if a difference *is* made, its effect will generally be injurious. The members
of your schools connected with the most respect-

able familes, and those coming from families
of less consideration, must be governed by the
same general rules, and intercourse with them
in the presence of the school, ought to be conducted on the same principles. They are
committed equally to your care and instruction,
and the same kind and conciliating language
must be addressed to all, or you fail of governing with due impartiality. If you are willing to
reprove one, and *unwilling* to reprove another,
it must be impossible to conceal the fact from
the children. They read the thoughts of teachers, almost as readily as they understand their
language. Let me suggest the necessity of
particular care on this point. Even though
you exercise *this*, pardon me for saying I shall
still have some anxiety, lest you should be influenced by some undue bias of mind toward
particular individuals.

5. *Govern mildly, but firmly.*

A habit of being fretful or peevish, will always make your company and attention disagreeable to children. No one desires the presence of a person, who habitually exhibits any
unkind feelings. Threats made in such a state
of mind are but little regarded, either by those
who make, or those who hear them. Promises made under such circumstances, are *not always* observed. I have heard expressions from
a teacher like these ;—" If you do so again I'll
whip your life out."—" I'll *ferule* you as long
as I can lift a rule," &c. &c. Now does the

scholar believe such a teacher? Does he expect him to keep his word? Ought he to expect it? Such threats never will be put into execution, and the children know it. If they do wrong, the teacher's *example* is before them, which they will be disposed to plead in extenuation of the fault.

A teacher, who indulges in anger or in any slighter degree of ill nature, must incur the necessity of making frequent confessions to the school, in order to secure even an imperfect degree of confidence. To do this is always humiliating, and very few are ready to acknowledge their errours, even when convinced it is their duty so to do. But without such readiness any instructions to scholars on moral obligation, will be of little weight.

It is the common effect of ill nature, to make him who indulges it unhappy. How then can the duties of the teacher be performed successfully, while in such a state of mind?

6. *Fulfil every engagement or promise.*

On this much must depend; for children are not slow to learn whether this is your principle or not. If you ever say to a child, you must be corrected for this fault, fail not to keep your word. If a request is denied *once*, let it be uniformly denied, unless circumstances change. If a scholar is required to do a thing, he ought to know at once that he *must* do it, and that there can be no excuse. When a teacher resolves to be obeyed in every thing, it is not difficult to convince the school of this determination. If convinced, every one will always expect to yield obedience as a matter of course. But if a rule is once *broken* and the teacher does not regard it, there is an end of quiet submission and cheerful obedience. I have before said no unreasonable laws should be made. It is therefore indispensable that all which are made should be regarded, and every promise should be faithfully *kept*.

7. *In order to secure obedience from others, it is indispensably necessary to govern yourselves.*

The importance and necessity of this has been implied in the previous remarks. Indeed this might, with propriety, have been placed as the first prerequisite to your success in the management of your school. " He who has no rule over his own spirit is like a city broken down and without walls." Self-government lies at the foundation of the exercise of government over others, in every situation. When I can control myself, I have little anxiety about being able to influence those who are committed to my care.

This direction extends to many things. The teacher must govern her passions—control her prejudices—restrain herself from holding up individuals or families as subjects of ridicule— and many times she must avoid saying *all* which might be said, without sacrificing truth. On one point, I wish to give a special charge.

Never mention the faults of a scholar, unless when forced to do it, as a correction or warning.

Many things, in the management of families may be proper subjects of animadversion, but I believe very little good can be accomplished by the teachers telling of them.   You will need to govern yourselves, constantly, with regard to these. Let every teacher be master of herself, and she will easily control the school.

LECTURE VII.

In the last lecture several suggestions were made on the subject of governing children in school. In this, I shall give some further advice on government and general management. The two subjects must necessarily be blended together.

Every thing in connection with the general management of a school, must have reference to the manner in which government is conducted ; for if this be irregular and imperfect, it is not possible for other things to be conducted as they should be. If there is not a judicious system of discipline, irregularity must extend farther, for it is impossible to introduce order, where this mainspring of harmony is not found. And if you fail in establishing your authority, you have little encouragement to attempt other salutary measures.

After you have fixed on a course of correct discipline, you are prepared to gain other important points, but not before. The first direction I wish to give here is, *see that every thing required is accomplished at the proper time.* The different exercises should have their appropriate amount of time allotted to them, and receive attention whenever that time arrives. If the school is *small,* still this is necessary to prevent misapplication and waste of time. If large, little which is valuable can be accomplished without it. When every thing is permitted to press on the attention of the teacher at once, what time is there for doing any thing as it should be done? If one thing is commenced and finished before another is introduced, opportunity will be furnished for all necessary exercises. Does the teacher attempt to prepare copies for the classes in penmanship, hear reading, and give answers to inquiries on other subjects, all at once, it is not possible to secure much benefit from any of them. All the energies of the mind are to be given to one subject, if we expect to be successful. He who engages in several different kinds of business at the same moment, will generally fail of paying a suitable degree of attention to either of them. "A time for every thing, and every thing at its time," is a maxim nowhere more important, than in directing the operations of a school. Disregard this, and constant irregularity and confusion will ensue.

2. *Give that attention to the different departments of labour, which their comparative importance demands.*

Various are the subjects which require your care. But some must necessarily claim more of it than others. If, while possessing different degrees of importance, they receive equal attention, some one of them must necessarily suffer. This is unavoidable. If

9

the less important receive the greater share of
attention, the injury will be still more serious.
Few subjects connected with the character and
happiness of children are, in my opinion, of
greater importance than that of cultivating early and cheerful submission, and obedience to
necessary rules of government. To accomplish this, then, must be a prominent object
from day to day. I would not imply that children are to be daily and hourly reproved for
little acts of carelessness, or trifling departures
from the path of rectitude. A child may easily be ruined by being restrained too much.
But I wish to say, that just as often as a disposition is manifested to resist rightful authority,
it should be met with the highest degree of decision and firmness. And if one thing calls
for attention more than any other, it must be
this. It demands constant attention, and if
you are so happy as to be successful, the
amount of benefit conferred on scholars, will
be incalculable.

A habit of thinking is of preeminent importance to children, and demands attention as a
second thing. It is generally true, that children who have never been deceived, are willing others should *think* for them ; thus they take
on trust, whatever is asserted by a kind teacher, whether right or wrong. "Why is this
true?" I asked a scholar yesterday, "Because
sir, *you said so*," was the reply. "But does
my assertion make it true?" "I don't know as

ers found in primary schools, whether taught by
males or females.   Several things have united
to occasion these results.   A very prominent
one is the ignorance of the instructers themselves; another reason is found in the small
degree of attention given to the exercise of
reading; and the careless manner in which it
is performed.   A third is found in the character of the books used for reading.   Those
books are often selected which contain lessons
presenting very little variety.   Every piece is
read alike in dull indistinct monotony, whether
it be prose, poetry, or dialogue.   You have it
in your power effectually to counteract some
of these evils, and apply a remedy to many, if
not all of them.   You can give sufficient time
to this department, and can make better selec-
tions for reading, than are frequently made.   So
far as qualified, it is in your power to adopt
that mode of teaching which will lead to distinctness in articulation, and the variety of tone
which the character of the lesson demands.
Among the younger classes who may be neces-
sitated to read with hesitation, *habits* may be
cultivated, which will lead to very happy results.   But in regard to those more advanced,
your task will be more difficult.   To them, too
much attention cannot easily be given.   The
great importance to almost every individual of
being able to read with propriety and correctness, places this part of your labour prominently
in view.   Whatever may be the future course

of the young, correct habits of reading furnish them with facilities for acqiuring knowledge, not furnished by any other single branch of study.

The other,studies to be pursued claim their proportionate share of attention, but it is unnecessary to enlarge here, as some directions on each will be given in a subsequent lecture.

3. Endeavour to make the school a pleasant and delightful place to children.

I shall be met here, very probably, with the remark, this is impossible under some, if not under all circumstances. I am not, however, disposed to admit this, for the following among many reasons.

1. Schools which have for a long time been entirely uninviting to children, have in a single month, been transformed into places of the highest pleasure by the well-directed efforts of the teacher. 2. It does not require greater resources, than all of you have at command, to provide for the entertainment and amusement of children at school. 3. The strong desire which the young manifest for each other's society, will be sufficient to make them happy in being collected together, provided there is nothing repulsive in the teacher, or school-room.

But how can we, under all circumstances, make the school for young scholars pleasant? I reply, 1. Be pleasant and kind yourselves. No direction is more important than this; for where is the child who does not love to be in the presence of a kind and affectionate friend?

9 *

2. Show that you are pleased, when the members of the school are made happy, and that to secure this, is a prominent object in all the arrangements you make.   3. Use as much exertion as is practicable for the convenience of the scholars.   4. Make every reasonable effort to ornament the school-room, and render it comfortable, neat and elegant.   5. Procure as many attracting objects as is possible, such as cards—pictures—specimens in botany, and geology or mineralogy.   6. Invite the *children* to join in furnishing those things which are designed for their amusement.   7. Let the studies be made intelligible and interesting, and the mode of teaching be such, as to throw a charm around every thing connected with the acquisition of knowledge.   And if you find children after this who prefer home, or idleness and play, to the attractions of the school-room, I have only to say that you will be surrounded by a class of children very different from any I have ever found.

It is not sufficient to pursue a dull and formal round of exercises; these can be attended with little benefit or fraught with little interest to your pupils.   But while I make this remark, I am very far from being an advocate for the course pursued by those teachers whose *chief* object is to amuse.   Such teachers are satisfied if children can be made happy, though but little knowledge is gained, and habits of thinking are not cultivated.   When a judicious course is pursued, children may be interested and pleased, while still their best good is consulted in every particular.

There is a class of nominal teachers, too numerous, if I may judge from the results of my own observation, whom I wish particularly to specify, and whose example I warn you to shun. If I seem uncourteous in my remarks, you will pardon me, remembering I plead the cause of the young—of those who cannot plead for themselves. I have visited many schools, and witnessed in them such a disregard to cleanliness, as not only to render the situation of the scholars exceedingly unpleasant, but also to destroy that purity of air so essential to the preservation of health. Week after week, leaves, paper, and rubbish of various kinds were permitted to accumulate on the floor, until it was difficult to decide of what materials it was originally composed. When I have intimated that a school-room ought to exhibit a very different appearance, the excuse has been very prompt, " *We have no broom, sir.*" In other houses I have been forced to the conviction, that the fashion of washing the room had not reached them. Coals and ashes from the hearth, and mud and dirt from the streets, had accumulated for years, and formed a paint on the floor which might be considered fire-proof. A thought of ornamenting the " home of childhood" had never penetrated the mind of either teacher or parent.

I will not say, what the appearance of the houses of these teachers, if they ever become the mistresses of families, will be; but I will say, that children confined for three or four months every year in such a room must unavoidably associate their uncomfortable accommodations with the studies they are required to pursue. I will say, farther, that parents and teachers who consent to have scholars thus situated, term after term, can have little to wonder at, if children furnish sad evidence of a distaste for study, or choose to wander in the fields, and play truant from the school. I can scarcely find it in my heart to blame them; for who can be delighted with that which is so revolting?

Every school-room ought to exhibit as much neatness, and, at least, as many attractions as the family parlour; and the teacher, who gives no attention to this subject, *is unfit to be a guide to infancy.* Let me say also in this connexion, that if a proper degree of attention is given to this subject by even *one* teacher, children will themselves be averse to negligence with regard to it in any succeeding one. The degree of attention which *you* may give to it, may be beneficial, long after you have retired from this field of labour.

4. Strive constantly to secure the confidence of children.

For this, you must furnish evidence that you are sincerely desirous of promoting their welfare, in all the efforts you may make. If you prove to them that your personal convenience or inconvenience have very little influence on your prohibitions or indulgences,—if you prove to them that you labour with interest and pleasure, whenever you can promote their improvement or happiness, it will be neither impracticable nor difficult to secure their confidence. The following brief suggestions may be important.

1. It is necessary for you to be deliberate in making decisions, which affect the circumstances of your scholars. Hasty decisions must not only prevent confidence in you, but must often lead you into errours, to correct which, may require much time and painful effort. It is generally true, that whatever is done in haste, is done imperfectly. You have little confidence in the opinion of that person, who gives it without investigation. And you cannot expect that your pupils will respect your opinions and decisions, formed in a similar manner. The first view of a subject is frequently essentially different from the second or third. If you form a permanent opinion from a mere glance, it will often be found erroneous.

Deliberation in commending or in punishing scholars is highly necessary. If a scholar.learns his lesson in an hour, and spends two in play, he does not deserve commendation so much as another, who studies all the time allowed him to obtain his lesson, and is still unable to recite it perfectly. If you are in haste to praise, or in haste to reprove, or in haste to punish, you must lose the confidence of those who are placed under your instruction. But let deliberation be your motto in all things, and you will avoid the evils of hasty decisions. I have somewhere met with an adage,—"think twice before you speak once;" this I think a very good rule for every teacher to adopt, together with this addition,—think *three times* before you *act* once.

2. Another means of securing the confidence of your school, is by being punctual in the discharge of every duty. The habits of some, at least, are to consult present convenience and inclination only. Show this propensity, and what foundation can you lay for confidence? You are employed to benefit others. Children are remarkably close observers of the habits of those around them. Let them frequently see you ten minutes too late,—let them be brought to believe that you have little regard to system,—let them find that you can promise and not perform,—in short, let them know that any trifling thing is sufficient to furnish an excuse for your irregularity,—and what confidence do you, or can you expect, they will have in you as their guide and director?

Always keep your word. If you have given a pledge of any kind, it is not only your duty to see it redeemed, but to see that it is redeemed at the proper time, When a promise has been made, it cannot be disregarded, without mani-

fest injury to those, who are more ready to copy the wrong, than to benefit by the good examples you may set before them.

Another means of gaining the confidence of
your juvenile charge, is the devotion of all your
time to them. The whole belongs to them, or
at least, all which can be employed for their
good. I do not say you can be *present with*
them through all the hours of the day. Much
preparation is necessary before you meet them
in the morning. Many things can be done
better, when they are not before you. Arrangements should be made for illustrating studies
and exciting interest in the branches you teach.
Many very important means of conferring benefit must be entirely neglected, if you devote to
the interests of your scholars, only that portion
of time, which is spent with them in the school-
room. And I wish here to bear testimony
against a practice, which I have frequently observed among instructresses, of engaging in man-
tuamaking, millinary, or other work, during the
whole of the time not actually spent with the
school. If the idea of *pecuniary* advantages
interests you more than any thing else, I beg
you to dismiss the thought of becoming instructers. Your task requires all your energies
and all your time, if you wish to perform it in
the best manner, and make your labours promote the best interests of the children of your
charge. If your great object is to do them
good, you must have their confidence. They

LECTURE VIII.

———

Several other subjects with reference to the general management of your schools, are worthy of attention, and will be suggested in this Lecture.

1. It is important not to confine children too long, or keep them too still.

I wish here to bear a decided testimony against a practice which too often prevails.

Children are sent to school in the morning, and, after they arrive there, are required to take their seats, and sit till noon, with the exception of being called up to read once or twice, and perhaps, of being permitted to go out once. They have an hour at noon for play, and then are confined again till the close of the school. They become tired, restless and cross; and no wonder that they should. To confine a sprightly child for six hours in a day to one place, without employment and with no change of scenery,—with nothing but a dull round of exercises, in which it takes little or no delight, is not only unreasonable and cruel, but it is a sure way to make the school an unpleasant place, and to make dolts of the scholars themselves. I have long ago ceased to wonder at

10

the lines of the poet, describing the infant school
boy

"With his satchel and his shining morning face,
Creeping like snail unwillingly to school."

It is indeed, a matter of surprise, that children
do not more frequently feel an aversion, so great,
that it can never be overcome in subsequent
years. They will often, indeed, attend school
with pleasure, from no other motive, than the
opportunity it affords them to play with their
little associates while going and returning, and
during the intermission. Aside from the facilities for amusement, the school would be a place
of no interest. By so much confinement they
suffer in their health, and more in their spirits.

A young child, one especially who is not able
to get lessons or study, ought never to be confined more than an hour at one time.* If pos-

* I give the following remarks from various authors,
on the importance of exercise, and the danger of too
much confinement. The benefit of teachers in large
towns, or instructers of schools continued through the
year, is especially regarded. Schools in the country,
where children walk a considerable distance every day,
and have the privilege of free exercise at home during
the greater part of the year, are not in so much danger
from the neglect of it.

"Exercise is universally acknowledged to be essential to the preservation of health. It is invariably
recommended by physicians, who, in their daily practice, have occasion to witness the melancholy effects of
those habits of inaction, which so generally prevail
among the female portion of society, more especially in
cities and large towns. With a view to diminish the
extent of the evil, several members of the medical profession, and other enlightened individuals have in the

sible some active exercise should be adopted in
the school-room. Marching, calisthenicks for

true spirit of philanthropy, published the results of their
experience on this important subject. In these valuable productions, the various afflicting consequences
which arise from the omission of adequate bodily exertion are detailed, their only efficient remedy is pointed
out, and its adoption earnestly recommended."
                                                  VOXRINO.
  " Every mother should be convinced that her *children
require a great deal of vigorous exercise.* They are as
fond of skipping and bounding about as other young
animals. You might as rationally attempt to restrain
the sportive gambols of a lamb or kitten as of a healthy
child. Nature has taught those exercises, which are
most conducive to little children's health and happiness,
and there is no need of other teaching. Keep them out
of danger and let them choose their own innocent sport.
It is delightful to observe the graceful, unstudied move-
ments of the little creatures while they are at play.
Their picturesque grouping and beautiful attitudes
have often called forth the admiration of the painter,
and taxed his skill in imitation. *Unfortunately, the re-
straints of the school-room soon destroy this charmi..g
ease and sweet gracefulness."*
                         Young Ladies' " Calisthenics."
  " We are far from thinking that three or four hours
a day devoted to health, would be lost from the period
of juvenile improvement : they would in fact prove so
much gain. A clear head and a happy heart are the
shortest road to all mental acquirements ; because they
convert toil into pleasant exercise, and leave the student the full and free use of every faculty. We do not
need a physician to tell us that dulness and inefficiency
of mind are the sure results of the neglect of exercise,
or that brilliancy and force of thought are the natural
fruits of activity."   Ibid.
  The Author begs leave to say to Instructresses generally, that " Letters on Calisthenics," published by H.
& F. J. Huntington, Hartford, Connecticut, ought to
be in the hands of every teacher.

girls, or marking on the Black-Board may be recommended.   But if this cannot be admitted, let
young children be sent *out* to amuse themselves,
while the older members are employed in recitation.   The presence of one, capable of directing their plays, or of admonishing them to avoid
danger, is always desirable, and under some
circumstances is indispensable.

2. It is highly important that all the school exercises should be arranged with such regard to
order and system, that every child may know
the time he is to be engaged in performing
each.

This is important from the following considerations.   A person who must be prepared for
doing a thing at a fixed hour, will be much
more likely to do it, than a person who expects to be called on sometime, but does not
know when the time will come.   If your scholars have no intimation of the particular time,
when they must have accomplished an exercise,
they will far more readily turn aside from their
preparation.   You may, therefore, make much
greater dependence, on having proper preparation made for reciting every lesson, when the
scholar knows the time, at which he will be
required to recite it.

Another reason, why this direction is important, is learned from considering the value
of habits of system and regularity.   Division of
time lays the foundation for system in pursuing
an object of importance.   If your scholars are

to give one hour to reading, another to geography and another to history, they know when to leave one subject and take up another. They establish a habit, which enables them to control their thoughts and fix them on whatever claims present attention. This is highly conducive to their progress in gaining and retaining knowledge.

A third reason for this direction is, it furnishes you with the means of giving a due proportion of attention to every scholar and every department of labour. But if you have no systematic arrangement of your daily exercises, one may receive too great a share of attention, while another is neglected.

3. The direction next in importance is this : Cultivate, as far as possible, among your scholars, habits of frankly acknowledging faults. In order to succeed in this, some effort on your part will be necessary. That effort will be successful, if rightly made. The first thing is to make a full confession to the school of your own errours. Let these be ever so trifling, if they have been observed by the school, or by any individual in it, let this acknowledgement be made before the whole school. This will lay the foundation for success in your efforts to lead the scholars to do the same.

Is it asked, how shall the object be secured ?

In reply, I recommend something like the following course.

10*

A fault has been committed by some one, but it is not known by what individual. Suppose a pane of glass has been broken in the window. Before asking for the author of the mischief, you may relate the story of Washington, who when a child " tried the edge of his hatchet on a choice cherry-tree in his father's garden."* When asked if he knew who had spoiled the tree, he replied " I can't tell a lie Pa, you know I can't tell a lie, I did it with my little hatchet." The teacher asks,—What did Washington do, when he had committed a fault ?

Children. He acknowledged it.

Teacher. Why did he not deny it ?

C. He could " not tell a lie."

T. Was he foolish for confessing it ?

C. O no : he did right.

T. Is it not probable he was punished when he owned it ?

C. No : his father said " run to arms, my dearest boy, run to my arms ; you have paid me a thousand fold for my tree, even though it had blossomed with silver and borne fruit of gold."

T. Was not Washington made unhappy by frankly confessing his faults ?

C. Surely not ; he was happy after he owned it.

* See Putnam's An. Reader, or Weems' Life of Washington.

T. Is it right for all children to acknowledge it, when they have done wrong?

C. Yes.

T. Can any one be happy, who commits a fault and then denies it?

C. We think not.

T. But if a parent or teacher does not *see* the child while he is doing mischief, will he not be more happy, if he denies it, and makes the teacher believe him innocent?

C. How can he be happy? He must tell a lie if he conceals a fault; and *he* knows he tells one, whether the teacher does or not.

T. If any child in this school should do mischief, will he be made happy by denying it?

C. No, he cannot.

T. All who think he will be unhappy, may raise their hands.

[Every hand is raised.]

When any one has done wrong, do you think he *will* cheerfully acknowledge it?

C. He ought to do it, and we think he will.

[The teacher may now mention in language like the following, what has been done.]

T. I perceive that since I went out, glass has been broken in the window. Perhaps the scholar or scholars who broke it, did it accidentally. But in whatever way it may have been done, I hope I shall have an exact account of it. The one who broke the glass may now inform me about it.

If, after pursuing such a course, you fail to obtain a frank acknowledgement from the author of the mischief, I have only to say you will be associated with a class of children, very different from any, I have ever found. I think no one who makes a faithful effort to comply with the direction last given, will *ever* fail of witnessing the most happy results. But if otherwise, in any given instance, the teacher will still have the happiness of knowing she has attempted to discharge an important duty.

4. Let it ever be a principle in your school to have every thing, that is commenced, pursued till it is finished.

In order to do this, some pre-requisites are indispensable. The first is to ascertain as nearly as possible, what the scholars can accomplish, before they are directed to that which you propose. The second is, assure yourselves that the subject is important to them and worthy of their attention. When you have established these points, you are prepared to decide, that the studies commenced, must be pursued till they are understood. When there are sufficient reasons to begin an enterprize, there are sufficient reasons for continuing and completing it.

Many teachers are disposed to yield to the frequent requests of children, for permission to take some new study, before accomplishing that in which they may have been engaged. To yield to their solicitations is highly injurious to

them, and often inconvenient to the teacher.
But my chief objection to it lies in this; no
young scholar ought to form a habit of thinking
that he is to study whatever he pleases without
advice from others; but, on the contrary, he
ought early to know that others must guide and
direct him.   Ignorant as he is, submission to
the decision of others is indispensable to *his*
greatest good.   If permitted to change his studies at will, every thing will soon become disgusting, and while he gets a smattering of all,
he is sure to acquire a *thorough* knowledge of
none.

5. Be cautious in promising rewards for accomplishing a given amount of study.

It is not my design to say that rewards are,
in all instances, injurious or improper.   I think,
on the contrary, that they *may*, under some circumstances, be beneficial, if given as a mark of
approbation for efforts made without any reference to them.   But whenever the child's application is graduated by the magnitude of the
expected reward, he is cultivating a habit at
variance with his best good.   He will soon
have no higher motive in studying.   And when
this becomes true, his advancement must be
slow, and his knowledge of little practical
utility.   If an artificial appetite is created, natural and proper digestion can hardly be expected.

"What will you give me if I get my lesson
well?" said little Myra to her instructer.   "I

make no promises, said the judicious teacher.
" But Ma always pays me for getting my lesson,"
continued the little prattler. " If your *Ma*
does," replied the instructer, " *I* cannot think it
proper. I hope all *my* scholars will have a
better motive and higher object in view. I wish
all to study from a love of learning, and a desire to be useful and happy." These, however,
were powerless motives with the little girl, and
of course her progress was not to be accele-
rated by them. But the teacher gained an
important lesson ; viz. that all who learn from
no other motive than the hope of reward, will
make very irregular and inefficient advances.

If rewards are *given*, they ought to be in
those instances, where there are fixed habits
of application, whether the proficiency of the
pupil is more or less rapid. In other cases
their effect is always doubtful,—generally pernicious.

6. Strive to improve favourable opportunities to make a lasting impression on the minds
of your scholars.

There are subjects on which instruction will
be of very little permanent value, if given in an
ordinary manner. And as circumstances will
occur during every district school, furnishing
opportunities to you to impart such instruction,
it is highly important, that these should be
carefully improved. Let me explain what I
mean :—

If you wish to teach children sympathy for

the poor,—if you wish to give them abhorrence
for lying, theft, profaneness, &c.—or if you
desire to impress them strongly with the value
of any habit,—the worth of any particular art
or improvement,—let each of these be distinctly fixed in the mind, and then inquire from
day to day, have I now a favourable opportunity to secure this or that particular object? If
favourable, how shall I improve it? By what
means shall I be most likely to succeed?

The ability to discover the most favourable
moments for making these impressions, and the
skill to improve them, are of very great value
to every teacher. By means of them, you may
transmit your influence to future generations, as
well as confer an important benefit on the children you instruct.

I can devise no better means of making you
acquainted with the whole subject to which I
ask your attention, than by relating the method
adopted by one with whose course I am acquainted.

Miss W. has written thus in her Note Book,
—" It must be my fixed and invariable purpose
to benefit EVERY CHILD placed under my instruction, as much as I have ability to do. I
must teach them the importance of submission—
I must inform them how to govern themselves—
I must cultivate a love of learning, and lead
them to form a habit of constant application to
the studies they are required to pursue—I must
promote cheerful obedience to parents, respect

to superiors, kindness and affection to associates and equals.—I wish to have every child habitually *honest* and scrupulously *just.*—I wish all to reverence the word of God, and regard its precepts as the rule of conduct.—I must labour to make a strong impression of the heinousness of lying, profaneness, intemperance, and other vices.—I wish the children to pity the afflicted and assist the needy.

"As some guide to me in obtaining results so desirable, I will adopt the following rules.

"1. If a child should die, I will endeavour to turn the attention of the others, as much as possible, to the manner in which they must live, in order to be prepared for a similar event themselves.

"2. If a house is burned, or destroyed by any means, or any similar occurrence takes place in the vicinity, I will strive to produce a conviction of our absolute dependance on the great Creator for the continuance of all our enjoyments. Personal accidents may be improved for the same purpose.

"If any particular crime is perpetrated in the vicinity, or is witnessed by the children, I will endeavour to make such an improvement of it, as shall produce the most desirable impression on their minds.

"4. I will watch with anxious and hourly solicitude from day to day, to improve all the little occurrences in the school, which may open the door for securing some one of the

things which I consider important, with regard
to the present and future happiness of my beloved pupils.

" 5. I will ask myself every morning when I
meet them, what can I do for these 'lambs'
to-day, that will do them good?

" 6. I will ask myself every evening, what
have I done, from which I can reasonably hope
some good will result?

" 7. I will read and reflect on the subjects
connected with my various duties as much as I
have opportunity.

" 8. As I am dependant on God for ability
to labour, and wisdom to guide, I will devote a
season every day to ask the blessing of Heaven
on my efforts."

When Miss W. entered the school, she usually addressed the children thus :—" Good
morning, my little friends.   Are you all good
children this morning?   All, who cannot recollect of having disobeyed their parents, may
hold up their hands.—All, who have been good
natured and pleasant, may hold up their hands.
—All, who have been kind to their brothers or
sisters, may hold up their hands.—All, who have
endeavoured to do all that I have requested of
you, may hold up their hands.   Now if any
scholar has held up a hand who ought not to
have done it, is that child happy?

C. No—certainly not.

T. Has such a child tried to deceive us?

C. Yes, Ma'am.

11

T. Is it very wicked to deceive?

C. It is. God has threatened, that all liars shall be dreadfully punished.

T. If a child has deceived us to-day, do you believe he ever will do it again?

C. We hope not ; and we hope no one has done it now.

T. I do not know as any one has; and I hope every one will be exceedingly careful to stop and reflect, before holding up a hand."

Remarks were made, varying with the different answers returned to the inquiries from day to day. If there were two or three, who had disobeyed parents, or had been unkind to brothers or sisters, such suggestions were made as the nature of the case demanded.

I will give another example of Miss W's manner. Two men drank freely of rum—they began to quarrel—then fought, and one of them took the life of the other. Several children were, by his death, deprived of a father, who was once temperate, and kind to them. The opportunity for some profitable instruction was thus improved.

T. You have all learned the sad news, I suppose, that Mr. N. has killed Mr. P. in a fit of intoxication. Do you wish me to talk with you about it this morning?

1st C. Yes.

2d C. What did he do it for?

3d C. Did Mr. P. try to hurt Mr. N. ?

4th C. Who let them have the rum?

5th C. Can drunkards go to heaven, Miss W.?

6th C. How sadly Mr. P's children must feel—I pity them very much.

T. All your questions deserve attention, but I can answer but one at a time. I will give you some account of these men to-day, and tell you how they came to this wretched state. When they were young men, they were both thought to be as respectable as any men in the place where they lived.   Mr. N. went into the army a few months during the last war, and as all the soldiers were allowed to have rum every day, he soon learned to love it.   When the war ended, he continued to use it daily, and in a year or two he had contracted such a thirst for it, that he drank to intoxication whenever he had an opportunity.   When influenced by spirit, he was, like all drunkards, quarrelsome and revengeful.

Mr. P. was the son of a farmer, who cultivated a large farm, and who constantly hired men to labour for him.   He furnished spirit for them ; and though he never became intemperate, in his own estimation, he set the example to his sons of using it freely.   In this way two of his sons have already been conducted to the drunkard's grave, after a life of wretchedness and shame.   The third is now dead, and has left the world in this most shocking manner.   Now, my children, see the wickedness of using ardent spirit.   It is a poison—

it destroys happiness—it kills the body, and murders the soul. And I wish you to remember what I say—almost every drunkard becomes such by drinking but a little at first. Every one, therefore, is in danger, who drinks any; and I hope you will determine never to taste of it while you live. Who of you intend to take my advice?

Nearly every hand is raised, and I am glad of it. I will talk with you about Mr. P's children to-morrow—don't you pity *them* very much?"

Such is the course Miss W. takes, and contrives to direct the attention of her scholars to those things which are of the first importance. Let me say, " go and do likewise," unless you can adopt a " better way."

LECTURE IX.

I PROCEED, in this lecture, to make suggestions on the mode of teaching. My first remark is, that a very large part of all the instruction you are to communicate must be oral. The age of your scholars renders this indispensable. Some will come under your instruction, who have never entered any school before. Others have attended school but a short time, and have derived but little benefit from the means of instruction, which have been enjoyed. It must, therefore, devolve on you to adopt such a course, as shall lay a foundation for acquiring knowledge hereafter, as well as to promote their present improvement.

I have before remarked, that an object of the first importance is, to teach children *to think*— to call into exercise their own powers of mind. For this purpose, various means may be used. The teacher will be obliged to tax her invention from day to day, and to vary her course according to the circumstances in which she is placed.

The following remarks on this subject, taken from Dr. Alcot's account of Mr. Olney's school at Hartford, Con. contain many very important suggestions.

" An eminent instructer observed, a few years since, that after all our improvements,
11*

there was still one sort of schools wanting, viz. *thinking schools.*

Every school, however, where the pupils are taught rationally, is in effect, a thinking school. Formerly, many teachers seemed to suppose their whole duty consisted in filling children's heads with words. The child who could commit the greatest number of verses or pages to memory in a given time, was considered the best scholar.

For this erroneous practice, another has recently been substituted, which is scarcely less pernicious. Finding that words did not always convey ideas, and justly supposing it important to make every thing presented to children perfectly intelligible,—instead of words, to give them ideas,—it was hence hastily concluded that they would be learned, in proportion to the *number* of ideas which could be crowded into their minds. This is a great mistake. As well might it be supposed that the physical frame of a child will grow exactly in proportion to the quantity of food which can be crammed into his stomach, as that the mind expands in exact proportion to the number of ideas or facts with which it is crowded. Nothing nourishes or gives vigour in either case, but what is, in a certain sense at least, digested. In both cases, more at a time than can be digested is not only useless, but injurious.

Considerable pains is taken in the Hartford school to make the children *think;* though not half as much as is desirable. There is still too much filling the mind with the ideas of others, instead of habituating the pupil to teach himself, and make those ideas his own. In order to have ideas our own, we must be led to originate them, as it were, for ourselves; we must learn how to arrange them, and when and where to apply them. A person might have the best chest of tools in the world, but would he therefore *of course* be a *mechanick*?

The familiar, common sense explanations and illustrations of science, which are here given from day to day, have a wonderful effect, so far as they go, in teaching the pupils to think, and invent, and originate for themselves. The following plan is sometimes adopted, both to teach them to think, and as a physical exercise.

They are requested in the first place to sit still a few moments, and try to recall some fact of which they have heard or read; or recollect something which has fallen within the range of their own observation. After a short interval of silence, those who have thought of something to say, raise their hands. The teacher then selects one from this number, who goes to the middle of the floor, and repeats, in a distinct voice, the fact which she has thought of. Sometimes they walk once round the room while they are speaking. The pupil then takes her seat, and another follows in the same manner. They are very fond of this exercise, and I never saw them weary of it; but they always

the opening of the school. They were required to think closely for ten minutes; the teacher informing them when the time was expired. After this, any one of them was liable to be called upon to give the narration. Some of them used to relate every thing in the most minute manner."

Another mode may be successfully adopted. The teacher, holding in her hand a fragment of a stone, asks,—

Children, do you see what I have in my hand?

C. Nothing but a piece of stone.

T. Well, what do you suppose I am going to do with it—can you think?

1st C. I don't know.

2d C. Talk to us about it.

3d C. Tell us to *think* about it.

T. Can any one of you think of any thing to say about it?

[A pause.]

T. Who made it?

C. God made it; for he made every thing.

T. Did he make it for any purpose?

C. He did; for nothing is made in vain.

T. Can you think of any use to which stones are applied? Each one who can think of any thing, may tell me.

C. To make walls.

To make door steps.

Houses are underpinned with stones.

Do not people pave streets with stones?

I have seen a *house* made of stones.

T. Any thing else?—*think.*

C. Mill-stones to grind corn and wheat with.

I went over a bridge once that was made of stones.

T. Can any one think of any thing else?

C. Hearths are sometimes made of stones.

Jambs are also made of marble, which is one kind of stone.

T. Who can think of any thing else for which stones are useful?

C. I remember of reading that Bunker-Hill Monument is made of stone.

The teacher may ask the question several times; and when no one can think of any other, she may explain the mode of obtaining lime from stone—the value of plaster stone as manure, &c.

At another time she holds up a nail, and asks, what is this, children?

C. A nail.

T. What is it made of?

C. Iron.

T. Can you tell me where iron comes from—does it grow as trees do?

C. No—it is obtained from the ground.

T. Can you think of any thing else that is made out of iron?

C. Yes—a knife, a chain, an axe, a crane, a hoe, a part of ploughs and harrows.

T. Can you think of any thing else?

C. Yes—the stove is made of iron.

T. Can any of you think of any thing else?

C. Yes—a horse shoe.

T. Any thing else?

When the teacher has elicited every answer that can be given by the children, she varies her questions, and inquires whether it is very useful —whether people could live in civilized society without it—or whether iron or copper is more useful. The conclusions they will be able to form will be very generally found correct. The chief benefit of this course is, the exercise of mind it gives to the children. They are led to think—to examine and to inquire, and will thus be led to form habits of reflection.

A knife, book, pen, piece of glass, watch, flower, stick, &c. may be used in the same manner, and the exercise will always receive attention.

The course may be varied, by proposing questions like the following.

Can any child mention any thing that is great? Why is —— great?

Who will mention something that is good? Why is —— good?

Mention something that is valuable? Why is —— valuable?

Can you mention any thing that is beautiful? Why is it beautiful?

Tell me of something that is mean—unkind —cowardly—wicked—virtuous—benevolent— lovely—praiseworthy, &c. &c.

In giving answers to these questions, children

will often discover reflection surprising to any
one who has never performed the experiment.
The teacher ought always to ask for the *reason*
why the particular thing possesses the character
ascribed to it by the child, and may remark as
freely on every subject as may be considered
necessary.

If it is asked, how much time should be occupied in lessons of this character? This must
always be determined by circumstances.   In a
school where the children are nearly all able to
pursue a regular study, and are prepared to
improve time profitably in getting lessons, a
much shorter portion of time should be thus
employed than in other schools, where but few
have learned to read.   In *every primary* school,
however, some part of both the morning and
afternoon ought to be thus occupied. ' If no more
than five minutes can be spent in this way, it
should be improved; but fifteen or twenty
minutes may in most cases be very usefully
devoted, in each part of the day.   An exercise
in arithmetick, having the same object in view,
has been conducted in many schools, with very
great benefit to the children.   I might easily
spend the time of a whole lecture in describing
various modes in which you may proceed; but
I will add the following only.

Take the numeral frame or arithmeticon,
or, if not possessed of either of these, take
pieces of paper, or any thing else which may
be seen by all the children at the same time,

and pointing to one at a time, let them count—then change the exercise and count by two and three, &c. As another exercise, they may be taught to add two to two, to four, to five, &c. continuing as far as they are able. Then add three to three, to four, &c. Exercises in subtracting, and the other fundamental rules, may be made equally simple; and children may, at a very early age, make some progress in them. Every teacher ought to have the North American Arithmetick, as a guide in these exercises. The arithmetical cards will, also, be found highly useful.

Another exercise, by which habits of thinking can be promoted, may be, defining words. This may be done by giving a word, and requiring them to tell its opposite. The teacher may ask, What is the opposite to cold? The children will at once say, hot. What is the opposite of great, good, pretty, virtue, knowledge, &c.? I think this is one of the best means of leading children to distinct ideas of the knowledge of words, and it is always pleasing to them. Many other means may be employed for making them acquainted with words. One that is well calculated to interest the attention, is that of giving them a word to think of, and then reading a little story, which will explain it. Let the word *cruelty* be given; then, to explain it, read the account of the treatment of Joseph by his brethren, and tell them that was cruel. The story of Absa-

12

lom's usurping the throne of his father, and going to war with him, after his father had treated him with great kindness, will be a proper illustration. The story of the trial and scourging of the Saviour, by the wicked Jews, will perhaps be a better illustration than either.

2. The next exercise, I wish to recommend, is in natural history. In this the youngest scholars may engage, and will always be found ready to give their attention. If not furnished with the infant school cards, every teacher should provide herself with as many pictures of animals, &c. as may be convenient. Whenever the children appear fatigued, they may without any previous notice be permitted to rise, or gather around you, while you proceed with a lesson. Many are furnished in the "Infant School Manual," which, I hope, every one employed in teaching, will possess. Much assistance may be derived from it.

A first lesson may be about the division, kinds, or classes, of animals. You may tell them the names of different classes and individuals, and also describe their most striking characteristicks; as, quadrupeds, or four-footed; bipeds, or two-footed; carnivorous, or those that feed on flesh, &c. &c.

Fowls, fishes, serpents, insects, animalcule, &c. may be described—trees may be divided into classes—vegetables may also be classed, and those on which we depend for food or clothing may be particularly examined. But it will be better, generally, to defer a very particular attention to these, till after a number of lessons have been given on animals.

The picture of a single animal may be sufficient to present at one time.

What animal does this picture represent?

C. A cow (or as the case may be.)

Is the cow a quadruped, or biped?

Is the cow carnivorous?

On what does she feed?

Where does the cow live?

Is she a valuable animal?

Why valuable?

Is she wild, or tame? ferocious, or gentle? large, or small? What does she furnish for our use? What is the flesh of cows good for? what is it called.

Is the skin of any use? Hair? Horns? Feet? Bones? Is any other part valuable?

Questions may be varied indefinitely, till every thing is said which will be useful. The questions above may be easily altered, so as to be applicable to *any* animal of which you may have a picture.*

* The following lessons are extracted from an interesting series, found in the " *Infant School Manual.*"

DEER.

What animal is this?

The Deer.

How does it appear?

Very beautiful and harmless, and runs very swiftly.

For what is it useful?

The skin makes a soft and strong leather, which is

Other subjects in natural history may be used in the same way. An orange, grape, filbert, or

made into gloves and shoes; their flesh makes delicious meat.

What is the meat called?

Venison. Its horns are useful in making knife-handles, and other articles. Butter and cheese are sometimes made of its milk.

To what age does it live?

35 or 40 years.

What does the deer use for food?

It eats the stalks, leaves, and moss of trees.

What are the other animals of the deer kind called?

Fallow deer, Reindeer, Roebuck, Moose, Elk.

Where are these animals found?

In almost all parts of the earth, where there are large forests for them to range.

DOG.

What is this?   The Dog.

For what is the Dog useful?

He is a faithful servant to man, and as he is permitted to accompany him, he feels proud, and above all other animals.—He is useful to defend his master's person and property.

Does the dog know more than most other animals?

He does; he loves and obeys his master, and always does what he is bid.

T. I hope my dear children will not suffer the dog to surpass them in obedience.

I'll never hurt a little dog,
    But stroke and pat his head;
I like to see the joy he shews,
    I like to see him fed.

Poor little dogs are very good,
    And very useful too,
For do you know that they will mind
    What they are told to do?

BEAVER.

What kind of animal is the Beaver?

It is amphibious.

some other vegetable, may be taken instead of
a picture, and, when they can be obtained, will
be preferable.

For what is the beaver remarkable?
For skill and industry,
In what does its conduct resemble man?
In forming Societies to do a great work. Two or
three hundred of them all work together in building
their houses, and when they have finished them, each
family keeps to its own house.
Where do they build their houses?
By the water side, as they are very fond of bathing.
How do they build them?
They make them very nice with three rooms, one
above another.
Of what do they make their houses?
Of sticks of wood. They plaster them with clay,
and keep them very clean. The houses are round like
an oven. Each beaver has a bed of moss to sleep on,
and a store of food.
What is their food?
The bark of trees and small sticks, which they pile
up very nicely.
Do they ever quarrel?
No, they live in peace, and appear quite happy.
Does it make children unhappy to quarrel?
It does; it is better to work, and live in peace, as the
beaver does.
Do men sometimes disturb their peace, and kill them?
They do, to get their skins, which have fur on them,
which is useful in making hats; they also procure from
beavers a medicine called castoreum, which is found in
bags of skin as large as an egg.
How large is the beaver?
It is as large as a common sized dog, but very differ-
ent in its form. Its teeth are remarkable for cutting.
It will cut off large trees with its teeth to make dams
across the water.
Who has taught the beaver to do these things?
It is God, who made all creatures, and guides them
by his wisdom.

12*

If any of the scholars have learned to read,
they may be requested to repeat from memory

THE CAMEL.

What ill looking creature is this?
It is a camel.
Is it naughty because it looks ugly?
O no, it is a very good animal.
What is it good for?
It will obey its master, and carry great loads of goods.
Of what other use is the camel?
It gives milk which is good for food, and its hair is
used to make clothing.
Where is this animal found?
In Asia and Africa.
How tall is the camel?
Six or seven feet.
Where is it most useful?
In the deserts of Arabia.
What is a desert?
It is a large country of sand, where no grass or trees
grow, and no streams of water run.
Can camels travel in the desert without drinking
water?
They can drink enough at one time to last them sev-
eral days.
How long does it take them to cross the desert?
Sometimes they travel several months before they
get across.
What do they do for drink then?
Their masters sometimes go out of their way to find
water at a distance.
Can camels smell water before they see it?
They will smell water a mile off, and travel very fast
till they come to it.
Does one man go alone with his camel and carry
goods across the desert?
No, they are afraid to go alone, because of the rob-
bers.
Who are these robbers?
Wicked men in Arabia, who catch people in the des-
erts, and take away their goods.

all they can recollect about an animal, mineral, or vegetable, which has been described. Several books containing such accounts ought to be found in every school.

Another exercise, to which you may direct the attention of the younger members of your school, is making letters, figures, &c. on a *black board* or slate. The former is an article of furniture indispensable in every school-room, and the latter should be furnished to every child, of whatever age. Variety in the exer-

How many men travel together in these deserts ?
Sometimes 1000 men with their camels go together.
What is such a company of men and camels called ?
A caravan.
How much can one camel carry ?
A large camel will carry 1000 pounds.
How do men put so great a load upon their high backs ?
The camel kneels down so low, when his master bids him, that it is easy to put on the load.
What will the camel do if they put too heavy a load on him ?
He will cry loudly, and will not rise till a part of it is taken off.
Do their masters drive them with a whip, as they do the horse ?
No, they do not whip them, they sing or whistle to make them go, and the louder they sing, the faster they will go.
Will they stop when their masters stop singing ?
They will. If their masters begin to sing to them, they must continue singing till night, or they cannot make them go.
What did Joseph's brethren do, when they saw such a company of men and camels coming ?
They drew up Joseph out of the pit and sold him to them.

cises of those who cannot read, is exceedingly important, and must be regarded, if you would make them happy.   Children may become prepared to engage in spelling words, by writing them on a slate, as early as they can spell orally; and, judging from experiments made, I know of few exercises either more useful, or more pleasant to them.

LECTURE X.

THE next subject on which I wish to remark, is the mode of teaching children to read. I have before said, that this is one of the most prominent departments of labour devolving upon you. I am happy to have the opportunity to furnish the following judicious remarks and suggestions, contained in a letter from a friend, who is a highly successful teacher in reading. No one who entertains just ideas of the importance of this branch, will think that an immoderate space is allotted to it.

"While all are ready to admit, that good reading is " *one of the very first of polite accomplishments,*" the little attention it receives in our common schools, furnishes matter for serious regret to every friend of the young. Almost every examination affords indisputable evidence, that, although other branches may have been faithfully taught, little improvement has been made in this. *Indistinct articulation, monotony, tones, a disregard of pauses, inflection, accent and emphasis,* and, in fact, every form of bad reading, are not only *tolerated, but actually encouraged by neglect !*

With the exception of organic defects, nearly all these faults must be ascribed to ignorance, or negligence, on the part of teachers, who, as if unsatisfied with what nature has already done in the formation of the organs of speech, are very apt to call upon her to perform their own irksome duties.

No argument is necessary, to prove, that reading does *imperatively,* demand the patient attention of every teacher.   The fact, that from our common schools, are to rise many of the future statesmen and orators of our country ; and the dependence of delivery upon early habits of reading, speak for themselves.   To the instructress, the subject presents its strongest claims.   *She* is to inculcate the rudiments of the art ; and, as her instructions are first given, they will be last forgotten.   Tones, formed under her direction, and cherished by her example, will, in all probability, continue through life.   If she succeeds in winning the affections of her pupils, her manner of reading, will be a model to them.   The features of different schools are so endlessly varied, that no universal plan of teaching the rhetorical elements can be devised.   Much, therefore, must be left to the teacher's discretion.   It is indispensable then, that a young lady engaged in teaching, should be herself, a good reader, and be thoroughly acquainted with the *principles* of correct reading.   She should be as familiar with the rules of articulation, inflection, and emphasis, as with the sounds of the alphabet, or the application of pauses.

Whenever practicable, these principles should

be acquired, with the aid of a living teacher, as mistakes would thus be avoided, and time saved.

Inability to obtain oral instruction need not, however, be a discouragement ; for in this, as in all other studies, persevering effort will surmount great obstacles. The Rhetorical Reader, or some other work of similar character, may be studied *privately*, with success.

Children in our common schools may in the following remarks, be considered under three divisions. The first, including all who are learning the alphabet, and reading the monosyllables :—The second, including those who read dissyllables, but hesitate upon long words ;— The third embracing all who read English Authors with tolerable readiness.

The task of teaching the alphabet in school is always unwelcome ; and when the number of scholars is large, the difficulty of uniting abecedarians in a class, on account of the variable progress of infant intellect, renders a teacher liable to devote to them, more than their due proportion of time.

This inconvenience might easily be removed, if parents would take pains to teach children the alphabet at *home*. Experience has repeatedly testified, that this is practicable in most instances ; and surely no affectionate mother can deem the time thus spent, misemployed or wearisome to her.

But as children *are* sent to school, before

they have learned their letters, it is highly important to inquire—What is the best manner of teaching the alphabet?

The analogical method is usually practiced, in which, the names, and forms of the letters—*a b c*, &c. are first taught, and next the combinations of vowels and consonants in order; as *ab, eb, ib, ba, da, ca*, &c. After this tedious, and, to the child, unmeaning process, he is pushed forward into polysyllables, and complex sentences, to which he attaches no ideas but those of weariness, and perplexity.

By this course, the anomalous sounds of letters are rendered familiar, and the regular sounds reduced to a simple scale, which is often committed to memory in the act of reading. Analogy, too, is an assistant of no small importance in this system. A child has learned that *b* followed by *a* spells *ba*. Therefore he intuitively knows that *d* and *a* spell *da*, *f* and *a*, *fa*. But while, perhaps, the mechanical use of letters may be taught in less time by this, than other methods, *thoughts* and *words* are not associated; and, as his only stimulant to further exertion is thus snatched from his grasp, the child is left disgusted, and discouraged at the outset.

Other methods, intended to obviate this infelicity are of late becoming popular.

Dice and polygons, with letters upon their sides; simple and painted cards, pictured primers, and various other toys, conspicuously displaying the alphabet, are used to render the forms and names familiar.* Children are by some teachers also taught with great success, to read upon the inductive plan, before learning the letters; although, the amount of time required seems to be an objection to its introduction into large schools.

For example, the child is shown the pictures of a man, dog, cat, cow, horse, and other familiar objects, with the name—"a man," "a dog," &c. underneath. The child is required to learn the word as well as the picture. As soon as these are easily distinguished, short sentences are placed before him; as, "a dog barks," "a man walks." Spelling also is taught by means of lettered cards, containing the letters of a word separate, and united together in parallel columns.

For a full explanation of this plan, and its modifications, teachers are referred to Parkhurst's excellent little work for children, entitled "Parkhurst's First Lessons in Reading." "Gallaudet's Picture, Reading, and Defining Book," "Hazen's Symbolical Primer," and "Lamb's and Worcester's Primer," are constructed on a similar plan and may be used. The use of dice, cards, &c. is recommended by Locke, but, as is remarked by the Author

* A card containing the alphabet may be put into the hand of one who knows the letters, with a direction to teach those younger, by calling on one after another to go and place a finger on any given letter. This mode has been practiced with success.

13

of the "Teacher's Guide," such inventions seem better adapted to the nursery, than to school rooms.

A new plan of instruction in any branch does not necessarily require a change of elementary books, and, as the *children* of the *poor* are frequently found in common schools, such a change should not be made needlessly.

Where no better course can be devised, the following is recommended, as it may be adopted in connection with any of the approved reading, and elementary books, now in use.

The alphabet, name and form, taught analogically, in the usual way, by being impressed on the memory in repeated rehearsals, while pictures, infant-school-cards and primers are used to awaken attention. As variety is always pleasing, children may sometimes march together, all saying the letters aloud,—sometimes sing an easy tune, perhaps " Auld Lang Syne," arranged to "a b c d, e f g h,"—and sometimes read, by themselves.

Monosyllabick sentences may be read, after the alphabet is learned ; and, if they can be selected in the form of interesting dialogue, they may with propriety engross considerable time.

At this early stage of education, natural defects, such as lisping, stammering, nasal enunciation, and inability to speak particular letters, as " *l, r, b, p, d, w,*" require attention. Faults of this kind, which, in riper years, would baffle the most skilful management, may be easily removed by a little care, at this age. The following suggestions, have all been tested by experiment, and for want of room, will be offered without theoretical explanation.

Let a lisper be instructed to hiss, or speak the *elementary sound* of " s," or soft " c," *with his tongue behind the upper teeth.* Lisping, and other faults, are often occasioned by a *web* or *string* under the tongue, which may be removed by a physician's lancet.

Some sounds, as of " *b, d,*" are more likely to produce stammering than others. These elements should be first ascertained, then carefully avoided, in all reading lessons. Easy, flowing poetry, and sentences in which the open vowels occur most frequently, should be read, with a full and loud voice, until the convulsive stoppage of the organs cease to appear.

When a child is unable to speak " *w, p,*" or any other letters, he should be directed to *imitate* by sight the *position* of the teacher's tongue, and other organs in making them.

Persons speaking with the *nasal twang*, are generally in the habit of breathing with the *mouth open.* Let the mouth be constantly closed, and, as the breath must then pass through the nostrils, they will become sufficiently enlarged, in a short time, to afford free passage to sound.

Most of the difficulties experienced by children, in trying to make clear and articulate sounds, arise, not from defective organs, but from the fact, that they do not know *how* to use them.

Children in the second division, i. e., those who are able to read monosyllables with ease, but are still liable to hesitate upon long words, should read *very slowly.* The most disagreeable tones, are formed and cultivated by the rapidity with which children are often allowed to read. They should spell frequently, dividing the words into syllables, as this will be of great importance in enabling them to speak each element distinctly.

So far as possible, their lessons in reading should be *colloquial,* and they should be permitted to criticise one another occasionally, and to imitate the teacher's voice, in repeating sentences. The use of stops, should also be impressed upon their minds, and they be carefully trained to make their pauses, naturally ; perhaps by counting aloud one, at a comma, two, at a semicolon, &c., until the pauses are familiar. They should understand, however, that pauses are subservient to *sense,* and that no exact time can be assigned to them.

The third division, should be instructed in the principles of rhetorical reading, either with or without a text book. Where it can be introduced, the Rhetorical Reader is recommended as a reading book, for this division. It should at least be in the hands of every teacher, as a guide to correct effort.

It would be needless, here to repeat the subjects of that work, in detail, but the order which it follows may be easily pursued in common schools.

The causes of defective articulation should be pointed out to pupils, with the difficulties and cautions to be regarded, in obtaining a distinct utterance.

Inflections* should be taught to a whole class at once, by learning them to make the

* N. B.—As it may be found necessary to explain the rules of inflection *orally* in a simplified form, I subjoin a few of them, with examples, reduced to the capacity of the youngest reader. The teacher is advised to *write out all the rules* commencing on page 29, of the Rhetorical Reader, in the same simple style, and to select copious examples of each, in the reading book of the school.

Rules 2d and 7th. When you ask a question, if you can answer it, so as to make sense, by saying "*yes*," or "*no*," you must turn your voice *up* on the last word in it; but, if you cannot make sense by saying "yes" or "no" after it, you must turn your voice *down* on the last word. Let us try it. "What is your name?" "yes." That does not make sense. Then you must turn your voice *down* on the last word. "Will you go?" "yes." Matt. xiii. 55th. "Is not this the carpenter's Son?" In these two questions you must turn your voice *up* on the last word. When you go home see if your parents do not *talk* so?

In most sentences, make the inflections on the word which you speak loudest, that is, the word which means most.

When you speak to a person, make the rising inflection on the name, as "John." "Men, Brethren, and Fathers, hearken."

When a man is sad, he makes the rising inflection.

When a man commands, blames, speaks in fear, or begs, he makes the falling inflection.

different inflections, simultaneously, upon different words as " màker—hárk—tĕmper—irŏny"
The rising, and falling, being the most simple,
should be first acquired and applied to direct,
and indirect questions, answers, &c.

After such attention to accent, as may be
found necessary, emphasis should be considered, with its distinctions of stress and inflection.
Modulation should be explained,—faults with
their remedies exemplified, and pitch, quantity,
fulness, loudness, compass of voice, rate of utterance, rhetorical pause, transition, expression,
and rhetorical dialogue, each practically illustrated.

Parents, who were taught to read in the " old
way," may feel opposed, at first, to the above
course.   But prejudices will soon vanish, if the
teacher is faithful.   The writer has seen the
course followed in summer and in winter
schools, in which children have become familiar with all its subjects; their natural tones,
and correct inflections would have put many a
teacher to the blush.

I cannot close these brief remarks, without
expressing the opinion that more time should
be spent in reading, in common schools, than
is commonly deemed sufficient.   As reading
stands first in importance, one hour, in each
part of the day, may under some circumstances
be devoted to this subject, without interfering
with other important studies."

A portion of your scholars are prepared to pursue Geography with advantage. The best mode of interesting children in it, and of making it beneficial to them, claims attention. Various suggestions for effecting this, have been made, some of them valuable, and others, having little merit. In the following hints, I shall attempt little more than to exhibit some of the results of my own experience, on this topick. It is an object of importance, in the first place, to have children obtain some distinct ideas of the relative size of different divisions of land, and also of the meaning of those terms which relate to the primary lessons that are to be learned. You may commence with giving some account of the yard, or garden, and may designate its boundaries and divisions.*

* The following may serve as an illustration of the first steps in commencing this study, with a young class.

Do you wish to know what a town is? I will tell you. It is a piece of land usually about six miles square; but sometimes larger and sometimes smaller. I will show you a picture of a town.

Boundaries mean the lines going round any thing. Thus the fence, round the yard, is the boundary of it. The line, that goes round a garden, field, farm, or any other piece of land, is the boundary. Towns are divided into house-lots, gardens, farms, &c. There are a great many such divisions in a town. The people who live in a town are called inhabitants.

Sometimes the land rises high, and such places are called hills. If the land rises very high, it is called a mountain. Mountains are commonly very rocky, and sometimes so steep that you cannot climb up to the top.

In almost every town there are streams of water, which run between the hills. If these are small, they

Children should spend considerable time in learning the geography of their own neighbourhood, for by acquiring distinct ideas of objects with which they are surrounded, they are much

are called brooks. When they are large, they are called rivers. Have you ever seen a river? Sometimes the brooks or rivers run into a low place called a valley or hollow; and then the water stays there and forms what is called a pond. If the quantity of water is large, it is a lake. There are hills, brooks, and ponds, in almost all towns; in a great many, there are rivers and mountains.

Now I will tell you about some other things. When a large number of people live in a place, it is called a city. There are a great many cities of which I mean to tell you the names hereafter. Did you ever see a city?

When a number of towns are united, they are called a county. In every county a town is selected, in which a court-house and jail are built. Courts are held in this town, which is called the shire town. A court is a place where lawsuits are settled.

When several counties are united together they form a state. A state therefore has several counties in it, and a great many towns, and commonly a city, or several cities. Several rivers and a number of mountains are found in almost every state.

A town or city is selected in every state, where a large house is built, called the state-house. All the towns and cities choose men to go to this house, every year, and make laws, and agree how the people shall be governed.

Several states are united together and are called a country, or republick. Perhaps you will understand me better, if I tell you that you live in a town, [or city,] and the town forms a part of a county, the county forms a part of a state, and the state forms a part of a country.

Now as I have told you so much, you must tell me the name of the town, [or city,] and county, and state in which you live. —*First Book of Geog.*

better prepared to be interested in a description of places, they have never seen. Indeed, without this, they can hardly be expected to have any correct impressions of the size and distance of the objects, with which they are unacquainted.

It is very important, that they are, from the *first*, accustomed to *make outline maps* of the countries over which they pass. However imperfect these maps may be, the learners are more decidedly benefitted in this way, than by any other mode, I have ever adopted, or have seen pursued by others. If one of the class is required to form an outline on the black-board, previous to every recitation, it will be useful.

The most familiar mode in teaching at every step, should be adopted, and all the interest excited, of which the subject is capable.

To young children, I think it is improper, generally, to give lessons which embrace very minute details; but the outlines, the great features of the science, may be thoroughly learned, and may be filled up as the memory becomes stronger, and the parts become more important to be known.

I have observed very favorable results produced, by asking scholars *many questions* occasionally, for them to correct. The attention of the children is excited, and they form a habit of thinking more rapidly, and answering more promptly. The following is a specimen of the course recommended.

T. What child in this class can tell me in what part of France, London is?

C. London is not in any part of *France,* but in the S. E. part of England.

T. In what part of Spain is Rome?

C. Rome is not in any part of Spain, but is in Italy.

T. In what part of England is Amsterdam?

C. It is not in any part.

T. Into what lake does the Thames empty?

Into what other river does the Amazon discharge its waters?

Which is the longest river in the U. States, the Niger or Euphrates?

On what ocean is Quebec?

On what island is Boston? &c. &c.

By asking such questions, the class will be much amused, and while one corrects the questions, all the others, will be more likely to retain the true answer, than if every question is proposed, in the usual method.

History is a branch of study which will be required in most summer schools. The mode of teaching it in a way, best adapted to the capacities of children, is of considerable importance, and requires your attention. The too common method, of putting a work containing little more than a detail of facts, into the hands of young scholars, and then requiring them to commit a succession of answers to given questions, has certainly very little to recommend it.

The story is not understood, and the answers are associated with the questions merely. I have not unfrequently seen scholars of more advanced age, who could answer nearly all of " Emerson's Questions," to Goodrich's History of the U. States, who, at the same time, could give no distinct and connected view of any one of the prominent subjects contained in the book. The *answers* were all that they thought of acquiring. Such knowledge is worth very little to any one, and can be of no benefit to a child of seven or eight years of age.

The first attempt to make children familiar with historical details, is by familiar stories. These have, invariably strong attractions for them, especially, stories of events, which transpired in places of which they have some knowledge. The first lessons should be those about which, they can acquire the most definite knowledge, and, with which they will be sufficiently interested, to effect an impression favorable to pursuing the study.

With young children, at least, history ought always to be pursued in connexion with geography, and I am happy to make you acquainted with the fact that there is *one book* combining both and written with reference to the mode of teaching which I recommend : I refer to the " First Book of History," by the author of " Peter Parley's Tales." The general use of this book, by the most forward members of summer schools, would be attended with very beneficial results. To all those who use it, further remarks on teaching history, will be unimportant.

Some of your scholars will be sufficiently advanced, to commence the study of Grammar, and there will be few of them, unable to learn *some* of the principles of it. My remarks will principally regard the first instruction which children receive. Very few scholars under the age of ten or twelve years, have a judgment sufficiently matured, to be able to understand the philosophy of grammar. All efforts therefore to instruct children in it will produce, not only a loss of time, but must give a distaste to the study of grammar, afterward. Put a grammar book into the hands of a scholar of eight or ten years of age, and require him to commit it all, to memory, and then ask him to apply all these unintelligible definitions, rules, and observations, and, if you do not see him sleep over his lesson, or hear him exclaim " I don't like to study grammar, it is so dry"—he will I am sure be a prodigy. Well do *I* remember the reflections occasioned by passing a long apprenticeship to such a teacher. And it has often been a matter of wonder, that I could ever become reconciled to the study.

The course I recommend will, I think cause the subject to be at least pleasant to children, and all the knowledge acquired by them will be easily retained.

The teacher may commence thus;—Children, do you ever hear persons talk improperly?

C. Yes, frequently.

T. Do you think it is because they do not know how to speak with propriety?

C. If they know what is proper, they will not continue to talk as they do.

T. Perhaps not, but I think very many use incorrect language, who know better. Do you think children ought to learn to speak properly?

C. Certainly, every one ought to do it.

T. Do you wish I should teach you something about it?

C. Yes, if we can understand it.

T. How many are wishing to learn? I see nearly every hand is raised—so I will begin, by telling you about a noun. All names are nouns. Man is a noun, because the word man is a name. Can you now tell me what a noun is?

C. A noun is a word which is a name.

T. Perhaps some of you can think of other nouns. You may tell me, if you do.

C. Chair, book, slate, table, boy, girl, stone, seat, house, window, door, paper, town, school, lesson.

T. You can tell me of a great many. I remember one 'of the cards says, "that the world is full of nouns." You may think of as many as you can before tomorrow, and then repeat them to me.

There are two sorts or kinds of nouns. One

14

is common and the other is proper.   Common
nouns are those names which may be applied
to any individual, of a class.   Proper nouns are
the names by which individuals are known
from all others.   Boy is a common noun, because it can be applied to *any* boy in the room,
or in the world.   Boston, is a name given to
one place, and is therefore a proper noun.
Can you tell me of any other common nouns ?

C. Dinner, children, pen, field, country,
&c. &c.

T. Who can think of a word, that is a proper noun ?

C. Mary, Susan, Alfred, Benjamin, &c.

A mode similar to this may be pursued, in
teaching the other parts of speech, and children
will treasure up definitions, which will be valuable hereafter.

Considerable time may be spent in proposing
sentences for correction by the scholars ; and
if any incorrect habits of speaking in the school,
are common, these should claim particular attention.   The following examples will illustrate
what I mean.

Teacher. John said, this morning, that he
hanged up his hat ; was that proper ?

C. No.   He *hung* up his hat.

T. I *seed* a man yesterday.

C. I *saw* a man yesterday.

T. He *brung* me a book.

C. He *brought* me a book.

T. Sally *shets* the door after her.

C. Sally *shuts* the door after her.

T. I *loves* a good scholar.

C. I *love* a good scholar.

T. Samuel and James rides to school.

C. Samuel and James ride to school, &c.

Hundreds of similar sentences may be proposed, and the exercise of correcting them, will be amusing and useful.*

Other branches of study may be pursued, but it will not be important to specify the particular mode of teaching them.   With those already specified, the instructress must spend a principal part of her time.   The same general rules may be adopted, with regard to such others, as may in a given case, be required.   I will add but a single remark. MAKE EVERY THING INTELLIGIBLE TO THE PUPIL, *and fail not to examine the learner, till you are satisfied the subject is distinctly understood.*

* For further directions on teaching grammar, I wish to refer teachers of summer schools to Mr. RAND's excellent little work, recently published.

LECTURE XI.

I HAVE now passed over the principal part of the ground, that I designed to occupy; but there are several things of some importance, not closely connected with the subjects already investigated. I shall therefore make this a miscellaneous lecture, throwing out some suggestions, in answer to various questions which have been proposed to me by instructers.

I. " Is it better to permit scholars to have a head in a class, and go above each other?"

This question includes a principle of extensive application, and it deserves particular attention.

Every arrangement in the school should have reference to impartial *justice.* If, in a class of scholars, all equally deserving, I hold out the expectation of reward to one only, I shall be chargeable with *injustice.* One only can enjoy the satisfaction of being " at the *head;*" half of the class may have performed the exercise as well as the one who enjoys this distinction. It is by no means improbable that the successful competitor may have been even less studious than most others in his class; or, that he is rewarded for the knowledge he has previously acquired. Generally, in a primary school, the scholars cannot be classed, so that each may have an equal chance for securing the reward. If, however, this *could* be done, I should be met by other objections. Whenever a scholar thinks more of "beating" than he does of gaining knowledge as a preparation for usefulness, there is little probability that he will cultivate any thing but his *memory*. He expects to insure success, by carefully cultivating this power. If he can repeat the given exercise, he is satisfied. Every person must readily perceive, that this will be far from the proper course of cultivating the young mind. All its powers should be improved.

Another result of this mode is seen in the unkind feelings not unfrequently entertained by one scholar towards another. When the mind is wrought up to a high pitch of excitement, and hopes are suddenly crushed, we are very naturally inclined to attribute our ill success to some unfairness in those who secure the meed after which we were striving. I make no plea in justification of this; *but it is a principle of our nature*, and must be taken into the account, in deciding on all questions which involve the subject of competition. Unimportant as it may seem to the superficial observer, I have known the foundation of ill-will, thus laid, extend from childhood to mature age, and it will probably be continued, till terminated by death.

The last objection I shall offer to the practice of permitting competition in school is, that it is *wholly unnecessary* for the purpose of securing

14*

a proper degree of attention to study. Whatever is *not* necessary, if it cannot be employed without some undesirable results, ought certainly to be discarded.

My uniform experience as an instructer has been, that an appeal to emulation or ambition is no more required in order to secure attention to study, than the excitement of anger, revenge, or other evil passions, for the same purpose.

II. "If children are not permitted to try to excel each other, or to have competition, how can they be led to make a proper application to their studies?"

An answer to this question has, in a former lecture, been furnished in general terms. But it may be proper to give more direct attention to it here.

The number of children is small, to whom the earnest endeavours of a judicious and kind teacher will not be a sufficient excitement to study. But the most important means, after making consistent effort to direct to proper studies and render them intelligible and interesting, are the following.

First, convince children that they are under high obligation to themselves, their country, their parents, and especially to their Creator, *to make the best improvement of their time.*

If it is asked, how this can be done, let me suggest a course like the following :—

Teacher. I have been thinking of a subject,

children, on which I wish to ask your opinion.
I hope every one will answer the questions I
shall ask, just as he thinks is right.

I am acquainted with two boys, John ·and
Charles. John says that he is very happy
when he learns all his lessons well, and con-
ducts properly; and, though he loves to play
sometimes, he never allows himself to do it, till
he has learned his lesson. Charles neglects his
book, whenever he can have an opportunity to
play. Now tell me which you think is more
happy.

Children. John.

T. All who think John is happier than
Charles, may raise their hands.—I believe
every hand is raised. But why do you decide
in favour of John?

C. Because he does right.

T. If children desire to be happy, is it the
best way for them to be faithful in getting all
their lessons, and in obeying their teachers or
parents?

C. It is.

T. All, who think so, may give the signal.—
I am happy to see that you all think alike, for
every hand is up. If the children of this
school wish to be happy, must they try to learn
as much as possible, and obey me and their
parents?

C. We must.

T. How many are of this opinion?

C. All of us.

T. Is it probable that Charles will gain the love of friends as much as John?

C. Certainly not.

T. Do you think Charles will be as useful in the world as John will be?

C. We think he will not.

T. What shall I say to a child in this school, whom I see idle? must I tell him that is the right way to be *happy*?

C. You must tell such, that it is the way to be *unhappy*.

T. I have another question. Do idle and inattentive scholars treat their parents kindly, or unkindly?

C. Unkindly, certainly.

T. Why?

C. Because parents provide instruction, and send their children to school, that they may learn, and it is unkind in children to waste time and misimprove these privileges.

T. Have any a *right* to be idle, when their parents expect them to improve their time in acquiring knowledge?

C. No, certainly not.

If a course like this is pursued, with regard to the obligation of children to themselves, parents, &c. and is repeated as often as it is found necessary, I cannot believe that the number of children is large, who will need other means used with them, to secure a proper attention to their studies.

It may be questioned by you, whether children will give answers of import similar to those I have written. In reply, I can say, that I have never known more than *one or two exceptions*, among hundreds who have been interrogated in a similar manner.

It is not difficult to convince children that they are accountable to their parents and Him who created them. This I would make use of as the second principle to insure application to study. And if teachers will pursue a proper mode of fixing this conviction in their minds, it will unquestionably be found highly salutary.

It is often useful to keep bills, in which every impropriety is registered, and also every perfect lesson is recorded. I recommend the practice.

III. "There are children in my school who are in the habit of telling *lies*. This is taught them by the example of their parents and others. How can I correct this fault?"

That such a fact should exist, is certainly very painful. It is not a solitary instance, and this renders it still more lamentable. But it must be met, and, if possible, a remedy be provided for the evil. I cannot promise that complete success will always attend the course I shall recommend. But I am confident, that something may be done towards it.

My first effort would be, to make the child acquainted, if he is not already, with the declarations of the BIBLE on the subject of lying. I have usually required a child, when proved guilty of this crime, to commit to memory and repeat to me those passages, which' speak directly on the subject. In some instances, where the habit has appeared inveterate, a child has been called on to repeat these *daily* for weeks, and at each time the heinousness of the crime of lying has been impressed on his mind.

It is highly important to convince a liar, that nothing beneficial can ever be gained by this vice. HE THAT TELLS LIES IS NOT BELIEVED WHEN HE SPEAKS THE TRUTH. It is not generally difficult to convince *children* of this; and when they are convinced, we may indulge the hope, at least, that they will be led to have some proper feelings with regard to the sin and folly of it.

If any of the children of your school are known to be profane, you may proceed in a similar way. The declarations of God on the subject ought, in the first instance, to be exhibited to those who are guilty of any of the crimes which are ruinous to the character and happiness of all.

The consequences of these sins, to those who commit them, and to those who are necessarily associated with them, should be clearly exhibited. What, you may ask, would be the consequence, if *all* should tell lies? How can business be transacted, if no dependance can be placed on each other? What benefit could you derive from attending school, if you could place no reliance on what *I* say to you?

But, generally, a child who is properly instructed with regard to his duty to God, may be deeply impressed with the idea of incurring his displeasure; and I have found no mode so efficacious as a direct appeal to this. He is accountable to God, and must be finally judged at his tribunal.

IV. " How shall I lead children to cultivate habits of civility and kindness towards each other?"

I know of nothing more efficacious than the EXAMPLE of the teacher. I always expect to see the manners of the instructer imitated by the school. If you are unkind, unsocial, or repulsive, you may expect the same in your scholars. If you are peevish, or selfish, you must expect them to imitate you. If you assume lordly airs, or speak only to command or threaten, then you must expect to see children following your example.

If such habits are already formed, they may be easily *corrected* by your example, and proper instruction. Familiar conversation, like the following, may be efficacious.

Teacher. I heard two children disputing the other day. They uttered such language as this, " I will"—" you wont"—" you lie"—" I'll knock you down"—I'll tell the teacher of you," &c.- Do you think they were happy?

Children. No, they could not be.

T. Why?

C. Such language is improper.

T. If I hear any such language here, what ought I to think of those who use it?

C. You must think those children are wicked and unmannerly.

C. How ought children to speak to each other?

C. Kindly.

T. How ought children at school to treat each other?

C. Affectionately.

T. What rule does our Saviour give for treating each other?

C. "Do unto others, as you would that others should do unto you."

T. Do you think that it pleases all who love children, to see them kind to each other?

C. Certainly.

Conversation of this kind may be indefinitely varied, and will lead children to reflect on *propriety* in their habits of intercourse with each other.

The following directions to the teacher are important.

1. Never *command* a child when the imperative manner can be avoided. It is always better to say " you *may*," than " you *shall* do it."

2. Treat children with respect.

3. Always speak as calmly to them, when you reprove, as when you commend them.

V. " What apparatus ought to be considered as indispensable in a summer school?"

In giving an answer to this question, I prefer to divide it. *First.* Is apparatus essential to the

highest success of the instructer's efforts? 2.
What articles are most necessary?

With regard to the first, I answer unhesitatingly in the *affirmative*. A faithful teacher may, it is true, confer benefit on her scholars without any; and she *may* do this, also, without *books*. But all will acknowledge that her efforts must be limited, if she depends wholly on oral instruction to benefit them.

Apparatus is of more importance to a *part* of the school than *books ;* for some are not old enough to use *these*, while *every child* is of sufficient age to be benefitted by particular articles of that. The people of every district are negligent of the best interests of their scholars, who do not furnish it.

Secondly. What articles are most necessary? I am not confident that I shall give the *best* answer that might be furnished to this question. I offer my opinion, requesting, at the same time, that you will not make too much dependence on its correctness.

1. A Black-board. One large, or two smaller ones, ought to be in every school-room in the country.

2. A small Globe. This has been provided in the excellent apparatus prepared by Mr. Holbrook.

3. The Arithmometer, and

4. Card of Geometrical Diagrams, &c. together with the. Map of the World and of the United States, accompanying the same set.

15

5. Several of the Infant School Cards, embracing some parts of Natural History.

The expense of all these will not exceed ten dollars, and can be furnished in the poorest district.

Several other articles are highly *useful*, and parents will richly find their account in providing them.

1. Mr. Holbrook's "Common School Set." Price $10.

2. The Season Machine, for showing the course of the seasons, day and night, &c. Price $3,25.

3. Black Globe, for drawing outlines of countries, oceans, seas, &c. Price $3,00.

4. Infant School Cards. Price about $8.

5. Geological Specimens. Price ——.

6. A small Library.

Let me, in conclusion, solicit all teachers to make faithful efforts to have these articles furnished for each primary school which they are employed to instruct.

QUESTIONS FOR REVIEW.

[Many of the following questions are designed to direct attention to the more important subjects, rather than to be answered in language taken from the book. Some of them may be answered without reference to the text.]

QUESTIONS ON LECTURE I.

1. What introductory remark does the author make?
2. What is the female teacher to cultivate?
3. Over what ought she to watch?
4. To what is the attention of the teacher directed?
5. To whom may a group of young children be an *uninteresting* assemblage?
6. Can the faithful *teacher* behold them with indifference?
7. Are they *less* interesting because they are young and ignorant?
8. What is said of Alexander, Bonaparte, and Washington?
9. What claim does the *age* of young children make on the primary teacher?
10. To what are children and youth exposed?
11. For what must the foundation be laid in childhood?
12. What will be the effect of habits very early formed?
13. Have primary teachers no farther duty than to teach the first principles of science?
14. What first claims attention in reference to this subject?
15. What ought to be the daily and hourly study of all *parents?*
16. Does every parent understand the nature of parental responsibility?
17. What will be the moral influence of such children as grow up unrestrained and untaught?

18. Can the teacher exert a great influence over the young?

19. What does the kind and affectionate teacher become in the estimation of a child?

20. Ought habits of discrimination to be cultivated?

21. What influence is the instructer exerting, by leading children to cultivate kind and affectionate feelings towards each other?

22. What puts the destiny of children very much in the hands of their teachers?

23. What have some female teachers appeared to think?

24. Can any be justified in entertaining such opinions?

25. What impressions remain the longest?

QUESTIONS ON LECTURE II.

1. With what inquiry does this lecture commence?
2. What is necessary in the first place?
3. In what may these objects be comprehended?
4. What is the great purpose of education?
5. Is implicit obedience, on the part of scholars, necessary?
6. For what do habits of submission in the nursery, family, and school, lay the foundation?
7. Is it right to control children merely for the sake of showing our power over them?
8. What is a second duty devolving on an instructer?
9. Is a habit of self-control important to every person?
10. Can it be acquired by young children?
11. What is a third object to be attained?
12. How may children be led to cultivate a habit of thinking?
13. Is this course usually pursued?
14. Is it more difficult to excite scholars to exercise their reasoning powers than the memory?
15. What is another part of our duty?
16. Does this subject usually receive that degree of attention, which its importance demands?
17. When did Washington receive his first lessons in military tactics?
18. What decided the future course of West?
19. Is it possible to lead even young children to cultivate habits of order?

20. What is the consequence of an imperfect foundation to an edifice?

21. Is it as easy to learn in a right manner, as in a wrong way?

22. What subjects of science ought you to be able to teach?

23. Can teachers benefit parents? Ought they to do it?

24. Are many parents ignorant of their duty to their children?

25. What instances of this have you seen?

QUESTIONS ON LECTURE III.

1. To what is attention directed in this lecture?

2. What are some things which render a person unfit for this important work?

3. What is the effect of intercourse with children?

4. What is the effect where responsibility is not realized?

5. What is said of the moral teacher? The physician?

6. What will be the effect of a want of interest in the society of children?

7. Will a child soon ascertain what feelings a teacher possesses towards him?

8. Is it necessary to *love children*, in order to secure their affection and confidence?

9. Ought a teacher to understand the manner in which children receive ideas?

10. Is ignorance of this, a reason why many are unsuccessful in communicating instruction?

11. How do children gain knowledge?

12. What course must a teacher pursue in order to ascertain how children exercise their minds?

13. What is the effect of an unintelligible mode of instruction?

14. Is a knowledge of human nature a necessary qualification of a teacher?

15. Are children all alike?

16. Is a person to whom the labour of teaching is irksome properly qualified to instruct the young?

17. What is the effect of impatience in a teacher?

18. What is indispensable in training young minds?

15*

QUESTIONS ON LECTURE IV.

1. What subjects are mentioned in the last lecture as disqualifying a teacher for usefulness?

2. Is it an important object to make children happy at school?

3. Is it right to *flatter* a child into obedience?

4. Does the influence of the teacher terminate when the child leaves the school room?

5. Is it important that a teacher should be able to enter into the sympathies of her pupils?

6. What effect does it have on the feelings of the child?

7. When is judicious instruction most efficacious?

8. Ought teachers to be acquainted with the character of the obstacles in the way of their success?

9. What is a prominent reason why schools so frequently fail of usefulness?

10. How is this obstacle to be surmounted by the teacher?

11. What is another obstacle?

12. How may this be overcome?

13. Are many parents ignorant of what a school should be?

14. Ought the indifference of parents, to serve as a discouragement to your exertions?

15. What are some difficulties of secondary importance?

16. What inquiry are teachers requested to make in regard to themselves.

17. What is the last qualification mentioned as indispensable to a teacher?

18. Is it possible to teach well without this?

19. What is to be understood by ability to govern?

20. How ought a proper capacity to govern to be considered?

21. What is said of the school of Miss G.?

22. What of Miss X?

23. What is the cause of the difference?

QUESTIONS ON LECTURE V.

1. What is necessary in the various departments of business?

2. What is said of theory without practice and practice without theory?

3. Does this apply to the primary teacher?

4. What literary qualifications ought the teacher to possess?

5. Is it sufficient to acquire merely the outlines of the few studies which the law specifies?

6. Ought a primary teacher to be acquainted with natural history?

7. Is this an interesting subject to the young?

8. Is ability to sing, highly important to a teacher?

9. Is this art attainable by nearly all?

10. Is it important for a teacher to be well acquainted with the principles of good reading?

11. Is an acquaintance with the principles of reading a common accomplishment?

12. What is often the course pursued in learning children to read?

13. What is the first object of reading?

14. Is a *thorough* knowledge of the English language important?

15. From what do children take their first lessons on language?

16. Are habits formed in childhood usually retained in after life?

17. What is said about arithmetick?

18. Is intellectual arithmetick a proper study for young children?

19. What is said of geography and history?

20. Are these studies always taught in the best manner?

21. What illustration is given?

22. Is history often taught in the same way?

23. Mention what is said of other studies?

QUESTIONS ON LECTURE VI.

1. What will be the first question asked by a teacher on entering the school room?

2. What one will follow?

3. Ought children to be governed as intelligent beings?

4. Are they able to distinguish between right and wrong?

5. What is the first direction given on the subject of governing a school?

6. What requisitions *are* reasonable?

7. What is said of partial and imperfect obedience?

8. Is it sufficient to regard the *present* welfare of pupils?

9. What is the second direction? Is it difficult?

10. Will children decide correctly on subjects of duty if properly instructed?

11. What illustration is given?

12. By pursuing the course marked out, will it be easy to comply with the direction given above?

13. What is the third direction?

14. Do the feelings of both teacher and pupils vary from day to day?

15. What will be the effect of neglecting uniformity in government?

16. What is the fourth direction?

17. Can a teacher have the same feelings towards all pupils?

18. Ought all, in school to be governed by the same general rules?

19. What is the fifth direction?

20. What will be the effect of being peevish or fretful?

21. What is the sixth direction? Seventh?

QUESTIONS ON LECTURE VII.

1. Why is a judicious system of discipline necessary in the general management of a school?

2. What direction is given with regard to alloting to each exercise its appropriate amount of time?

3. What is the second general direction on this part of the subject?

4. What is the most important subject in the management of a school?

5. Is it possible to restrain a child too much?

6. What does a disposition to resist rightful authority on the part of a child, require from the teacher?

7. What subject demands attention as a second thing?

8. Are children generally disposed to believe their teacher's opinions to be right, and thus avoid thinking for themselves?

9. What influence will such a habit have on the child?

10. What subject is next in importance?

11. Why are there so few good readers in common schools?

12. What can the instructer do to surmount the obstacles to correct habits of reading?

13. Why should this be made a prominent object?

14. What is the third general direction for the management of a school?

15. Is it possible to make school a delightful place to children?

16. What reasons are mentioned in support of the opinion that this is practicable?

17. How can this object be accomplished?

18. Should it be the sole object of the instructer to render scholars happy?

19. What will be the unavoidable consequences of a neglect of order and neatness in a school room?

20. What is the fourth general direction?

21. What general principles of conduct are necessary to the accomplishment of this object?

22. Is deliberation in making decisions requisite?

23. What is the effect of hasty decisions?

24. What is a good rule for every teacher to adopt?

25. Can confidence be secured, when there is a want of punctuality on the part of the teacher?

26. How much of the teacher's time ought to be devoted to the interests of the school?

27. Can any thing be done to promote the improvement of the children, when the teacher is not with them?

28. Does the fact, that the compensation is not what it should be, afford any excuse for unfaithfulness?

QUESTIONS ON LECTURE VIII.

1. What is suggested with regard to the unnecessary confinement of children?

2. What is the common practice?

3. What are some of the inevitable consequences of such a course?

4. How may these evils be obviated?

5. What direction is given with regard to order and system in the arrangement of exercises?

6. What is the first consideration which renders this direction important?

7. What is the second? Third?

8. What is the third direction of this lecture?

9. Will it require effort to cultivate this habit?

10. What is a prerequisite on the part of the teacher?

11. How shall the object under consideration be obtained?

12. What illustration is given?

13. What is the fourth direction?

14. What prerequisites are indispensable in order to be prepared to do this?

15. What evils will result from allowing a child to change his studies at will?

16. What is the fifth direction?

17. Are rewards always injurious?

18. To what cases should they be restricted?

19. What is the sixth direction?

20. What questions should the teacher propose to herself from day to day?

21. What course is recommended with reference to this subject?

22. What illustrations are given?

QUESTIONS ON LECTURE IX.

1. What is the first remark on the mode of teaching?

2. What is one of the subjects of first importance?

3. What means must be used to induce a habit of thinking?

4. What kind of schools were said by an eminent instructer to be wanting?

5. What was formerly supposed to constitute the whole duty of a teacher?

6, What other erroneous practice has been more recently substituted?

7. What plans are adopted in the Hartford school to teach the pupils to think?

8. What other modes may be adopted with success?

9. How much time should be devoted to exercises of this character?

10. What arithmetical exercises are recommended?

11. What is the plan recommended for defining words?

12. Is the study of natural history adapted to the capacities of young children?

13. What mode should be pursued in teaching it?

14. Is the black-board an important article in a school-room?

15. What is the next subject to which attention is called?

QUESTIONS ON LECTURE X.

1. What are the first ideas which should be impressed on the minds of children in the study of geography?

2. Of what part of the world should they first acquire a knowledge?

3. What exercise is particularly recommended to fix the situation and outlines of places in the memory?

4. What parts of this science are adapted to the young mind?

5. What plan has been found useful in exciting the attention of children?

6. Is history to be taught in summer schools?

7. What is the usual manner of pursuing this branch?

8. What results from such a mode? •

9. Are children pleased with hearing stories?

10. In connection with what other science should history be pursued?

11. What book is recommended as written with reference to this mode of teaching?

12. How far is the study of grammar adapted to the capacities of young children?

13. What objections are there to the common mode of teaching grammar?

14. What advantages does the course recommended by the author possess?

15. How is this course illustrated?